How To

Living & Working in Paris

Living & Working in Paris

Your first-hand introduction to this capital city

ALAN HART

How To Books

Published by How To Books Ltd,
3 Newtec Place, Magdalen Road,
Oxford OX4 1RE, United Kingdom.
Tel: (01865) 793806. Fax: (01865) 248780.
email: info@howtobooks.co.uk
http://www.howtobooks.co.uk

First edition 2001

British Library Cataloguing in Publication Data.
A catalogue record for this book is available from
the British Library.

Edited by Peter Williams
Cover design by Shireen Nathoo Design
Cover image by PhotoDisc
Map drawn by Nicki Arvill

Produced for How To Books by Deer Park Productions
Typeset by Kestrel Data, Exeter
Printed and bound by Cromwell Press Ltd, Trowbridge, Wiltshire

NOTE: The material contained in this book is set out in good
faith for general guidance and no liability can be accepted
for loss or expense incurred as a result of relying in particular
circumstances on statements made in the book. Laws and
regulations are complex and liable to change, and readers should
check the current position with the relevant authorities before
making personal arrangements.

Contents

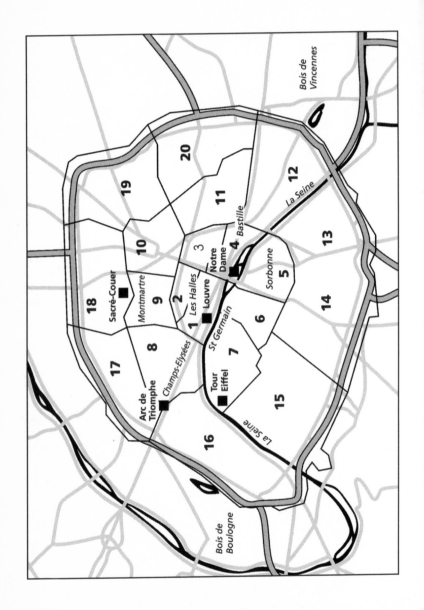

Preface

On a dull grey day in October 2000, I sat in a typical Parisian café at the Place du Trocadéro opposite the Eiffel Tower with Gyles Lewis and Nikki Read of How To Books and tried to imagine what this book might be, and how it would be different from the hundreds if not thousands of other guide books to the French capital. The more that we talked, the more the concept of this book became clear to us all. First and foremost, it should be noted that this is not a traditional guide-book, with a quick-fix whistle-stop tour of the main sites. A guide very definitely pushes you from pillar to post in order for you to successfully complete your tour.

This book is designed to be what almost everybody needs to really feel at home in a new town or city – a companion – to accompany you, to inform you, to support you, and hopefully to reassure you as you find your own path to Parisian happiness, and overcome the shock of a rich, exciting new culture. I hope that it may also provoke you or intrigue you enough to try one or two things which you may only ever have heard about before arriving.

Culture shock comes in many shapes and forms. Ten years ago, on my first night in Paris, freshly arrived from London and the land of sliced bread, and trying to feign Parisian *savoir-faire* of which I did not have an ounce, I nonchalantly told my new boss who was also my neighbour that I was 'just popping out to buy some bread for the morning'. With a typically wry little smile, Dr Martin Draper gave me my first lesson in the French way of life by reminding me that this was something I was going to have to get used to doing each morning, not the night before.

As with my earlier book, *Living and Working in France*, the aim of this book is to help you settle into Parisian life as easily and rapidly as possible, avoiding the pitfalls and getting the most out of your time in Paris. Finding friends, especially through expatriate associations where you will find people experiencing the same kinds of situations as you will face, is an extremely important step; but avoid the risk and temptation of sinking into an expatriate ghetto where French is spoken only falteringly if at all and your native manners ride rough-shod over the very sophisticated Parisian lifestyle. Learning the language still remains the secret of success in Paris, and a good control of the language is rewarded by respect, friendship and compliments about your accent which form 'part of your charm'. Importantly for you as a new arrival, a grasp of the language will also help you to overcome your initial linguistic frustrations, and to combat a normal but not inevitable sense of loneliness at separation from family and friends.

The sources I have used for this book are all cited, and I have as far as possible tried to let Paris and the Parisians speak for themselves via the endless and overwhelming number of surveys and articles written about the city and its population in the last year. The main sources have been the principal right-wing and left-wing newspapers and magazines – *Le Figaro, Le Monde, Libération, L'Express* and *Le Point*. But Paris is also endowed with a number of excellent chroniclers of its own. Amongst these are *Zurban, À nous Paris, Time Out in Paris* and a number of other journals, all of which I have consulted. I also drew upon the 2000 edition of the American Embassy's resource pack for new arrivals in Paris. Finally, I have consulted extensively the French government websites listed in this book, and I highly recommend you to do the same. Many of these sites are well translated into English.

My first book was dedicated with love and thanks to the congregation of St George's Church who brought me to Paris and supported me through the difficult days of cultural adjustment. This book is dedicated to all my friends, and especially those close friends and colleagues who have helped me to make my home in Paris.

Alan Hart

1

Introducing 21st Century Paris

There are hundreds if not thousands of books which recount the fascinating origins and history of Paris and the Parisians. The history of Paris is written in stone and in street-names across the city, and hardly any stone is turned in Paris without unearthing some part of the flamboyant city's bloody and glorious history.

Reading one or more of the histories of Paris and exploring its monuments and ancient sites will thoroughly enrich any visitor or newcomer to the French capital. But it will also provide the back-drop for the passions which still run high in present-day Paris, a city of 2,147,857 people according to the 1999 census figures. Almost a third (631,000) of these have come to Paris since the last census in 1990, although the overall population is down by 26,500, and half of the population is now in the 25 to 39 year old age range. The foreign community has declined by 10%, now accounting for 14.5% of the population, and whilst the number of under-15 year olds has remained stable, the over-60s (20%) have declined. Paris is younger, more French, less populated but still as popular as ever. Even if the number of foreign residents has declined, the cosmopolitan nature of the city remains with the huge influx of tourists to the capital of the world's top tourist attraction. (Source: Insee quoted in *Zurban*, 22 November 2000).

You should note that these figures are only for inhabitants of the 20 arrondissements of Paris itself, and so the overall population of 'greater Paris' with the suburbs and the commuter towns of the Île de France is much higher. If you do opt for living beyond the city limits, or find yourself there by force of circumstance, it will not necessarily be a 'lesser experience'.

Disparities between different **communes** in the Paris region in terms of age and nationality or ethnic origin are very high. The theme of **mixité sociale**, seeking to create a social equilibrium, is one of the most contentious on-going sagas of French society and politics. Everybody talks about it, but the anthropological reality is that human beings are just as tribal in Paris as they are elsewhere, and like attracts like. However, there have been serious population shifts which have upset the centuries-old political and social pattern of Paris, and these are creating some of the most interesting lifestyle opportunities in Paris.

VOUS ÊTES PARISIEN?

Depending who asks you this question and in what context, it could be a compliment or an insult. Residents of the French capital are the ones that other French nationals love to hate: either because they are jealous, or because they have had a bad experience in the French capital at the hands of the cosmopolitan and sometimes cunning and callous capital-dwellers.

Ask Parisians how they define themselves and you will receive any number of answers. The popular French comic Virginie Lemoine, a native of the **populaire** and now trendy *quartiers* of Abbesses and Ménilmontant, said recently that she detests the view of Parisians as anything other than people who enjoy living in the city, no matter what their age or background (*Á nous Paris*, April 2001). The authors of the perennially popular *Paris Insiders Guide* defined Parisianism as 'a form of snobbery . . . not automatically accessible to those living in Paris, or . . . born in Paris . . . a way of thinking, of having a good time, of laughing and speaking, and of being well-up on everything, which only exists in Paris' (*Paris Insiders Guide* 2000, International Welcome to Paris). What everyone is agreed on then is that to be a Parisian is to possess that certain *je ne sais quoi* which tantalises the rest of the world.

In point of fact, Parisians are big-city dwellers like any others. If you are a happy Londoner or a happy New Yorker, you will soon get the hang of the city. You will learn the knacks and pick up the habits fairly rapidly, and soon start to form your own, which will allow you to settle comfortably in the city. Paris is no less friendly than any other comparable city, and is indeed a lot more friendly than some other major French towns and cities where foreigners can feel frozen out. Paris is so cosmopolitan that it is always possible to find your niche eventually. But to make the city work for you, you also have to make an effort to be open to new ways and styles. Don't try to turn the tide, but go with the flow. With a city as diverse as Paris, there are several 'flows' to go with, so you should be able to feel at home.

UNDERSTANDING THE FRENCH PEOPLE

If you are coming to live in Paris, you will be surrounded by one of the most complex peoples on the face of the earth. The essential problem with understanding the French is that they are 'neither fish nor fowl', neither Latin nor Anglo-Saxon, but a mix of the two cultures. From the former they take their romanticism, a large part of their looks, their religion, and their love of intrigue and tendency to corruption and lawlessness, ranging from a minor shrug of the shoulders and cheeky grin when ticked off for speeding to an alarming tendency amongst politicians for grand fraud. From the Anglo-Saxons they have acquired the other half of their looks, much of their culture, and commercial brilliance hampered by their innate need to argue about everything.

The contentious nature of the French, who are unable to agree on anything amongst themselves, was neatly summed up recently by Paris' first-ever Green Party mayor, the new mayor of the second arrondissement Jacques Boutault: 'The Greens are Gauls! As soon as they are together, they cannot stop themselves from arguing amongst themselves, but when they are under attack from the exterior, they band together' (*Le Parisien*, 15 March 2001) echoing the famous words of General de Gaulle about his compatriots when he was president, 'How can you expect a nation to agree on anything in peacetime when they have over three hundred types of cheese?' Any resemblance to the antics of Asterix the Gaul and his companions is more than passing and fictional; the French love the cartoon character who best reflects their past but also their current character.

'Asterix contra mundi'

The fact that Asterix has an enduring appeal to the French may perhaps explain the new popularity of the anti-globalisation (**mondialisation**) campaigner José Bové, who bears more than a mild physical similarity to the fictional character. Bové's popularity explains much about the French character, which otherwise remains incomprehensible to foreigners and especially to Anglo-Saxons. The problem that France has with Europe, and indeed with the rest of the world, has a number of origins.

First, it is due to the fact that the French believe passionately in **l'exception française**, the French exception in politics and culture. They truly believe that they have lessons to teach the rest of the world, without necessarily having anything to learn. This results not only from the exceptional intelligence and richness of the French culture, but also from a little Corsican general who is still revered in France, Napoléon. His military successes, along with subsequent colonial developments (which France still nurtures in one form or another), have given the French a sense of superiority which can and does grate on foreign nerves. This all explains why, for instance, the French have more court rulings outstanding against them for infringements of European law than any other European Union state. The French see the European Union not as a coalition of states reaching consensus on various issues (consensus being an almost unknown concept in France), but as the Francisation of Europe.

Second, it stems from a sense of 'victimisation', and of constant attack from the English-speaking nations and their common language. The French rightly complain that English is too dominant as a language in the world, but have yet to produce a convincing argument why their language should replace it. Bové's attacks on multinationals have struck a chord with his fellow citizens precisely because he stands for the individualism they cherish in the face of multinational companies.

The third reason for the seeming arrogance of the French is that they fear foreigners. According to a survey in October 2000, 60% of the French population think that there are too many foreigners in France, and 43% consider themselves to be 'a little' racist. Of the 26% who consider themselves not to be racist, the majority consider that immigrants are a source of cultural enrichment.

Read in isolation, these statistics might seem alarming, but they go a long way to identifying the complexity of the French character. After all, one half of the population dreams of moving to Paris, and after a few years in the city, they dream of moving out and buying a home in the places they originally wanted to escape from. How can you reason with a mentality like that?! The answer is that you cannot. You simply have to take it all in your stride, make allowances, and try to be sensitive. In so doing you will disarm the French, who do take time to get to know and to accept newcomers, French and foreign alike. You will overcome their reticence, their *froideur*, their seeming arrogance; but first of all you have to learn the rules of the game and then play to win.

DISCOVERING PARIS BY NUMBERS

The city of Paris is divided into 20 districts or local municipalities known as **arrondissements** (see map on page 10), described in the following chapter. Certain **quartiers** of Paris – e.g. the Marais, or Les Halles – spread over more than one arrondissement. Other quartiers – e.g. La Butte Montmartre or La Butte aux Cailles – are pockets in individual arrondissements.

The arrondissements of Paris curl out from the centre where the city grew from the river banks and islands, marshlands and fields out to a first city limit (the 1st to 6th arrondissements), then spreading to the east beyond the Bastille and to the west into the 7th and 8th arrondissements. The sick and the infidels – Protestant, Arab or Jew, or simply non-French – were kept to the outlying districts of the 9th and 10th arrondissements, and later brought within the city limits by the series of Grands Boulevards.

The villages of Montmartre, Batignolles and Belleville to the north, Auteuil, Chaillot and Passy to the west, and the Butte aux Cailles to the south were gradually pulled into the city limits, as newer areas such as Montparnasse grew up to house the influx of new workers. Whilst the south and west became generally calm areas favoured by the bourgeoisie and aristocracy, the 'red' arrondissements to the north and east – the 13th, 18th, 19th and 20th arrondissements – were villages transformed into the first Parisian dormitory towns (**cités dortoirs**) which became hot-beds of political radicalism for the working classes expelled from the renovated city centre.

These defining lines are still largely operational today, and the bourgeois technocrats who rule Paris in the 21st century still have the same reaction to the most recent arrondissements and their problems as Victor Hugo in the 19th century: 'The wall which walls in Paris makes Paris murmur.' *Le mur murant Paris rend Paris murmurant.* Despite its transport network and much talk, Paris remains a socially disjointed city, but every arrondissement has its positive as well as its negative points.

TRACING POPULATION PATTERNS

The year 2000 has provided an extraordinary amount of new information on the social geography of Paris. To some extent, it confirms what guidebook writers have been saying for years about the growth of certain **quartiers branchés** (trendy districts).

But a global view of the surveys commissioned by the left-wing and right-wing press, together with figures inadvertently released concerning the number of **PACS** (*Pactes de solidarité civile*, a civil contract roughly equivalent to common-law marriage and open to heterosexual and homosexual couples since November 1999), confirm a very clear **rive droite – rive gauche**, north – south-of-the-river and east – west divide in Paris, which has shown the depth of the impact of both urban regeneration and social mutation. The results of the municipal elections in March 2001 have also confirmed the ebb of the traditional Catholic bourgeoisie in western Paris, and their replacement by the rising tide of the 'BoBo' and 'LiLi' generation in eastern Paris, which some social commentators have seen as a 'battle' between the traditional and new bourgeoisies. Paris is now split down the middle, with the eastern arrondissements under Socialist control and a minority of large western arrondissements under the control of the right-wing RPR.

Introducing Bobo and Lili

Who or what are the BoBos and Lilis? Writing in the left-wing newspaper *Libération* on 8 January 2001, the geographer Christophe Guilluy described the BoBos as the 'bohemian middle-class . . . on the American model, resulting from the merger of the artistic and intellectual worlds and the business world . . . Individualistic, multi-cultural, environmentally-concerned, addicted to liberal values, alien to notions of 'class war' [found in the traditional French socialist movement] a new bourgeoisie, [middle-class], less well-off, younger, and more intellectual . . . than their political rivals in the well-off traditional bourgeoisie, . . . [The BoBos] are more concerned about questions of lifestyle and quality of life . . . but still display typical right-wing concerns about taxation and crime', preferring to preach a multi-cultural society than to practise it when it comes to sending their children to school in still largely immigrant renovated areas to the east and south of Paris where the BoBo presence is most heavily felt. The following day in *Le Monde*, the journalist Pierre Georges summed up – or perhaps dismissed – the BoBos as 'Left-wing hearts and society and right-wing wallets. Free-thinking morals and liberal politics [*Libertaires et libéraux* = Lili].'

The overall conclusion has been that this group now form a volatile political class – naturally drawn to the Right but most often successfully appealed to by the new softer (fiscally-friendly, generally 'green' and socially-aware) Socialist approach of Lionel Jospin. Commentators believe that the BoBos and LiLis control the political balance of not only Paris, but also most major French cities. By now British readers at least will have recognised that the French version of the Islington '*Guardian* reader' has been born.

Understanding urban renewal

One thing that the 'BoBo' specialists themselves have noticed is that in seeking to break down ghettos in former slum areas by encouraging the settlement of the 'BoBo' element, a new 'BoBo ghetto' mentality has grown up.

Libération (9 February 2001) half-mockingly defined the process by which a quartier achieves BoBodom, as the following:

1. A dynamic underground movement moves in. Exactly what this is is left to our imaginations . . .

2. The trendy élite follows on.

3. Up-and-coming Parisians follow the trendy élite and the dynamic underground.

4. Rougher elements from the generally poor suburbs in the Seine-St Denis (93) départment follow on.

5. The provincial French come to visit.

6. And then tours are organised of the new **quartier à la mode** for Japanese tourist groups!

Quite what is represented by the starting point, the 'dynamic Underground' that everybody is following is left unclear, although one is led to believe it can only be artists, musicians or perhaps journalists and their friends.

FINDING YOUR NICHE

The shift in population patterns makes it possible to offer general suggestions and guidelines as to which areas of Paris now are populated by which social 'type' of person. The 5th, 6th, 7th, 8th, 15th (with the highest population), 16th, and part of the 17th arrondissement (in a roughly triangular section from Villiers to Péreire to the Étoile) now appear to house the traditional family units, whilst the 'BoBo' couples and families have colonised the

11th, 12th, 13th, 14th, the Batignolles secteur in the 17th, the 18th from the Mairie to Pigalle and Place de Clichy, the 19th, and parts of the 20th arrondissement.

The largest number of PACS recorded in Paris were in the 11th and 18th arrondissements, which both house significant young professional and gay communities. The small 1st, 2nd, 3rd and 4th arrondissements also have similar populations, with high property prices tending to restrict access to those with higher incomes content to pay more for less space in order to live in the city centre (i.e. single people or dual-income-no-kids couples), than families of three or more. These four arrondissements do, however, contain an extreme mix of traditional bourgeois families and traditionally non-bourgeois types, and are pretty cosmopolitan. The 9th arrondissement is a mixed bag of styles from the 'BoBo' element between Trinité and Pigalle, to the more traditional bourgeoisie on either extremity of the arrondissement, whilst the 10th is drawing a distinctly 'BoBo' crowd into the renovated more chic areas.

Ethnic Paris
The British, North American, Irish or other European Union communities are not concentrated in any particular area, with the exception of a strong Portuguese community in the 14th arrondissement, the largest European community in Paris.

The African and especially North African (**maghrébin**) immigrant communities are most strongly concentrated in the poorer areas of the 10th, the northern halves of the 17th and 18th arrondissements, and the further extremities of the 19th and 20th arrondissements. The Chinese and Vietnamese communities are heavily concentrated in the 13th near to Place d'Italie and in the 19th at Belleville, and a small now mainly commercial community in the northern Marais in the 3rd arrondissement. Jewish quarters exist in the 4th arrondissement around rue des Rosiers, and also in the 9th around rue du Faubourg Montmartre; but Jewish families, synagogues and kosher restaurants can be found across Paris.

This thumb-nail sketch of social distribution in Paris may well explain why you have access to fewer facilities for your kids than your neighbours across the street in a different arrondissement where the focus is less on young childless professionals and more on young families. This will also to some extent help you to situate yourself in Paris if you adopt an 'alternative lifestyle' – gay or straight cohabitation with or without children. In so doing I may be guilty of contributing to the creation of social ghettos; but I hope that I will also be helping you to settle quickly into an area that best reflects your personal culture.

What is clear is that Paris is a city on the move, and so you may well find yourself drawn to different areas at different stages in your Parisian life. Plans for future development have been included at the end of this chapter to help you if Paris is where you hope to be in years to come, or if you wish to keep a corner of Paris for yourself when you return to your original or next home. Enjoy exploring the city and its suburbs, and remember that even if all that you learn from a visit to a new area is that you really do not feel at home there, you are wiser nonetheless.

UNDERSTANDING HOW PARIS WORKS

To some extent, Paris is like a very large French residential building owned in **copropriété** (see later chapters on accomodation). The individual owners (arrondissements) are responsible for a share of the overall costs according to the size of their 'appartement', plus their own expenses such as local crèches, cultural centres or sporting facilities. The copropriété (the **Mairie de Paris**) looks after maintaining the **parties communes**: the lighting, the cleaning, city-owned and subsidised housing, some of the most well-known monuments.

Parisians elect their local councillors and ultimately their city council every six years, with the most recent elections having taken place in March 2001. The French electoral system provides for a two-round race, unless an electoral list gains 50% or more of the votes cast in the first round. After a second-round vote, the winners gain 50% of available seats, and the rest are distributed proportionally to the other parties that have gained 5% or more. In the second round, only parties that have gained a minimum of 10% can go forward, but political alliances are allowed. The 163 municipal councillors are drawn from the winning electoral lists, and it is these councillors who ultimately vote in the mayor of Paris, a post created in 1977 and held by Jacques Chirac until his election as president in 1995.

The **Conseil de Paris**, presided over by the mayor, sets the city budget and agenda, leads attempts to attract major events such as the World Cup or the Olympics, organises major festivities such as the Millennium New Year celebrations, and distributes millions of francs of grants to associations and projects. The local mayors (the products generally of the direct election of the voters, or at least coalitions of like-minded groups) and local councils in the arrondissements are responsible for providing and administering local facilities, from schools to cultural and sports centres. Nonetheless, it is the City of Paris which controls the vast number of social priority housing together with a highly contentious and desirable collection of 'grace-and-favour' appartments across the capital, even if some administrative rôle is given to local councils.

Chirac transformed Paris into a huge money-making machine to finance his right-wing RPR party, and it was his number two, Jean Tiberi, who took over the helm when Chirac moved into the Presidential Palace. The result was an explosive series of corruption scandals involving most of France's leading politicians, who also have electoral strong-holds on the Paris City Council. Parisians have now made clear that they want a mayor who concentrates less on the national arena and more on the city and its needs. In 2001 control of Paris fell to the Socialists, led by Bertrand Delanoë, for the first time since the aborted Revolution in 1871!

Voting in Paris
European Union nationals resident in France are entitled and encouraged to vote in municipal and European elections. They can even be elected as local councillors, as long as they are not an elected politician at the same time in their home country. The procedure for registering is surprisingly easy for a country which adores complicated and bureaucratic paperwork:

1. You must register before the 31st December prior to the election at your local town hall (**mairie**).

2. Take along a valid **carte de séjour** (residence permit) which will indicate your nationality.

3. Take along either a rent receipt (**quittance de loyer**), or a telephone or EDF bill with your name and address.

4. Officially you should provide a written document stating that you have not had your voting rights removed in your home country. In practice, you simply sign the appropriate statement on the form **sur l'honneur**.

5. If you are living **chez** somebody else, you will have to provide a signed statement from that person stating that you are living there.

6. Electoral cards (**cartes d'électeur**) are sent out a few weeks before the election, and you need to take these along with you (plus your carte de séjour) in order to vote.

In April 2001 the new mayor of Paris, Bertrand Delanoë, announced the creation of a Council for Foreign Residents of Paris. For the time being, details of what this is or how it will function are scant, but it does seem to be a positive indication of the rôle and importance which Delanoë intends to place on foreign Parisians and their requirements and suggestions.

PARISIAN PRIORITIES

From late 2000 up until the municipal elections in March 2001, Parisians were endlessly surveyed, analysed and polled as to their local and global priorities. Several priorities show the Parisian 'Nimbyism' (Not-in-my-backyard') attitude which in a nation that makes moaning a national sport often places the Parisians at the top of the league. Nonetheless, you can expect to see movement on a number of these areas which may impact your choice of where to live.

- **Security** The out-of-sight out-of-mind concrete towers (**cités**) relied on by a generation of urban planners to house the poorest, principally immigrant, communities have provided a bad harvest of excluded ghettoised and often violent young people. Violent crime is as much a reality in central Paris where the pickings are easy as in the home 'territories' where gang fights are increasing. Rest assured Paris is not down-town Rio mixed with the Bronx. But you need to learn a certain street-wise attitude rapidly to deal with situations which take much longer to recover from than to occur.

- **Transport** All the political parties are in favour of a ring of tramways around the outer boulevards of Paris near to the **périphérique**, offering yet another cleaner layer to the Parisian public transport system, but possibly increasing congestion.

- **The environment** More bike lanes, more parks and open spaces, and less delivery vans to the bottle-neck medieval streets of central Paris are all priorities. Paris has a serious pollution problem, especially in summer. Do not under-estimate this if you have a respiratory problem, and if so stick to the greener areas of the city to the east or west, or to the garden suburbs. Plans to cover the railway tracks will con-siderably change the urban landscape in northern Paris.

- **Housing** Everybody is fed up with a lack of reasonably-priced easily-accessible housing, which does not necessitate pro-ducing five years of pay-slips for yourself, your wife, your mother, and her father, together with a declaration signed in blood guaranteeing that you *will* pay the rent. Landlords have become more and more exacting in their qualifying demands for tenants, to the point of quite simply invading personal privacy. The waiting lists for municipal social priority housing are extremely long, and so now the cry is for more such housing to meet the needs of new arrivals, young families (fewer in Paris itself) and low-paid workers.

- **Crèches and educational facilities** Paris lacks municipal child-care facilities, which together with a lack of affordable accommodation is forcing young families out of the city and into the suburbs. School class sizes are also a source of concern, and there are firm plans in hand for ameliorating the situation in some of the more densely populated areas, even if other areas are still being left waiting.

- **Four-legged foulers** Paris is renowned for an extremely high number of pet dogs, from the forbidden pitbull terriers of the **cités** to the tiny Yorkshire terriers camouflaged in the fur coats of the ladies of the 16th arrondissement. Naturally our four-legged friends have their 'needs', and owners provide the opportunity for these to be met by regular walking. The problem is that nobody has the slightest intention of clearing up after the deed is done. The city council has developed a major pooper-scoop industrial plan, but this does not seem to be working (or perhaps the dogs need to change their diets). Rather like traffic congestion, this is something that Parisians want everybody else to act on but have little intention of dealing with themselves.

THE CHANGING FACE OF PARIS

For many people, Paris is an 'eternal city' in the same way as other European masterpieces such as Florence or Rome. But the truth is that it is, in the words of T. S. Elliott, 'still, and still moving' – beautifully preserved but constantly renewing its skyline, horizon and perspectives. The Eiffel Tower, the Centre Pompidou, the Louvre Pyramides or the Grande Arche at La Défense have each in their day drawn the wrath of contemporary critics before being absorbed into the rich tapestry which gives Paris its mythical charm.

The threads which form the Paris 'tapestry' are the variety of lifestyles found in each **quartier** of the arrondissements of Paris. Almost no arrondissement fits into a single mould, although some are more uniform than others, and it is easier to identify social patterns in some parts of Paris than in others. The renovation, restoration or 'gentrification' of large parts of Paris has already changed popular conceptions, and will continue to do so in the next few years as new life returns to certain **quartiers** and new settlements develop their own style.

However, one important point to note is that where several arrondissements and styles meet, danger-points are often but not always found. The junction of the 8th, 16th and chic 17th at Place de l'Étoile is problematic only in terms of the traffic around the Arc de Triomphe. But the collisions between the 8th, 9th, 17th and 18th at Place de Clichy, and the 3rd, 10th and 11th at Place de la République, make for more unstable and sometimes unsettling mixes, especially at night, as each arrondissement adds its own ingredient to the communal pot.

RECLAIMING THE CITY – THE NEW QUARTIERS

President François Mitterrand left an indelible mark on Paris with his pharaonic constructions to mark his 14-year reign, such as the Pyramids at the Louvre, the Grande Arche at La Défense, or the new Opéra at Bastille. His rival and eventual successor, Jacques Chirac, who was mayor of Paris up until his election to the presidency in 1995, took the helm of a plan of urban regeneration which has been characterised by not only restoration but innovation. In the 12th arrondissement around Bercy, the 13th arrondissement behind the new Bibliothèque François Mitterrand, or again in the 17th arrondissement at Porte d'Asnières or at Porte de la Villette in the 19th arrondissement, new apartments have sprung up on derelict lands left by urban change and decay.

These new quartiers have largely still to establish a real style of their own, as they balance the state requirements of social mix between social priority housing and private, often luxury, developments. The hand of the favoured master-planner Christian de Potzamparc, will also be felt in these new areas, with his three-phase vision of city-planning and exceptions making rules such as the spectacular 'Flower Tower' planned for the Porte d'Asnières. But the new **ZAC (zone d'aménagement concerté)** quartiers do definitely offer an interesting opportunity for those willing to contribute to the definition of the quartiers' styles.

LOOKING TO THE FUTURE

The transformation of Paris which these new projects represent is only part of the story, however. Yet more large zones of renovation and initiative are being created in the heart of the city, as army barracks and hospitals close in a gradual process of centralisation which will fundamentally change the neighbouring areas of Paris. In the ultra-chic 7th arrondissement, just behind *Le Bon Marché* and surrounded by conventual calm and politicians' and diplomats' apartments, is the ancient Hôpital Laënnec dating from the 17th century, which was closed as part of a centralisation programme focussing on the large number of hospitals across the Rive Gauche. The other hospitals, Broussais in the 14th and Boucicaut in the 15th, have now also closed to be amalgamated into the new super-hospital Européen Georges Pompidou. The result is that three excellent development opportunities have been created in the heart of Paris, but not without their own personal difficulties.

Further in the future, the Paris-VI university itself is the other **grand chantier** (great building site) which will transform the face of central Paris. The modern rabbit warren at Jussieu, best known for its futuristic towers, dominating the quaint and luxurious 5th arrondissement which is also the traditional seat of Parisian learning and home to the Sorbonne itself, is stuffed full with asbestos and is closed for renovation. The 20,000 students and staff are currently homeless, waiting for their new campus in the 13th in the development area behind the Bibliothèque François

Mitterrand. Once the work at Jussieu is complete, the site is likely to be dismantled as a university. What will happen next is any-body's guess, and is obviously a highly political decision. But within the next decade, it could become an important area of redevelopment in central Paris, with a prime location virtually on the river bank.

THE GREAT PARISIAN COVER-UP

Many of the new projects have been established on land sold off by the SNCF, and in areas abandoned for generations to the poorest working classes because of their proximity to the long dark gashes on the Parisian landscape which represent the rail-ways. At the Gare d'Austerlitz plans are now well advanced to cover over these tracks, and there is fierce debate over whether to do the same behind Gare de l'Est and Gare du Nord. Opponents say that in so doing, the quartiers will lose their working-class origins, ironically from railway lines built by British engineers and workers in the 19th century. Proponents of the cover-ups say that the new open spaces that will be created will transform the poor quartiers and offer wide open spaces to over-crowded Paris.

Meanwhile the inhabitants of the areas closest to the 35-kilometre-long Paris ring-road, the **périphérique**, are now seriously demanding that similar schemes be applied to the ring-road – the busiest in Europe, transporting 1.2 million vehicles a day. Not only would this change radically the levels of noise and car pollution in these areas and provide vast open spaces for sports grounds and parks, but it would also have a far more profound social effect on the 'crown of thorns', (Philippe Mermet in *Libération*, 6 February 2001) which surrounds Paris – the **banlieues** (suburbs). They are home to 985,000 people living in a band 800m wide around the périphérique – a population the size of Brussels and larger than France's third city Marseilles – often characterised by urban problems. But the sheer immensity of the project and the cost involved means that little is likely to happen until towards the end of the first decade of the 21st century except in isolated sections.

2

Making a Successful Move

To make a success of your move to Paris, you need to plan as much as possible. Remembering to bring the right papers with you to Paris and then to the right appointment in your earliest days will save you many headaches later on.

Four important points to remember are:

- Moving home is reckoned to be one of the most stressful experiences known to humans, along with death and divorce. You will have a hiccup or two somewhere along the line even if you plan well. Try to minimise the threats to your sanity and also retain what the French most admire in foreigners – their sense of humour!

- To the French, bureaucracy is not a means to an end but a way of life. The typical French civil servant really could not care less how many times you have turned up at his/her counter to ask for your carte de séjour or driving licence – they literally have all day to sit there and find reasons to make you come back and keep them busy tomorrow. Preparing yourself well will allow you to get off the administrative roundabout as quickly as possible, but it cannot be avoided altogether.

- Losing your temper is on the whole very counter-productive with the French administration. You might as well tell the wind not to blow in your face. Stay calm; try to smile even if you are developing a deep personal loathing for the person across the counter; and avoid screaming fits unless you happen to speak extremely good French and really know your way round the system. The average French civil servant has nothing approaching British or American expectations of service.

- Take a good supply of reading material and always arrive early at French administrative centres.

A successful move falls into three categories: before, during and immediately after your arrival.

1. PREPARING BEFORE YOUR DEPARTURE

Preparing the paperwork

Passports
Under the new internal arrangements (the Schengen Agreement) within the European Union, (EU) EU citizens can enter France with just a national identity card. However, **British citizens need a valid British passport in order to enter France** (or indeed any other country covered by the Schengen Agreement), as the United Kingdom does not adhere to the Agreement.

Commonwealth citizens with residency rights in the UK are not recognised as British citizens under EU regulations. You will therefore be subject to entry requirements related to your country of origin. **Channel Islanders and Manx citizens** are not included either in the EU provisions, unless they, or a parent or grand-parent, were born in the UK, or they have been resident in the UK for five years.

Visas and residence permits
EU citizens do not require visas in order to enter France. Regulations for visas for non-EU citizens vary, and you will need to check current regulations with the French Embassy or Consulate nearest to you. For non-EU citizens, a number of different visas are available:

- **Visa de transit** Allows three days' travel across France by train.

- **Visa de circulation** Often given to business people. This allows several stays of up to 90 days, with a maximum of 180 days in any one year. This visa is normally valid for three years.

- **Visa de court-séjour** A sort-stay visa valid for up to 90 days, permitting re-entry to France during that period.

- **Visa de long-séjour** A long-stay visa for those studying, working or living in France for more than 90 days. You must already have this visa if you decide to stay for a longer period than originally intended. Otherwise, you will be obliged to return to your home country in order to apply for this visa.

Minimum requirements for Americans seeking visas to live and work in France include a valid passport; several passport-size black and white photographs; proof of your financial means and ability to support yourself during your stay in France and also support any dependents you may have; and your work contract with French Labour Ministry approval. Full details are given later in the chapters on finding employment in France.

All foreigners intending to reside in France for more than three months **must** obtain a residence permit (carte de séjour). This includes EU and non-EU citizens. Temporary residence permits for non-EU nationals are normally valid for up to one year. For EU citizens, the temporary permit is normally valid for the length of your employment contract.

Driving papers
You are obliged to carry your papers with you whenever you are driving a vehicle in France. Failure to produce them can lead to a fine. You can bring a car into France for up to six months in any one year without having to complete customs formalities. See Chapter 3 for further details on licences, car importation and car registration.

Professional papers
Take with you all relevant professional certificates, diplomas, etc. which may be required if you are setting up your own business. You will also need to enquire at your nearest French Consulate about the **carte de commerçant** required in some cases by those seeking to establish their own business.

Personal papers
You should bring with you copies of income tax documents for the last four years, and of any documents relating to investments and stocks and bonds. Receipts for your moving expenses, if they are not reimbursed by your employer, may be needed for tax purposes.

Pet papers
To import domestic pets, make sure that you have the animal's vaccination certificates and medical register up to date and ready

for inspection. This should include a rabies vaccination certificate not more than six months old. Importing domestic cats and dogs into France is not difficult. However, if you have a pet snake or something else in that line, you will need to enquire about import regulations at the French Consulate.

The British Government recently issued a consultation document on quarantine regulations for animals entering or re-entering the UK. There are six possible courses of action being considered, from no change at all, to free movement of animals with valid rabies vaccination certificates.

Documents checklist
Check that you have all of the following papers ready as you prepare for your departure.

☐ Valid passport.

☐ Valid visa for non-EU citizens.

☐ Full 'certified' copies of your birth certificate, that of your spouse, and those of your children.

☐ Full 'certified' copy of your marriage certificate.

☐ Valid driving licence.

☐ Car registration and insurance papers.

☐ *Carte de commerçant* if this is required and professional certificates.

☐ Au pairs need their **Déclaration d'Engagement** from their employer. Non-EU citizens will also be asked for a medical certificate.

☐ Students should bring with them evidence of admission to a study course.

☐ Bank statements, tax declarations and other financial documents. Proof of your financial resources may be demanded before you are granted a residence permit, depending on your nationality and occupation.

☐ Vaccination certificates for your pets.

Import rules and regulations

Detailed rules about the importation of household goods should be discussed with the customs section of the French consulate. If you use a professional moving firm, they should also be able to inform you about necessary customs formalities.

- For EU citizens, goods on which you have already paid VAT in another EU member country are exempt from VAT payments when imported into France. This should be specified on the 'CMR' form provided by a professional removal firm. If you have receipts which show that VAT has already been paid, it is wise to have these available for inspection if required. You should also prepare an itemised inventory of your effects, both for customs inspection, and in case of an insurance claim.

- Non-EU citizens are also exempt from VAT payments on their belongings, *providing that* they have been in their possession more than six months, *and* that VAT has been paid in another EU country. You will be required by the French customs officials to produce receipts to this effect. Items purchased less than six months before your arrival, and outside of the EU area, will be subject to VAT payment. You have one year from the date of your arrival in France to import your possessions before they become subject to VAT payment. You must obtain a stamped **Certificat de Changement de Domicile** from your 'home' French Consulate, and your detailed inventory must also be stamped by the same consular authorities. There are restrictions on what is considered duty-free, and you should check with the French Consular services which of your personal effects and possessions may be subject to tax upon importation to France.

- Arrangements for the importation of vehicles are given in Chapter 3.

- There are restrictions on which plants can be imported into France, although a limited number of plants can be included amongst your personal effects. If in doubt, contact the Service de la Protection des Végétaux, 175, rue de Chevaleret, 75646 Paris Cedex 13. Tel. 01 45 84 13 13.

- Works of art and collectors' items may require special import licences, and firearms and ammunitions also. Medicines and medical products, except for prescribed drugs, may also be subject to special regulations. For all of these items, you must contact the French Consulate for further information. You can also contact the French customs office at the Centre des Renseignements des Douanes, 238, quai de Bercy, 75572 Paris Cedex 12. Tel 01 40 01 02 06.

Preparing financially

It can cost a lot of money to set up your new home in France. If you rent an apartment or house, you will have to pay two months' rent in advance as a deposit (and up to three months for commercial premises), and also the rent for the first month – i.e. three months, rent in advance.

If you use an agency to find your new home, there will also be their fee to pay, normally equivalent to one month's rent. You will then have the cost of electricity and gas connections and the rental of a telephone line to pay as well.

It can be difficult to secure a rental contract from French landlords if you are a foreigner. Even young French couples are asked for written guarantees, either from their parents or their employers as a precaution against unpaid rents and bills. Make sure that you bring a significant sum of money with you to cover both these initial expenses, and day-to-day living expenses. Driving licences and residence permits also have to be paid for.

Preparing culturally

Many people come to France specifically to improve their French, or quite simply to learn the language for the first time. You will find that a grasp of the most basic phrases and words will help you enormously when you arrive. Do not count on everybody speaking English to you; many can, but not everybody will. You will certainly need to understand what is being said to you when you apply for your residence permit, for example.

You will integrate more rapidly and increase your own personal standing with French people if they see that you are trying your best to communicate with them in their own language.

● Try hard to find time to study basic grammar, phrases and vocabulary before you come to France. If you have the opportunity, an evening or conversation class would be a very good idea.

- Bring a good dictionary with you (not necessarily the most expensive), and also a good phrase book.

You should also try to find out something about the country to which you are moving. There are plenty of excellent introductions to French history and culture available in bookshops. The varied and generally very good French press is also widely available. Reading articles on current life in France will not only help you understand your new environment, but will also improve your language skills.

2. MAKING THE BASIC MOVES

Registering at your Embassy
British citizens are not required to register at the Embassy or the nearest Consulate-General. However, if you use the consular services for other reasons (e.g. information purposes), it may be as well to register. Details of British Embassy and Consular services can be found on the website www.amb-grandebretagne.fr.

When you arrive in France, you will need to obtain a **fiche d'état civil**, which is an official document translated by an officially-recognised translator which will combine translations of your birth certificate, your marriage certificate, the birth certificate of your spouse, and the birth certificates of your children.

This service is offered in Paris by your country's consulate, at a fee. Ring and check the price in advance. In the suburbs and provinces it can also be performed at the local town hall (**mairie**), where a fee will also be charged. You must use one of these two services, and not a private translator. You will need to bring with you:

- Your passport, and that of your spouse and children if they are to be included on the same fiche.

- A salmon-coloured 'certified' copy of your birth certificate, obtained from the registry office in the UK where your birth was registered. You will also need similar copies of your spouse's and children's birth certificates if they are to be included on the same fiche.

- A green-coloured 'certified' copy of your marriage certificate if applicable, obtained from either the church or registry office in the UK where your marriage was registered.

NB: Photocopies are **not** acceptable. It must be an 'original' certified copy.

You need your fiche d'état civil in order to apply for your social security card and residence permit. Children born in France should be registered immediately in order to preserve the child's claim to native citizenship. New passports can be obtained via your consulate. The official information regarding applications for residence permits does not now require fiches d'état civil, but is as well to have one ready as the difference between what is required and what is demanded is often considerable.

American citizens are not obliged to register at their Paris Embassy but are strongly advised to do so. This will not only help establish your rights as a US citizen in France, but will also make it easier to deal later with the re-issue of passports, emergency situations which may occur which involve contacting your family in the USA, and also ease the registration of any children born in France with US citizenship.

Obtaining your residence permit

If you intend to stay in France more than three months, you must apply for a residence permit (**carte de séjour**). Failure to apply for your permit within three months of arrival is a serious offence. Fines for failing to have a carte de séjour are from 3000FF to 12000FF.

Citizens of a member country of the EU have the right to a residence permit if they have a job in France, or can prove they have the financial resources to support themselves. The permit will normally initially be valid for five years, unless the holder has a temporary job with a contract for a year or less. EU citizen rights are not granted to Australians with British residency rights, and there are certain restrictions on inhabitants of the Channel Islands and the Isle of Man. You must have a full British passport in order to qualify. You can either apply by post or in person for the carte de séjour.

Citizens of non-EU countries need a long-term visa (**visa de long séjour**) before arrival in France. Residence permits will not be issued without the appropriate visas. Americans and Canadians do not need entry visas for France, but Australians do need entry visas. **In Paris** you will need to ask your Consulate which police centre (**centre d'acceuil des étrangers**) you need to apply to, which will depend on where you live. **Outside Paris**, you should initially apply to the local town hall (**mairie**) who may refer you to a **préfecture** (police headquarters) for that département.

The bureaucracy you encounter to obtain your carte can be agony. It is advisable to take several copies of all your documents with you, a good book, and allow plenty of time. You will receive a temporary carte (**récépissé de demande de carte de séjour**) initially, proving you have applied, which is valid for three months. This will eventually be replaced by your permanent carte.

Checklist: Documents needed by an EU citizen to obtain a carte de séjour
The following is a list of documents which are usually required no matter what your nationality or status. **Regulations often change, so check the precise requirements with your local préfecture or mairie**.

☐ Your full birth certificate (the salmon-pink 'certified' copy you used for your fiche d'état civil:)

☐ Your passport

☐ Your fiche d'état civil (no longer officially required but it is better to be prepared with a copy, quickest and most useful way to establish a carte de séjour for all the family)

☐ Four passport sized black and white photographs

☐ Either the rental contract on your apartment; or a bill from France Telecom or Électricité de France (EDF) in your name showing your address; or a **certificat d'hébergement** from the person who is lodging you dated in the last three months plus a copy of their carte nationale d'identité or carte de séjour (if they are also non-French).

☐ If you are in paid employment, either: two copies of your **lettre d'embauche** (job offer) on headed paper from your employer; or your original contract plus a copy and three most recent pay slips if you have already begun work.

☐ For various categories of self-employed workers, you will be required to provide proof that you have taken the correct administrative steps to establish your business legally in France. Take advice upon this point.

☐ If you are retired you must be able to prove your financial ability to support yourself and your dependents. You must also prove that you have sufficient health insurance cover.

Once you have all the necessary documentation, and if you are living in one of the 20 Paris arrondissements, then you need to go to the Préfecture de Paris 9, boulevard du Palais, 75004 Paris, open non-stop Monday to Friday 08h30-17h00 M° Cité. Tel. 01 53 71 51 68. (www.prefecture-police-paris.interieur.gouv.fr in French).

Cartes de séjour are normally limited to the length of your 'guaranteed' stay (i.e. the length of your employment contract) in France. Cards are normally initially issued for five years, then renewed for ten years. Student cartes de séjour are normally limited to one year, and are renewable. Further details are given for applications for student cartes de séjour in the chapter on education, and the préfecture website has a page in English explaining student application procedures.

Managing your money

French money
The French franc is divided into 100 centimes. It is abbreviated to FF to distinguish it from the Swiss franc (SF) and the Belgian franc (BF). Obtain a selection of French money from a bank or foreign currency exchange before leaving for France. It is a good idea to familiarise yourself with the different coins and notes before you arrive in France. Notes and coins exist in the following denominations:

• Notes (or bills): 20, 50, 100, 200 and 500. Beware of forgeries, and check for water-marks. Many shops now have detectors which recognise forged notes.

• Coins: 5, 10, 20 centimes; ½, 1, 2, 5, 10, and 20 francs.

• Currency exchange offices are located in airports, railway stations and most banks. If you have the time and the choice, compare exchange rates to find the most favourable rate, and also check to see how much commission you will be charged. In central Paris, you will find many currency exchanges centred around the rue Scribe and the Place de l'Opéra near the bus stops for Roissy airport.

Introducing the Single Currency (The Euro)

On 1 January 1999, a Europe-wide financial and cultural revolution began. France is one of the principal countries leading the introduction of the single European currency, which will be known as the **Euro**. The Ministry of Economy, Finance and Industry has published a free leaflet available in all banks and post offices explaining how and when the new currency will be introduced.

Both French Francs and the Euro are now common currency in France. Prices, salaries, rents and taxes will all be published in both currencies, as banks and businesses make the conversions necessary for the total abolition of the French Franc on January 1st 2002. The French stock market has operated only in Euros since 1 January 1999.

The exact value of the Euro is 6.5597 FF. On 1 January 2002, the conversion to the Euro will be complete and all financial transactions will take place in Euros. All French currency will be replaced by new coins and notes on 19 February 2002.

The Euro is available in the following denominations:

- Notes (or bills): 5, 10, 20, 50, 100, 200 and 500 Euros. Any remaining French Francs notes can be exchanged for Euros at the Banque de France until 1 January 2012.

- Coins: 1 and 2 Euros, and 1, 2, 5, 10, 20 and 50 cents representing one hundredths of Euros. French cents will still carry the mark 'RF' to distinguish them as coins issued in France.

The Euro timetable

1. On 1 July 2001 chequebooks in Euros were issued to all French chequebook account holders.

2. In September 2001 the major French banks will start to issue bank statements only in Euros.

3. On 15 December 2001 you will be able to buy 100FF worth of Euros in cash at French banks.

4. La Poste will adapt all their cash distributors to Euros by 31 December 2001 in order to allow you to withdraw Euros on 1 January 2001.

5. On 1 January 2002, all bank accounts will be automatically converted into Euros. All existing financial contracts and arrangements will remain valid, but will be calculated in the new currency. Payments by standing order (*virement*) and cheque and all credit card transactions will be in Euros. Euros will become common currency.

6. The French Franc will gradually disappear by 17 February 2002. At this date the double display of prices in Euros and Francs will also cease. You will be able to trade in your Francs for Euros until 20 June 2002.

7. After that date, it will still be possible to convert Francs to Euros for coins until 2005, and for notes until 2012, but only at the Banque de France.

The Euro will be valid in all countries which participate in the European Monetary Union scheme. At first this will be a core group of countries, principally composed of France, Germany, the Benelux countries, Italy and Spain. The scheme allows for other countries to join the system when they meet certain economic criteria. The United Kingdom will not be a founder member of the Euro currency.

Information about the Euro can be obtained in France on a free help-line telephone number: 0800 01 2002, or on the internet at www.euro.gouv.fr.

French Banks
There are four principal French banks: (Banque Nationale de Paris) BNP-Paribas, Crédit Agricole, Crédit Lyonnais, and Société Générale. Of the major British and American banks, Barclays is the best represented in France with about 100 branches in Paris and across France. Citibank has a number of branches in Paris, and Société Générale on the Boulevard Haussmann has an English-speaking international client service.

To gain access to banks in France, press the bell outside the street door. When the green light flashes, enter and wait until the door closes. Then press the second bell, and open the door when the second green light flashes. Follow the system in reverse to get out again. Despite the security, the atmosphere inside is normally more relaxed!

Opening times
French banks are generally open from 09h00 to 16h30 Monday to
Friday. Many French banks in cities and large towns are now also
open on Saturdays. Lunch hours generally run from 12h30 until
14h00. Banks are closed on all public holidays, and may close for
le pont (a day between a public holiday and a weekend). In
smaller country towns, banks may close on Mondays if they are
open on Saturdays.

Opening a French bank account
- You will become accustomed to red-tape and paperwork in
  France. However, opening a bank account is one of the easiest
  steps to take. There are two options:

- A non-resident account (**compte non-résident**). Previously
  there were many restrictions on these accounts. However,
  these restrictions generally do not apply any longer. But whilst
  you can negotiate loans to buy a car or a house, you may not
  have an overdraft facility (**découvert**). This kind of account
  would be appropriate if you buy a second home in France.

- An ordinary current account. If you are resident in France, or
  are working principally in France, then you will normally be
  able to open a current account entitling you to a cheque book
  and a **carte bleue**, the standard French debit card.

- To open your account, take the following original items, plus
  copies of each:

- Passport, or residency permit (for resident accounts)

- Proof of address (**justificatif de domicile**). This can either be a
  copy of your rental agreement, or a telephone or electricity bill
  with your name and address on it.

You will sign customary account-opening forms and give a speci-
men signature to permit the payment of cheques written by you.

How the system operates
- Some banks may make you wait to receive your **carte bleue**.
  However, they will give you a cash card which will allow you
  to use the bank's automatic cash dispensers. You can use
  your card not only to withdraw cash, but also to give you
  a statement of the balance of your account (**solde**), and also a

statement of the most recent transactions on your account (**relevé**). Some banks also offer other services such as ordering cheque books, paying in cheques, etc.

- Cheques normally take about three days to clear once they have been paid into an account. This can take longer if they are drawn on an account (**compensable**) in a more distant town or city, or from another bank. Nonetheless, the date that will appear on your monthly statement (**relevé de compte**) is the date on which the cheque was deposited into your account.

- Cheques are used almost as frequently as cash in France for payment. To fill out a French cheque, write the amount in figures in the top right-hand corner, and then in words on the first (and second if necessary) lines of the cheque. Then fill out the name of the person or company to whom you wish to pay the cheque. Remember to sign the cheque in the space provided on the bottom right-hand corner, and to fill in the date and town where you wrote the cheque. Many shops now have machines which automatically fill out the amount of the cheque, date, place and to whom it is payable. You can cash a cheque at any branch of your own bank. Simply make it payable to yourself. **A piece of official identification is normally required to endorse cheques, and is always required when cashing a cheque in the bank**. There are no cheque cards in France. Cheques in Euros will be very similar in layout and operation to cheques in French Francs.

- Cheques can only be stopped in France in the case of loss or theft of your cheque book. They cannot be stopped because of unsatisfactory goods or services.

- A cash deposit (**versement d'espèces**) into your account will normally be registered much more rapidly than a cheque deposit. Banks normally have a separate counter (**guichet**) for cash deposits and withdrawals.

- Direct debits (**prélèvements**) can be used to pay for many services in France, including taxes, electricity bills, telephone bills and rent.

- **It is illegal to be over-drawn in France without a prior agreement with the bank, or to exceed your overdraft limit. There can be serious consequences if you break this rule**. You may be placed on the Debtors List at the Banque de France, and be refused credit in the future.

- There is no reason at all why you should close your bank account in your home country. It is probably a good idea to keep a reserve sum of money in your national currency in order to avoid conversion rates when you return home.

- You should also consider opening a deposit account in order to save for tax bills (which for the first year are a large lump sum) or to provide yourself with some form of security in time of trouble. The main accounts are the **Codevi** (limited to a maximum of 30.000FF) with instant access; the **Plan d'Épargne Logement (PEL),** with minimum savings periods of 18 months or five years; and the **Plan d'Épargne Actions (PEA),** composed of shares and investment funds managed by the bank. Each of these has different implications, including tax exemptions, so you need to discuss them with your bank.

- Changing banks can be a very expensive process if you decide to transfer your accounts to another bank. Unless you are wealthy, French banks will react coolly to threats of a change of bank if you are dissatisfied with the service offered.

Credit and debit cards
The principal French debit card is the **carte bleue Visa**, issued by all major French banks. This will give you the right to draw money from all cash dispensers in France, and is the most widely recognised and used of all cards. As with cheques, the carte bleue widely replaces cash. Payment is normally accepted for amounts over 100FF. You will have your own PIN number, which not only gives access to cash distributors, but also is essential for paying for goods in shops and restaurants.

The carte bleue debits funds immediately from your account (like the British Switch or Connect cards), and is not a credit card. Standard credit cards are generally accepted, with Visa being the most widely accepted. If the sign of your own credit card is not displayed at the entrance to a restaurant, you may wish to check it is accepted *before* spending any money! Many stores and commercial groups have their own credit cards.

Some British credit cards without micro-chips are refused in France, although they *are* valid. If your card is refused, you should politely insist.

> **IF YOU LOSE YOUR CARD OR IT IS STOLEN:**
> **telephone 08 36 69 08 80.**
> Other emergency numbers can now be found on most
> cash dispensers if the card is stolen whilst you are out.
> You must cancel the card immediately, and report the
> loss or theft to the police, and to your bank. All of this
> should be done as quickly as possible to avoid fraudulent
> use of your card. French banks will arrange replacement
> cartes bleues fairly rapidly.

Tipping

There are no definite tipping rules, but generally the following
people are tipped: porters, taxi drivers, doormen, room service,
waiters, cloakroom attendants, hairdressers and lavatory
attendants. Taxi drivers are usually given 10-15% and hairdressers
10%

In restaurants the service is usually included, in which case the
bill will read 'TTC' (**toutes taxes comprises**). If you have received
good service, it is customary to leave a tip nonetheless for the
waiter. Never leave centimes as a tip. This is considered very
insulting, and it would be better to leave no tip at all than to leave
centimes.

You should tip the **concierge** of your apartment building at
Christmas, depending on the level of service you have received.
This is an annual tip and should be in the region of 150FF
depending on your financial capacity. Should you live in a small
garret at the top of the building, a smaller gift will be equally
appreciated. Around Christmas, others will call on you for their
'Christmas Box' – postmen, refuse collectors, and the local fire-
fighters. You are not obliged to give money to these people, and
such collections are strictly speaking illegal. However, it is up to
you to decide on the level of your own personal generosity.

Learning to tell French time

In France, the 24 hour clock is used: for example 1.20pm is written
as 13h20, 8.00am is 08h00, and 5.30pm is 17h30. The French
working day usually begins at 9h00 and finishes at 18h00. The long
French lunch hour is still widely observed from 12h30 until 14h00.
Even if only a shorter period is actually taken for lunch, many
offices will be closed to the public during this whole period.

Early mornings are generally busy with the rush to the office or school, but less so in the school holidays. It is a good idea to buy yourself a French diary which lists the school holidays and French bank holidays. School holiday dates vary from region to region, and bank holidays considerably affect work patterns.

3. STARTING TO REALLY LIVE IN PARIS

Keeping in touch

During the first days in France, you may well be excited but you may also be suffering from loneliness linked to dislocation, as may the family and friends you left behind. Keeping in touch even when you have no permanent home is not difficult and is very reassuring for all concerned.

Public telephones

Coin-operated telephones are now only found in cafés, hotels, restaurants and some cinemas. Otherwise, all public telephones are generally operated by phone-cards (**télécartes**), sold in post offices and tobacconists (**tabacs**). Rates are cheaper after 21h30, on official holidays and Sundays. Long distance rates vary according to distance. Local call rates normally offer fairly generous amounts of time for the rate charged.

France is divided into five area codes, numbered from 01 (for Paris) to 05 (for the south-west). Dial the area code plus the eight-figure number to reach your correspondent. For international calls dial 00 plus country code plus city code plus telephone number.

Mobile phones

The French went from initial wariness to total obsession with mobile phones, with over 3.5 million subscribers by June 1997. There are a wide variety of systems available covering the whole country, including well-known British makes. If you bring a foreign-based mobile phone to France, remember the following rules for use:

- To make a call, dial as if you are a local subscriber. Dial your correspondent's number in the same way as you would do on a normal telephone. Include international dialling codes where appropriate.

- Calls made to other British-based mobile phones must be made using the international dialling codes, even if your correspondent is also in France. For instance if you are in Caen, and you want to call your friend in Paris who has a British-based mobile phone, dial 00 44, then your friend's normal mobile phone number but without the 0 at the beginning of the number. Be careful using this system as you will be faced with very high phone bills as a result.

Call-back systems
Call-back systems are readily available in France. Details of subscription rates and services can be found in 'international' magazines. Savings on international rates are often at least 30 per cent.

The postal system
As in the UK, post offices offer many more services than simply the post. Main post offices are normally open 08h00 to 19h00 Monday to Friday, and from 08h00 to noon on Saturdays. In Paris, the main post office in the rue du Louvre is open 24 hours. Stamps can also be purchased at tobacconists' shops.

Automatic franking machines inside post offices, including scales for weighing letters and small packages, dispense labels (**étiquettes**) for the appropriate value. Using these can help you to avoid the often considerable queues for assistance at the counter. Postage rates differ with destination and weight.

If you wish to send a registered letter (**lettre recommandée**), there are a number of options:

- with no proof of delivery and no declared value, but with a proof of despatch – **sans avis de réception**

- with proof of delivery (which will be sent back to you signed and dated), a proof of despatch, but no declared value – **accusé de réception**

- with declared value – **avec valeur déclarée.**

Chronopost is the French equivalent of Datapost in the UK, and next-day delivery is normally guaranteed throughout France.

France uses a five-digit code system, with the code written before the name of the town or city. The first two digits indicate the department, and the last three indicate the city. For instance, the 8th arrondissement of Paris is 75008 (75 for Paris, 008 for the 8th arrondissement).

Fax
All regular fax services are available throughout France, including both Group 3, and the faster but rarer Group 4. You can easily have a fax line installed in your home or office, but the machine must be 'approved' (**agréé**) by France Telecom. All the major fax distributors are present in France.

Most major towns and cities have shops where fax machines can be rented or purchased, from smaller phone-fax machines through to larger laser printer machines. If you buy or rent a machine, check on the cost and availability of after-sales service and supplies.

Internet
France is well connected to all major internet systems and services, and is participating fully in the multi-media revolution. This is both through home-grown material, and a strong American presence in the French market. You should have no problem connecting your existing equipment to French outlets. Several 'cyber cafés' have recently opened in central Paris, allowing consumers to surf the net over lunch or a coffee. La Poste also offers free e-mail addresses. For more details ask at any post office.

Learning the language
In order to get the most out of your time in France, you simply *must* study French and learn to speak it as well as you possibly can. If you do not, you will almost certainly find yourself con-siderably restricted and you will definitely feel left out. The French place a very high priority on their language, and their opinion of you as a foreigner will depend to a significant degree on whether you speak their language. Although they may criticise your less-than-perfect attempts to speak French, they will respect you far more for having tried than if you insist on speaking English.

There are now literally hundreds of language schools in and around Paris, and indeed throughout France. They provide tuition at all levels, from basic to advanced, and many offer courses in business French. Try looking in the Yellow Pages (**Pages Jaunes**) or the local phone book or free Paris guides such as *France-USA*

Contacts (FUSAC). Welcome offices, consulates, churches and clubs often have details or advertisements from schools and private tutors. You may prefer to use a private tutor at first if you are shy of speaking French in public.

You may also see offers of 'conversation exchange', whereby you trade an hour of English for an hour of French conversation. This could be a good way to meet people, and you could try joining a conversation group.

Try to listen to as much French TV and radio as possible, so that you start to become used to the sound of the language, and the way in which it is used. Also, try reading one of the more accessible French newspapers such as *Libération* or *Le Parisien*, in order to develop your vocabulary.

When you go shopping, read everything, paying particular attention to labels. Make an effort to go to some small local shops, and learn to ask for the items you buy. After a while you will be able to carry on a simple conversation with the shopkeepers, who are often happy to help and advise their loyal customers.

Finally, do not be afraid to make mistakes (**faux pas**). Use French whenever you can, and try to forget the natural dread of saying the wrong thing. A sense of humour is essential, and the ability to laugh at your own mistakes. Mastering the French language is a question of confidence, no matter what level you are starting from. Just as when you learn to walk you must expect to stumble every now and then, so when you are learning to speak French you must not be too upset by unintentional errors. By and large, your efforts will be rewarded with respect, an understanding smile and a little patient help.

The Media

Radio
Under French law, at least 40% of air-time every day must be devoted to French music on commercial music radio stations. There are a wide variety of stations available throughout France. The leading 'classic' radio stations are France-Inter (current events, music and discussions), France-Culture (arts and literature), France-Musique (classical music and jazz) and Radio Classique.

In Paris, if you buy a copy of *Pariscope* at any kiosk, you will instantly have a free frequency guide to all the major Parisian radio stations at the back of the magazine. The Parisian radio stations are, not surprisingly, the most trendy. The most popular stations for the 18- to 30- somethings are Europe 2, Nova, Voltage, and the Parisian Gay radio station FG, which is highly popular for young people of all persuasions with DJ interviews, exhibition reviews, shopping recommendations, etc (although the later the hour, the more you may be shocked). Nostalgie and Chérie FM churn out selections of 'Golden Oldies', including French disco and ballads – a good preparation for your first invitations to French parties. RTL2 and OuiFM will appeal to rock fans and easy listening lovers.

For those who are pining for the cricket commentary or *The Archers*, it is still relatively easy to receive the BBC World Service and Radio 4 throughout France.

Television
Foreign TV sets do not work in France, so you will need to buy or rent when you arrive. There are six TV channels available throughout France:

- TF1 is privately-owned. It generally has the 'big name' news presenters and TV journalists. Otherwise, the quality of programmes is variable, with many poor-quality game-shows and '**réalité**' shows (e.g. tracing missing relatives).

- France 2 is still under state control. This is the main heavyweight rival to TF1. There is a generally higher standard of varied programmes.

- FR3 is also still under state control. It produces regional programmes and news reports. Programming is similar to France 2.

- Canal+ is a private pay channel. For part of the day everybody is able to receive their programmes, and part of the day (normally the most interesting part) you must take out a private subscription for a receiver. Many good quality films, and the popular satirical but caustic puppet show *Les Guignols* (a French institution) appear on Canal +.

- *La Cinq/Arte* – These two stations share a frequency, Arte taking over at 19h00. The latter is a Franco-German company. An intellectual channel, with good documentaries, no game-shows, and films in original languages (**version originale** or

v.o.) including English. They also show English comedy series in v.o.

- M6 is considered a 'lightweight' channel in comparison with the others. Nonetheless, there is a good selection of films and reports (especially on Sunday evenings), and a much younger dynamic feel to the presentation.

On French TV there is a coding system with different symbols on the screen indicating the level of parental consent advisable for various films and programmes. The main programme for the evening normally begins about 20h45, after the news and weather broadcast.

Satellite television, offering a wide variety of channels from sport to history, and including the BBC and leading American channels, is now widely available throughout France. Check to find out if your building is cabled (**câblé**), and ask neighbours about how and where to subscribe. The cable TV stations available include American and 'packaged' BBC programmes, including many popular soap-operas broadcast both subtitled and dubbed. Amongst the best cable TV channels are Paris Première (general arts, lots of v.o. English/American films, and Fashion Week specials), Téva (for v.o. American sitcoms), and channels such as Odyssey for general interest programmes. The French equivalent to CNN is LCI, the continuous news channel. (Watching a repetitive channel does have the advantage of allowing you to learn vocabulary and expression.) MTV is available also, and the French equivalent, MCM.

Newspapers and magazines
France has a very wide variety of newspapers and magazines. Regional newspapers are often given greater prominence in France than is the case in the UK. The principal national French newspapers are:

- *Le Figaro* – right-wing, conservative, but a good general read.

- *Le Monde* – independent, centre-left, regarded as 'the Intellectual's newspaper' for both the right and left wing. Takes some getting used to, but worth the effort.

- *Libération* – young, centre-left and trendy. Good arts coverage.

- *L'Humanité* – the ailing mouth-piece of the Communist party.

- *Le Parisien* – sensational headlines, most akin to the English tabloids but much softer.

- *Le Canard Enchaîné* – the scourge of the political establishment, satirical but serious. A bit heavy going until you get into French politics.

Les Echos and *La Tribune* are the business newspapers equivalent to the *Financial Times*; *L'Équipe* is the popular sports newspaper; *La Croix* is run by the French Catholic church. Magazines such as *L'Événement, Marianne, Le Point, L'Express,* and *Le Nouvel Observateur* offer good broad-ranging weekly news coverage from a variety of political perspectives.

The foreign press is widely available every day in France, but at a more elevated cost. One way to save money is to take out a subscription to your favourite newspaper, which often leads to considerable savings. Telephone the newspaper of your choice before leaving the country to ask about subscriptions if you will be in France for a considerable length of time. Almost all major newspapers are now available in internet versions.

3

Travelling Around Paris

Paris is a beautiful city in which to stroll, and indeed has always been intended by its urban planners as a city for strolling, from the grand avenues feeding off the Place de l'Étoile, to the covered pavements of the rue de Rivoli or the Place des Vosges, to the 19th century Grands Boulevards which cut across the Right Bank of the city. It is undoubtedly the best way to get to know the city and enjoy it in both its splendour and its more intimate corners. However, when you are tired or in a hurry, or the weather does not lend itself to a gentle wander or the distances are too great, there are many options for travelling around Paris by public or private transport.

INTRODUCING PARISIAN PUBLIC TRANSPORT

The Paris extensive public transport system is controlled by the **RATP**, *Régie Autonome des Transports Parisiens* – also known to Parisians during the regular strikes as '*Rentre-Avec-Tes-Pieds*', 'Go home on foot'. In spite of the French national hobby of striking, the RATP services offer an excellent public service with **Métro** stations at an average distance of 500m apart in central Paris, the RER (*Réseau Express Régional*) offering fast links from the furthest suburbs into the heart of Paris and between central Paris locations, a dense network of buses and also a small number of night-buses, plus fast links to the Paris airports at Orly and Roissy. In addition to these services, local **SNCF** (French national railways, *Société Nationale des Chemins de Fer*) services also provide commuter services from the suburbs to all the main Paris stations, where there are interchanges onto the Métro or RER.

Even with a four-fold transport service, the French are still addicted to driving to work every day, if only so that they can complain about pollution and traffic jams before, during and after their journeys. When the RATP and/or the SNCF decide to go on strike, the situation only becomes worse. Given the congestion in Paris and the difficulty of finding parking spaces, free or otherwise, you would be well-advised to stick to using public transport in Paris.

Maps of the bus, RER and Métro systems are available free in Métro stations at the ticket office, and at tourist offices. A recorded 24-hour multi-language (including English) telephone information line on all services operated by the RATP can be called on 08 36 68 41 14. In 2001 the RATP launched a new campaign to inform and enable passengers with special needs and limited mobility to use the public transport system. Several buses and Métro and RER stations are now equipped with entries/exits for wheelchairs. This access plan can be down-loaded from the excellent fully bilingual RATP website (www.ratp.fr) which is linked to the Paris Tourist Office website and has many excellent links.

USING THE UNDERGROUND

The Métro

- In central Paris stations are close together, and trains run 20 hours a day from 05h30 until 01h30. Several lines fork at particular stations. To determine what is the final destination of the train and which stations are therefore served, check the electronic indicators on both the platform and on the front of the train as it arrives. The final destination should be highlighted.

- Generally the Métro is clearly marked, well lit, quiet and clean. The basic structure of the Métro is a series of concentric circles with spokes at intervals, enabling you to change from one line to another.

- One ticket is good for the length of any one trip, providing you have bought the correct ticket. It is cheaper to buy a book of ten tickets (**carnet**) than to buy tickets individually. Tickets can either be bought at the ticket offices (**guichets**) or from automatic vending machines accepting either coins or credit cards. For information on travel passes, see below.

- In Métro ticket halls and sometimes on the platforms (**quais**), you will find local street-maps with alphabetical street indexes and major buildings (e.g. schools, churches, government offices, post offices) will all be indicated. You will also find the

Métro exits indicated on these **plans du quartier** so that you can take the correct exit to arrive as quickly as possible at your destination.

Enjoying your journey
The Parisian underground system, the Métro, is one of the best in the world. It was founded in 1900 in time for the Universal Exhibition and following the example of London's Underground (which it currently surpasses considerably in terms of quality, cost and service). Many of the original wrought-iron Métro entrances by the architect Guimard are considered works of art, such as the Place des Abbesses and Porte Dauphine, and a new 'Guimard' exit was restored to Châtelet Métro station in 2000 at the Place St-Opportune exit. Less grandiose but equally atmospheric contemporary creations can be found scattered across the city. With their orange torch-lamps, yellow name-plates with swirling Art Nouveau script in green picking out the discoloured green copper, these Métro exits have become one of the most enduring symbols of romantic and exuberant *Belle Époque* Paris.

Stations built in the 1970s and 1980s Parisian reconstructions, notably Châtelet and Montparnasse, are vast warrens; one wrong turn or change of line (**correspondance**), and you are lost for 15 to 20 minutes on moving walkways and a search for the **sortie** (exit) which can feel like a TV challenge game-show.

To celebrate the centenary of the Métro in 2000, a new exit was designed for Palais-Royal (in front of the Comédie-Française) with hundreds of glowing colours – it has received universal praise as a new work of art. Direct access from the Palais-Royal Métro leads you into the Carrousel du Louvre and a short-cut to the underground entrance to the Louvre beside the inverted pyramid, thus avoiding the spiralling crowds on the square above. At nearby Louvre-Rivoli, treasures from the over-flowing stores of the Louvre line the platform.

Many central Paris Métro stations have themed decorations linked to their location: the Revolutionary Declaration of Rights at Concorde, the scene of both great and gory revolutionary acts; the history of the Paris City Council and City Hall at Hôtel de Ville; from Passy to Bir-Hakeim you have a wonderful view of the Eiffel Tower as you cross over the river; whilst you are plunged into submarine copper cleanliness at Arts-et-Métiers, where the décor celebrates the neighbouring renowned higher education colleges for engineers and architects.

The brand new automated line 14 from Madeleine to the new Bibliothèque-Nationale-François-Mitterrand (BNFM) is a state-of-the-art masterpiece, with crowd safety doors, spacious stations, lifts, underground gardens, and the chance to ride in the traditional driver's place at the front of the driver-less trains. One other great advantage of this line is that it sweeps under Paris and the Seine in only 15 minutes, including stops in the renovated **quartier** of Bercy with its entertainment and sports attractions. The intention is to extend the line to St-Lazare in the north-west, and further south-east into the 13th arrondissement. Small branch services serve the 19th and 20th arrondissements, linking them to main Métro lines serving north, east and central Paris.

RER or Rapid Regional Transit

The RER (**Réseau Express Régional**) is a more recent and very modern system with underground trains running deeper than the Métro. It is an express system with fewer central Paris stops, but which reaches much further out into the Paris suburbs. Fares vary according to distance, and the RER runs from 05h30 until a little after midnight. A number of central Métro stations have inter-sections with the RER, although the RER and Métro stations do not always have the same name (e.g. Opéra Métro = Auber RER).

There are now five RER lines (A to E), and each one forks at least once. As with the London Underground, you will find 'fast' trains not stopping at all suburban stations. You also need to be sure that the train you board is going to the correct final destination. Electronic boards on the platforms indicate both the final destination and stations where the train will stop. They also indicate if it is a short of long train, so that you can position yourself on the platform accordingly, as well as the waiting time for the train.

To transit from one system to another, you need to pass through dividing barriers. If you have a travel pass (e.g. **Carte Orange**) you will be able to make the transition without any problem.

To exit from any RER station, you must either use the same ticket you used to get into the system (at which point it becomes obsolete if it is a single ticket or use a new ticket if you have managed to lose your original ticket. If you have lost your ticket, you may have difficulty leaving the system at main stations (e.g. Châtelet, La Défense), as both full-length barriers and ticket controllers will prevent the only other possible methods – squeezing through with a friend or crawling under/jumping over the barriers.

There is no difference between Métro and RER tickets.

TAKING LOCAL TRAINS

The French state railway company (**SNCF**) runs local services with frequent stops in the suburbs (**banlieues**) of Paris. These operate at roughly the same times as the RER and Métro. Regular green bus/Métro/RER tickets are not valid on the SNCF local lines, and you must purchase yellow tickets from the guichets or vending machines. These tickets will indicate your final destination on both tickets if you buy a return ticket, e.g. Paris-St Lazare – Versailles, will appear on both tickets.

Before boarding the train, you must validate (**composter**) the ticket, as with all SNCF tickets. To do this, insert the corner of the ticket into one of the orange machines at the head of the platform, and when the green arrow lights up and you hear a clunk, one corner of the ticket will be automatically removed and the date stamped on the reverse side. The ticket is now valid and you can safely board the train. You must repeat this process with your return ticket before joining the train.

TAKING THE BUS

There is an extensive bus network in Paris. The right lane of the streets is reserved for buses, so buses move fairly well. Passengers queue up at the bus stop (**arrêt de bus**) as in the UK. Inside the bus there is a chart of the route and the stops, with information on how many tickets are needed for each distance travelled. Time-tables are posted at bus stops, and most also have simple **plans du quartier**. Certain lines run until 0h30 in the morning, but mostly the last bus is about 21h00. Partial services stopping part-way on the bus route are indicated by a line through the final destination. The major stops on a bus route are also indicated on the sides of the buses.

Bus and Métro tickets are identical. However, they are more expensive when purchased from the bus driver. You should punch the ticket in the machine provided to validate it (**composter**) when getting on the bus, unless you have purchased a travel pass (see below).

Once you are on the bus, to request the driver to stop use the red buttons. If you have to fight your way out of the bus because of over-crowding, and the doors close and the driver is preparing to pull away, just shout '**la porte, s'il vous plaît**'. You will normally find a volunteer chorus also chimes in at this point. Remember to board the bus at the front and leave at the rear (if possible), unless it is an extended bus with three sets of doors.

There are a number of night-buses (**noctambus**) which serve Paris, leaving from the Place du Châtelet every hour on the half-hour, until the Métro opens once again at 05h30. You can use your **Carte Orange** pass on these buses, but you cannot use ordinary bus tickets. Individual tickets can be purchased from the driver at a cost of 15FF each.

Travelling across Paris by bus may not always be the quickest way to travel, but it can be one of the most enjoyable. It also allows you to familiarise yourself with the sights and the city. Try the **Number 67** bus from the Place Pigalle at the foot of Montmartre, down alongside the Louvre, along the Seine river bank, across the Île St-Louis, and down into the 5th arrondissement. On the **Number 29** bus from Opéra, when the sun shines the open-air final section of the bus provides an ideal platform to view and be viewed as you cross the trendy fashion districts in Les Halles and the Marais. The **Number 72** bus from Porte St-Cloud to the Hôtel de Ville sticks to the right river bank to give you great views of the Eiffel Tower, Place de la Concorde, the Musée d'Orsay, Notre Dame, and finally the Hôtel de Ville.

The Montmartre **trolley bus** (*Montmartrobus*) leaving from the Place Pigalle is especially adapted to the steep hill as it winds its way through the village to the Mairie, and a similar bus is now planned for the narrow streets of the Marais. Also in Montmartre is Paris' only **funicular railway**, once again designed to save your legs and help you to enjoy the view from the terrace of the Sacré Coeur. Get out at Anvers Métro, and walk up the rue de Steinkerque, and take the **funiculaire** from the gardens at the foot of Sacré Coeur. Walking down through the old village is a lot less painful than walking up through it!

There is one other bus service of note in Paris, but not where you would expect to find it. The **Batobus** is a summer seasonal river bus service on the Seine running through central Paris. This service first achieved notoriety as a method of travelling to work in central Paris during the severe strikes of 1995, and has become a popular service since then. Cheaper than the *bateaux-mouches* who glide by with their multi-lingual commentaries (which you can always hear in any case), the Batobus is a very pleasant way to enjoy a day-time Paris river cruise at a reasonable price. Boarding points are dotted along both river banks.

CHOOSING YOUR TRAVEL PASS

All of these services are operated by the RATP, and regular transport passes and tickets can be used. A single RATP ticket (**billet**) currently costs 8FF, and a **carnet** (10 tickets) costs 58FF.

If you intend using a public transport on a regular basis, or even for occasional short periods from one day to one week, the most economical and convenient way to use the system is by buying a pass. A free pamphlet in French outlining the passes available and current prices is available at all Métro stations.

1. The **Carte Intégrale** is an annual travel pass for RATP services, the regional SNCF trains, and partner services, in the zones chosen. The card is personal, and can be replaced should it be lost or stolen. You can pay in one lump sum, or by monthly standing order. Some major stations sell this card, but otherwise it can only be purchased by post. Current prices range from 2915FF/year or 265FF/month for zones 1 and 2 (central Paris), to 8327FF/year or 757FF/month for those living in zone 8 in the furthest commuter towns.

2. The **Carte Imagine 'R'** is an annual travel pass for travellers aged under 26 and reserved for school and higher education students. It is valid in the selected zones Monday to Friday, and throughout the Île de France on weekends and public holidays. It can be paid for in one lump sum or by monthly installments. For zones 1 and 2 the annual cost is 1532FF, or 170FF/month, up to 4745/FF year for zones 1 to 8 or 521,65FF/month

3. The **Carte Orange** is the Paris travelcard covering bus, Métro and RER. Price varies according to the number of zones you wish to include. Zones 1 and 2 cover the whole of central Paris, up to the end of almost all Métro lines, but the business district of La Défense is in zone 3. Check at your local station to see

which zone you live in. The current monthly cost for zones 1 and 2 is 285FF, and for zones 1 to 3 it is 378FF. If you go outside your zone, you have to buy a ticket for the whole journey – you cannot simply buy an extra-ticket to 'add on' to your Carte Orange.

When you buy your Carte for the first time, take one passport size photo with you, and ask for a *coupon orange*. Stick the photo to this, fill in your name and address, and write the number of the coupon onto the white ticket printed with the month and the date. Otherwise, the Carte Orange is invalid and you could face a heavy fine.

You will be supplied with a small holder for the coupon and the carte, and you can ask for a free Métro map at the same time to insert into the back of the holder. Always remember to take back your ticket once you have passed through the Métro or RER barriers. Never put your ticket into the punching machines on buses, but do show the pass to the driver.

4. The **carte hebdomadaire** is used in the same way as the Carte Orange, and is valid for one week from Monday to Sunday. For zones 1 and 2, the cost is 85FF/week, and for zones 1 to 3 it is 113FF.

5. The **carte mobilis** is a one-day travelcard, which can be adapted to cover certain zones and not others. For zones 1 and 2 the cost is 32FF/day, and for zones 1 to 3 the cost is 42FF. This ticket should be validated (**composté**). The **ticket jeune** for travellers under 26 is a weekend travelcard for Saturday and Sunday, and public holidays. The cost for zones 1 and 2 is 20FF/ticket.

There are a number of other passes available for tourists each year which give unlimited travel for a period of days. Ask about these at any Métro stations, or at your hotel or welcome centre. Of particular note is the latest offer from the RATP, '**Paris Visite**' which offers one-day or short visit travelcards (two, three or five days) covering all public transport in Paris described in this section and in addition offers a 'cheque-book' of 14 money-saving offers for entry to museums and Disneyland Paris and also a free cinema entry at the Grand Rex cinema. For more details telephone 0836 38 77 14 or see the special website www.parisvisite.tm.fr

The Carte Intégrale and Carte Imagine 'R' are reimbursed by

almost all employers at 50%. Most employers will require you to hand over your monthly tickets at the end of their validity as proof of purchase and use. Families with three or more children are entitled to reduced-rate travel by requesting a **Carte Famille Nombreuse**. Ask at Métro stations for details.

TRAVELLING TO AND FROM THE AIRPORTS

If you use public transport to travel to either Orly or Roissy, you must either have the travel pass covering the correct number of zones (1 to 4 for Orly, 1 to 5 for Roissy), or buy the necessary ticket(s). RER Ligne C goes to Orly, and RER Ligne B goes to Charles-de-Gaulle-Roissy. The Orlyval train is not included in any travel pass, and the cost from Paris to Orly is 57FF.

Buses to the airports run from the following places:

- The RATP Roissybus (same rules for travel passes as for the RER) from rue Scribe beside the Opéra-Garnier. A single ticket costs 48FF.

- Air France buses from Place de l'Étoile (beside the Arc de Triomphe), and Porte Maillot (beside the Palais des Congrès) also serve Roissy. Tickets are purchased on the bus, and prices are comparable to the Roissybus.

- The RATP Orlybus leaves from Denfert-Rochereau Métro in southern Paris. The same rules apply as for the Roissybus. The cost of a one-way ticket is 35FF.

Air France also operates buses to Orly leaving from Invalides Métro in central Paris. The RER also leaves from this station for Orly.

TAKING THE TRAM IN PARIS

One of the universally popular themes of the Paris municipal elections in 2001 was the redevelopment of the Paris tramway (streetcar) service. At the moment two small inter-suburban lines link northern and western Paris. But with successful tramway developments in several major French cities already achieved, ecologically minded Parisians are calling for the return of an extensive tramway system to Paris. Obviously this will take quite some time to achieve if it is finally launched as a project, but the plan is to run a ring around Paris parallel to the périphérique. In many respects this is 'old lamps for new', as not only was Paris well-endowed with trams in the past, but it also had a railway ring known as **la petite ceinture** which emerges here and there in grassy disarray in the outer arrondissements. The first Parisian trams are planned for the outer reaches of the 14th, 15th and 20th arrondissements in 2005 to 2006.

AVOIDING PROBLEMS IN PUBLIC TRANSPORT

1. Travel passes must be shown with the accompanying coupon (e.g. orange), with your photo and name. The number on your coupon should be written on the appropriate line on the pass. Failure to do so can lead to a heavy on-the-spot fine of up to 200FF.

2. Cartes Oranges can be purchased from the 20th day of the month, valid for the following month. Avoid long delays by buying your ticket in advance of the first of the month.

3. Travel passes are personal and not transferable. Avoid aiding passengers without their tickets or passes to enter or leave stations. Ticket controllers (sometimes accompanied by the police) often wait discreetly around the corner from ticket barriers. Aiding other people to enter or leave the system illegally can lead to you being fined also.

4. Do not put Cartes Oranges, Intégrales, or Imagine 'R' into the validating machines on buses. Otherwise they become invalid!

5. Certain stations are more dangerous than others. Take great care at all the major train stations, and especially Gare du Nord and Gare de l'Est; Châtelet-les-Halles and Montparnasse on the RER, especially in the long corridors; Métro ligne 4 from Strasbourg-St-Denis to the end of the line, Porte de Clignancourt; Pigalle to Porte de la Chapelle; Place de Clichy to the northern ends of ligne 13 and to Nation on ligne 2; and République. These stations should be used with caution after night-fall.

6. Many stations have lifts, including some of the key tourist spots at Montmartre. Take care at these stations. The lifts are

probably preferable to taking the stairs, even if you feel threatened, as the journey time is much shorter.

7. You can be attacked anywhere on the system, and pick-pocketing is rife in the Métro and RER. Always be vigilant, even in 'safe' areas like the 7th arrondissement.

8. **NEVER** leave your baggage unattended or ask a stranger to guard it for you, even for a moment. This rule especially applies at the main train stations, and certainly Gare du Nord and Gare de l'Est.

9. RER trains are often double-decker. There is plenty of room to move around within trains if you feel threatened. On buses, if for any reason you feel unsafe, stay near the front and the driver.

10. There are alarm buttons on the platforms of all Métro stations and RERs and in many corridors, and within the trains themselves. These have direct links to the ticket offices at stations, and to the train driver.

11. Most central Paris stations have France Telecom card phones on their platforms and at their exits. These can be operated using ordinary French phone cards, and calls to the emergency services are of course free.

12. The RATP have introduced their own uniformed police force, complete with guard-dogs. You will also see many police and uniformed soldiers with rifles in central Paris stations. The police and military presences are part of the *Vigipirate* anti-terrorist campaign, but also have successfully reduced crime in the underground system.

13. Unlucky 13 sometimes turns out to be a winner . . . The RATP Lost Property Office (**Bureau des Objets Trouvés**) is to be found at the Police Station at 36, rue des Morillons, 75015. Tel. 01 40 30 52 00 (M°Convention), next to the Parc Georges Brassens. The office is open 08h30-17h00 Monday and Wednesday; 08h30-20h00 Tuesday and Thursday (except in July and August when the hours change to 08h00-17h00); 08h30-17h30 on Fridays; and closed on weekends and bank holidays.

'What are they talking about?'

Phrases you will often hear announced over the Métro loud-speakers include:

- '*Les pick-pockets sont susceptibles d'agir dans cette station. Veuillez veillir à vos affaires personnelles.*' – 'Pickpockets are at large in this station. Take care of your personal belongings.'

- '*Suite à un mouvement social, le service est très perturbé/interrompu sur la ligne 1 entre Étoile et Bastille/sur toute la ligne.*' – 'As a result of strike action, the service is very disrupted/has ceased on Line 1 between Étoile and Bastille/on the whole line.'

- '*Suite à un incident voyageur à St-Germain-des-Prés, le service est momentanément suspendu entre . . .*' – 'Following an incident involving a passenger at St-Germain-des-Prés, the service is temporarily suspended.' This phrase is used to cover anything from drunks on the tracks, to brawls, to suicides.

- '*Suite à une manifestation, les stations Franklin Roosevelt, Champs-Élysées-Clemenceau, et Alma-Marceau sont fermées au public. Les correspondances sont assurées.*' – 'As a result of a public demonstration, Franklin Roosevelt, Champs-Elysées Clemenceau, and Alma-Marceau stations are closed to the public (i.e. no entries or exits). You can still change lines and trains here if you are already in the underground.'

TAKING TAXIS IN PARIS

In Paris, like everywhere else in the world, taxis are harder to find in the rush hour or bad weather. You can normally find a taxi by simply hailing one down on a busy main street, or by going to a **stationnement de taxi** (taxi rank). You will often find taxis waiting for fares outside nightclubs, well-known hotels or theatres.

In Paris, when the sign on top of the cab is not lit up, the taxi is occupied. When it is lit, the taxi is for hire. If you have ordered the taxi, the meter will be running when the taxi arrives, as you pay for the service from the moment the driver has accepted the call to collect you. Make sure if you catch a taxi in the street that the previous fare has been cleared from the meter. Day and night rates should be displayed, and many taxi drivers have standard rates for a trip to the airports near Paris. Tipping is generally 10%.

Fially, bear in mind that all taxis will take three passengers, but very few will accept four passengers without prior request by telephone. Extra charges are made for large amounts of luggage, including perhaps the 'excess baggage' of a fourth passenger, if you do manage to squeeze them in!

DRIVING IN PARIS

Without a doubt the Place de l'Étoile with its centre-piece, the Arc de Triomphe, is the most notorious symbol of one of the world's best-known bad habits, and one which probably ranks in the top three bad habits that the French admit to about themselves – Parisian driving. Bad-tempered; bad-mannered; always right; always trying to force their way through; always arguing; convinced that pedestrian crossings are to be used for 'target practice'; driving through inconvenient red lights; always blocking each other in parking spaces; driving along the pavements in circumstances which suit; constantly blasting the car horn . . . if you really feel the need to join this circus, probably the first piece of advice I should give you is to find a good psychiatrist.

Your number-plates will determine not just the reaction but the variety of insult you receive: only those ending in 75, the departmental code of Paris, will escape abuse within the city. But then again, when you drive out to the suburbs and *provinces*, where manners are generally more courteous, drivers give way, and quaint customs such as stopping at pedestrian crossings are still observed, you might have a hard time with one or two locals who have scores to settle over ancient Parisian traffic battle-scars.

Parking in Paris is *spécial* in the French sense of the word. Many people would say that the best advice would be to bring along a can-opener to manoeuvre yourself in and out of the available slots, or to escape from the mess somebody else has made of your neat parking. A resident's parking permit (**vignette de stationnement résidentiel**) can be obtained from your local town hall, which gives you the right to preferential parking rates and access. If you receive a parking fine, you need to buy the appropriate fiscal stamp (**timbre fiscal**) at a tobacconist's, affix the stamp and send the payment. Failure to do so in the specified time limit will lead to an increased fine. If your car is towed away, you will need to make enquiries at the nearest commissariat to find out which car pound is holding your car, and you may well have to pay costs as well as a fine.

Driving papers

You must always carry your driving licence when driving, as well as the original registration document and the car insurance documents. You must be at least 18 years old to drive in France.

Although the annual car tax (**vignette**) has been abolished for individuals, if you have a company car and that car is hired, all the documents for the car will be in the name of the car lease company and your employer. In this case, the car should display the valid vignette for the calendar year. This can normally be arranged through either your employer or the car company. If you are stopped and your papers are checked, you could be fined for not displaying the vignette, assuming that you, your employer or their car supplier have purchased it!

British drivers in France

Officially, it is no longer necessary to exchange a British driving licence (**permis de conduire**) for a French licence if you are resident in France. However, the delay between the announcement of this decision and its application has created an unclear situation. Check with your local *préfecture* when you arrive to see if you need to exchange your licence, as the official decree appears to be being 'progressively implemented'. Under the old regulations, a British licence had to be exchanged within one year of arrival.

Applications for international driver's licences (valid for three years), if necessary, should be made at your local *préfecture*. You should note, however, that international licences are not valid in the bearer's country of residence. British citizens visiting France can drive with a UK driving licence.

American drivers in France

US visitors who stay in France less than 90 days can drive in France with a valid US licence although it is advisable to carry a translation of their licence. Residents (who have either a *carte de séjour* or *carte de résident*) can drive in France for up to one year from the start date of their residence permit. In this case either a 'sworn' translation or an international driver's licence is also obligatory. American students may drive with an American licence throughout the duration of their studies.

Ten American states have official agreements with France allowing holders of state licences to exchange their licences for French licences. These are: Colorado, Connecticut, Florida, Illinois, Kansas, Kentucky, Michigan, New Hampshire, Pennsylvania and South Carolina. You have up to one year to exchange your American licence for a French **permis de conduire**. In practice, you should allow up to three months to exchange licences. The whole process takes place at the Préfecture de Police on Ile de la Cité (M°CiteC.) and needs to be completed before the end of the first year of residence.

You need to obtain and complete the necessary form from the Préfecture; provide your US driver's licence with a notarised translation into French; a proof of your current address (rental agreement or EDF or France Telecom bill); a photocopy of both sides of your *carte de séjour*; and two passport size photographs. Make sure you have originals and copies available of all of these documents.

If you hold a US licence from another state, you must take the two-part French driving test (part-written part-practical) after a series of lessons from a recognised French driving school which will allow you to fulfill the obligation to take the test in a dual-control car. Some concessions are made for the fact that your knowledge of French may be limited when you take the practical test, and a translator may be allowed to accompany you.

Replacing a lost licence
If you lose your licence or it is stolen, you must report it at the nearest police station to where the incident happened. They will give you a receipt valid for two months, which acts as a temporary licence. During that period go to your local *préfecture* and request a new licence. Take with you:

- the receipt of your declaration of loss or theft

- a piece of official identity

- the completed form requesting a duplicate licence

- a proof of residency (e.g. tenancy agreement, electricity bill, etc.)

- three passport size photos.

It can take three to six weeks to obtain your new licence. You will also have to pay the appropriate fee.

Lost or stolen US driving licences can only be replaced by the Department of Motor Vehicles in the driver's home state.

Importing a car

You can import a car for a period of up to six months in one year without completing customs formalities. A new or used car on which VAT (TVA in France) has already been paid in another EU country can be imported into France by a French resident free of French VAT.

Otherwise, VAT is payable *immediately* upon entry into France. You can pay at the point of importation or at your local tax office. You will then be issued with a customs certificate (*Certificat de Douane 846A*) permitting you to register the vehicle in France. The same form will also be required even if VAT has already been paid, to prove that this obligation has been met.

Tourists (anyone staying no more than 90 days) can bring a car or motorbike into France duty-free and retain their foreign number plates but must display a US driving disk beside the licence plates if from the USA. Cars brought in for more than three months need French licence plates, which requires registering the car.

US temporary residents who hold a *carte de séjour temporaire* are exempted from customs duties if they can show:

a) that they will stay in France less than one year
b) that they have a permanent residence outside France
c) that they have lived outside of France for at least one year
d) that they have owned the vehicle for at least six months.

Long-term residents are not entitled to exemption from customs duties on imported vehicles, and the car must carry French licence plates and be registered in France. You should also ensure the full payment of all duties on the vehicle in the country of export.

Registering a car in France

Registering an imported car
Imported vehicles must be registered in France within three months of entry. To do this, you must contact the local **Direction Régionale de l'Industrie, de la Recherche et de l'Environnement**

(DRIRE). After the local vehicle inspection centre (**Inspection des Mines**) has checked that your car meets French construction and use regulations, you will receive a certificate from DRIRE which will allow you to apply for the registration certificate (**Certificat d'Immatriculation** more normally known as a **carte grise**). This happens at the Préfecture, or the Préfecture de Police, or local mairie in Paris. They will provide a checklist of documents required, which are:

1. Proof of origin of the vehicle or copy of the certificate of sale.

2. The foreign registration document.

3. The customs certificate 846A (see above).

4. A manufacturer's certificate of construction. This is available from a local car dealer, the French importer, or the manufacturer. *Officially* it is no longer required, but it may be asked for. It can also be very expensive. The point of the document is to prove that the vehicle meets European safety standards.

5. A completed request for a registration card form (**Demande de Certificat d'Immatriculation d'un Véhicule**), available from the Préfecture, or the Préfecture de Police, or the local mairie in Paris. This document should be accompanied by your *carte de séjour*, passport and proof of residence.

6. A technical test certificate if your vehicle is more than four years old. All vintage vehicles and vehicles over four years old are subject to regular testing every two years.

Once you finally receive your car registration, new number plates must be installed within 48 hours. They can be made up and fitted at local garages for a small fee. The last two numbers of your new registration will refer always to the département in which the car is registered.

Registering a new car
You have 15 days in which to register a newly purchased car. You will need a new form to apply for a new **carte grise**, the certificate of sale, the technical certificate from the **Inspection des Mines**, a piece of official identity (e.g. *carte de séjour*) and a proof of residency less than three months old (e.g. electricity or telephone bill in your name).

Registering a second-hand car

Once again you have 15 days in which to register. Vehicles less than 10 years old cost the same to register as new vehicles; those which are more than 10 years old cost half as much to register. You will need ID and proof of residence (as above), and the **carte grise barrée** (old registration document of the car) supplied by the former owner.

Cars more than four years old must also have the necessary technical certificate dating from less than six months before the purchase. You also need a **certificat de situation administrative** supplied by the seller.

Moving home

Even if you stay in the same département, you must change the address on your *carte grise*. This is free, and can be done immediately at the local mairie or préfecture, by presenting a new proof of residence and your *carte grise*. If you fail to do this, you could face a fine of 600FF.

Replacing your carte grise

If you lose your *carte* or it is stolen, you must report it to the police. You will be issued with a temporary document which will allow you to use your car. It will also allow you to apply for a new *carte*. You will need an official piece of identity, a proof of residency, the receipt of your police statement of loss, the form requesting a duplicate *carte*, and the necessary technical certificate for vehicles more than four years old.

Selling your car

If you decide to sell your car once you have moved to France, you must supply the following documents to the buyers before the sale is complete and legal:

1. The **certificat de vente** – it is your responsibility to obtain this from the préfecture or sous-préfecture.

2. The **carte grise barrée** i.e. 'crossed-out'. You must write across the carte in indelible ink *'vendue le . . .'* (sold on . . .) and fill in the date. You must then sign the amended *carte*.

3. If the car is more than four years old, a technical certificate dated less than six months before the date of the sale proving that the car is roadworthy (see above).

4. A **certificat de situation administrative** To obtain this, go to your local préfecture with your *carte grise*. You will need to submit the registration number of the vehicle, the model, and the power of the engine. The certificate will show that there are no outstanding fines relating to the vehicle.

Within 15 days of the sale of the car, you must hand in the second copy of the *certificat de vente* at the préfecture at which it was previously registered. Restrictions apply on the sale of cars imported duty-free which are regulated by the French Customs Office.

Insurance

Fully comprehensive insurance is advisable to cover the costs of breakdown or accidents. Third-party motor insurance for unlimited liability is compulsory in France. You will need to shop around to find the best policies and prices. Third-party insurance is required for the import of cars whether they are occupied or not, and if you opt to take out a policy before arrival you must have proof ready for French Customs at the point of entry (land or sea). The Customs Offices themselves offer temporary insurance for up to 30 days at these same points of entry.

Fuel

Garages are placed at intervals of 24km along all motorways, and are to be found across the city centre. Many of the Parisian and suburban garages are self-service. '*Faites le plein, s'il vous plaît*' means 'Fill her up, please', if you do find yourself being served.

Leaded petrol is now sold only in one grade (**essence super**). Unleaded is sold in two grades: **essence sans plomb**, and **super sans plomb**. The minimum quantity that you can buy is five litres. Diesel (**gazole**) is cheaper and readily available.

France was the starting point of a European consumer fightback against rising fuel prices in 2000. A favourite tactic in any industrial French dispute in order to bring pressure on the government is to block access to petrol refineries, and if possible, Paris itself. The result is always panic buying, and long queues at the pumps. If trouble seems to be looming, then think ahead and try and keep a small reserve in your own parking lot if you have one.

Road rules

The most important thing you need to remember is that in France you drive on the right! Equally important is the fact that in built-up areas, you must give way to traffic coming from the right – the famous *priorité à droite* rule. In less built-up areas, traffic on main roads has priority over traffic from side roads. The exception to the rule of priority is at roundabouts. Traffic entering the roundabout has priority, EXCEPT when signs such as *Cédez le passage* (give way) or *Vous n'avez pas la priorité* are displayed.

Health and safety precautions

- Seat belts are obligatory in France, including in the rear of the car if they are installed. You can face an on-the-spot fine if you disobey this rule.

- Random tests are made for drink-driving in France, which is a major killer on the roads. The legal limit is now 80mg of alcohol per 100ml of blood – not much more than one glass of wine. You may face an on-the-spot fine, a court appearance, or a driving ban if you are found guilty. The best solution is not to drink alcohol at all when driving.

- Speed limits are reduced in bad weather. Generally on toll motorways (**autoroutes à péage**) the maximum speed is 130kph, and 110kph in bad weather. The minimum speed in the outside (overtaking) lane is 80kph during daylight on flat roads with good visibility. For dual carriageways and toll-free motorways, the limit is 110kph; for other 'departmental' roads the limit is 90kph; and for roads in built-up areas the limit is 50kph. The limit on ring-roads is 80kph.

- Cars made in the UK and Ireland must adjust their headlights in order not to dazzle on-coming traffic. Headlight converters made from pre-cut black masking tape must be fitted over the headlights. If another driver flashes his headlights at you it is to indicate that he has priority and that you should give way.

- If you break down, try to move the car to the side of the road and flash your hazard warning lights. The red warning triangle should be placed 30m behind your car (100m on motorways). Emergency phones (**postes d'appel d'urgence**) are at 4km intervals on main roads, and every 2km on motorways.

- If you have an accident, you should call the police immediately by dialling 17. The ambulance service will also be alerted if necessary. You and the other parties must complete and exchange an accident statement form (**constat à l'amiable**) and exchange insurance details. If possible, persuade witnesses (**témoins**) to remain and make statements.

Pollution controls

In recent years, pollution has become a major problem in Paris and other major cities. To combat this problem, regulations are enforced each year (or sometimes simply threatened), whereby you can only drive on alternate days. This depends on the last two numbers before the letters in a number plate. On one day, only even numbers (**pairs**) will be allowed to drive; the next day it will be the turn of the uneven numbers (**impairs**). Listen out for warnings on the TV and radio.

Also read carefully the following sections on cycling and roller-blading in Paris. The river banks of the Seine at street-level are reserved for cyclists and bladers on Sundays for most of the day, as are the quais Valmy and Jemmapes along the Canal St-Martin. This movement will certainly spread across Paris in the coming years.

OTHER FORMS OF TRANSPORT

Non-motorised forms of transport – bikes, roller-blades and 'scooters – have experienced a real rise in popularity since the near-general strike of 1995. In addition, the ecological benefits of these forms of transport, and their beneficial health aspects – counter-balanced by lung-fulls of good old Parisian exhaust fumes – have all led to a huge rise not only in use of these forms of transport, but in street planning to cope with the rise in popularity.

Cycling

Cycle lanes now run the length and breadth of the city with protective barriers to stop encroachments from motorised vehicles. Cross-country biking (VTT) is also a popular sport at weekends and on vacation. On Sundays, the banks of the Seine are reserved for bladers and cyclists, as are the banks of the Canal St-Martin running from République to the Porte de la Villette at the northern tip of Paris. The Bois de Boulogne and the Bois de Vincennes respectively to the west and the east of the city centre also provide plenty of good space for fans of open-air pedal-powered propulsion with regular weekend closings to four-wheel traffic.

If you have your own bike, you can take it on the RER lines A and B in the carriages marked with bike signs at weekends, and on weekdays from 09h00-16h30, and after 19h00 (i.e. not in rush-hour). Métro line 1 can also be used on Sundays up until 16h30, although Louvre-Rivoli and La Défense are not accessible. For more information call Maison Roue Libre (95bis, rue Rambuteau 75004) Tel. 01 53 46 43 77.

Roller-blading

Roller-blading is now recognised as an official form of transport, and draft legislation is before the French parliament to provide an official framework for bladers, resulting from Paris' unique position as the roller-blade capital of Europe. The number of French bladers is estimated at about 4 million.

Most Friday nights throughout the year, an enormous free rally of bladers (up to 22,000!) known as Friday Night Fever moves through Paris over variable courses of 20 to 25km (for experienced rollers only), leaving Place d'Italie at 22h00, and returning there at about 01h00. The whole event is under the official protection of the special cycle and roller-blade units of the Paris Police Force, and has become one of the major social events in Paris for bladers.

A Beginners Mega-Blade (**Rollers et Coquillages**) leaves from Boulevard Bourdon at Bastille every Sunday at about 14h00 (Tel. 01 44 54 07 44). These 'junior' events for the less-experienced also attract up to 10,000 people, and last about 3 to 4 hours. For more information check out the following website and its links: http://paris.roller.online.fr. The Paris Rollerblade Association (which has information in English) can also be contacted at Paris Roller, 62, rue Dulong, 75017 Paris. Tel. 01 43 36 89 81.

The latest craze of the **trottinette** as it is known in French, the push-pedal scooter can also be found across Paris at many of the same shops and websites as roller-blades. **Skate-boarding** is also still a popular past-time.

4

Looking at Health and Welfare

There used to be a joke amongst British expatriates that the standard remedy for any medical problem in France is to prescribe suppositories. This is not only untrue, but distracts from the reality that French healthcare is generally of a very high standard. Critics might retaliate, however, that this is because the French are a nation of hypochondriacs, which at times it is hard to dispute.

JOINING THE SOCIAL SECURITY SYSTEM

For British citizens, it is essential that you obtain copies of the Department of Social Security pamphlets 'Social Security Abroad' NI38, and 'Your social security insurance, benefits and health care rights in the European Community' SA29. Both of these comprehensive pamphlets are free from: Department of Social Security, Overseas Branch, Newcastle upon Tyne, NE98 1YX. Separate leaflets are available from the Northern Ireland Social Security Agency International Services at 24-42, Corporation Street, Belfast BT1 3DP.

If you are living and working in France, you are obliged to join the French **Sécurité Sociale**, covering pensions, sickness and healthcare, and unemployment. Generally, you will need certified copies of your birth and marriage certificates, as for your *carte de séjour*. Check with your employer and/or your local social security office.

The official telephone information line for the Paris Health Authority, the **Caisse Primaire d'Assurance Maladie de Paris (CPAM de Paris)** is 0810 75 33 75, and the website can be found at www.cpam-paris.fr. The site is in French only, and a little dense in comparison to some of the other official French sites, but it does contain plenty of useful links and hints for those who have a sufficient level of French.

- If you are in regular employment in France, you should automatically join the **Sécurité Sociale** through your employer. Both you and your employer must make regular contributions to ensure that you and your dependants are adequately covered. This rule applies to all foreigners who have obtained their *carte de séjour*, visa, etc.

- If for any reason the enrollment (**inscription**) to the **Sécu** (as it is generally known for short) is not organised by your employer, you should go to your local **caisse** (each arrondissement and commune has their own local branch). You will need to take with you a piece of official ID, a **relevé d'identité bancaire** also known as an **RIB** (bank account details, available from your bank) and your pay slips. These last documents are essential to show that your employer has been making the necessary contributions on your behalf to the Social Security service.

- If you are in paid employment in France, and are therefore enrolled in the French Social Security system, your spouse, partner (if they are totally dependent on you financially), your children under 16 years of age, or up to 20 years of age if they are studying, are all covered by your social security payments for standard medical treatment and reimbursement.

- If you are self-employed, you pay a percentage of your taxable income as your contribution which will then be deductable for Income Tax purposes. Self-employed workers are not covered in the same way as employed workers by the *Sécurité Sociale*. It is therefore important that you join the appropriate scheme as soon as possible after arriving in France. See Chapter 16 for further information.

- If you are a UK national sent to work in France for less than 12 months, you will normally remain insured under the UK National Insurance scheme. You or your employer should obtain the appropriate forms (E101 and E111) from the DSS Overseas Branch, Newcastle upon Tyne, NE98 1YX, before coming to France. These prove that you remain insured under the British system, and entitle you to emergency medical care.

- For those working as au pairs, your employer is obliged to make the necessary declaration and payments on your behalf to the Social Security administration service (URSSAF). This will provide you with basic rights and coverage.

- If you are unemployed and come to France to look for work, see Chapter 13 for further information.

- If you are a student and an EU citizen, you will need to obtain the form E111. See Chapter 5 for full details.

Introducing the *Carte Vitale*

The *Sécurité Sociale* is notoriously slow in issuing numbers, the card known as the **Carte Vitale**, and reimbursement. You may have to wait some time until you receive your card demonstrating your eligibility to use state services, and for reimbursement. Medical treatment will only be reimbursed after proof that you have worked 200 hours in the previous three months. This can include time worked in the UK. If so, form E104 available from the DSS in Newcastle upon Tyne will need to be completed and submitted by your French employer.

In 1999 the **Couverture Médicale Universale** guaranteed minimum health care to all 'stable' French residents. In parallel to this move, efforts have been made in recent years to reduce the paperwork involved in the reimbursement process by the introduction of the **Carte Vitale** which is now issued to all subscribers to the CPAM de Paris. Once your rights have been validated (i.e. you have joined the system), they remain valid throughout the time that you are a legal French resident. The end-date on your card will simply indicate when the card needs to be renewed and/or brought up to date.

However, if your card carries specific prescription exoneration rights, etc., then the end-date indicated will refer to the moment when your rights and needs in this respect will be reconsidered by the *Sécu*. If you lose this card or it is stolen, or for some reason you never receive it, you have to make a **déclaration sur l'honneur** in writing to your *caisse* in order to be issued with a new card.

*What is the **Carte Vitale** and how do you use it?*
The **Carte Vitale** is a personalised medical record on a credit-card sized 'chip' (**puce**), which allows doctors and other health service professionals to register their acts and details of your files on a central system. The plan is that in 2002 the brown **feuilles de soin** (see below) will disappear and reimbursement will become a paper-less process. However, you should not count on this

becoming an immediate reality. The cost and practical implications of depriving the French of two of their favourite hobbies – procuring medicines and medical treatment, and filling out forms – are proving colossal, and there is much resistance from health service professionals to the costs they themselves are facing in converting to the new system.

The *Carte Vitale* is now accepted by over 1500 doctors in Paris who are equipped with the necessary card readers, as well as hundreds of other health professionals and hospitals within the state-run sector. For all of these services, the card will send the required information through to a central data bank which will automatically register the need to reimburse you for the cost of the transaction, which you must still pay in full.

You should note that the *Carte Vitale* **is not a form of payment and you are still required to settle the full fee at the end of your appointment.** The difference is that you do not have to send the forms through the post to the *Sécurité Sociale*, so there is less paperwork and less chance of lost and unreimbursed claims.

Updating your Carte Vitale
You can make updates to the information on your *Carte Vitale*. Theoretically you can do this yourself but the lack of information and facilities available to do so mean that in practice you need to go to your *caisse* in order to make the changes. There are almost 150 sites in Paris (hospitals, local *caisses*, pension withdrawal centres and family support centres) which have computer terminals (**bornes**) which allow you to check the accuracy of the information on your card. They do not give access to medical records.

- If you move home, you may well move to a different local *caisse*. You will need to make contact with your new *caisse* to ask them to update your *carte* with your new address and perhaps also new bank details.

- If you acquire some form of exemption or medical assistance, this should be registered on your new card also.

- Children acquire their rights from their parents already in the system. New mothers need to present both a demand in writing for the *inscription* of their children, plus the birth certificate (**extrait d'acte de naissance**) and the *livret de famille* (see below), at their local caisse. All reimbursements concerning the children will then be made into the same bank account as for the mother or father (as you wish).

Working abroad for a fixed period

Medical records
If you inform the UK DSS Contributions Department that you are going to live or work abroad for a limited period (e.g. because you or your partner have been seconded), they will automatically inform the National Health Service Central Register. They will amend the Central Index of Patients which helps to determine funding for each Family Health Service Authority (FHSA).

The FHSA will in turn withdraw your medical records from your General Practitioner about nine months after your departure. Your records will either be held until you return or re-register with a new doctor, or until they are destroyed. Records are normally held for at least six years.

If you are going abroad for a limited period and plan to return to your current home area, it may be useful to inform your General Practitioner of both your departure and your anticipated return date. This will avoid your records being withdrawn unnecessarily.

Maintaining British social security rights
The DSS pamphlet NI38 explains in detail how to go about maintaining your British social security rights (if you have them) whilst working abroad. It is very important that you read this pamphlet and take advice based on the information which it provides. This can affect your eligibility for state benefits upon your return to the UK, and your pension rights later in life.

Voluntary contributions can also be made in some circumstances, but these will not automatically entitle you to French social security benefits. They will simply guarantee your right to apply for British benefits.

IMMUNISATION

Standard immunisations are always worthwhile, although there are no particular dangers associated with life in France. All vaccines are available on prescription in France from chemists' shops, and can be administered by qualified doctors. If you arrange immunisations yourself, you can ask your doctor to write you a prescription in order to obtain reimbursment from the *Sécurité Sociale*. However, you will generally have to pay a fee to the doctor, so it is best to ask him or her to write the prescription when they administer the immunisation.

GOING TO THE GENERAL PRACTITIONER

In France you are not limited to registering with one general practitioner in your area. You are free to consult as many doctors as you wish, as often as you wish, wherever you wish. The French frequently take advantage of this system to ask for second or even third opinions, but it is not really advisable unless you doubt the competence or approach of your doctor.

Sticking to one doctor allows him or her to get to know you and your problems better. The Government is now actively encouraging doctors and patients to build 'exclusive' relationships, to cut back on the amount of money spent reimbursing multiple doctors' appointment fees. Your chosen GP may also be designated as your **médecin-référent**, which means that he or she will coordinate all your medical cover and also prescribe generic medicines (see below). This system can also have certain financial advantages. To find out more, you need to contact your local *caisse*.

Each time you visit the doctor, you will be asked to pay a consultation fee (**honoraire**) currently of either 115FF or 140FF – the price depends on the system the doctor works within (see below). Make sure that the doctor completes and signs a brown **feuille de soin**, as you will need to reclaim this cost. The level at which you will be reimbursed for standard doctors' fees is currently 70% for doctors who are **conventionné**. Prices increase for home calls, night calls, Sundays and bank holidays. There are also small charges for medical acts such as cleaning and dressing a wound, administering injections, etc.

Over 1500 Parisian doctors from specialists to general practitioners are now accepting the **Carte Vitale**, which allows an automatic registration of your visit and activates a claim for reimbursement from the *Sécurité Sociale*.

GOING TO THE CHEMIST

At the chemist's shop (**pharmacie**), indicated by a green cross, hand over the prescription (**ordonnance**) and the **feuille de soin** to the pharmacist. Once your medicines have been prepared, you will be asked to pay in full. The pharmacist should enter the cost of the drugs on the reverse side of the **feuille de soin**, and also stick on the small labels (**vignettes**) from the medicine boxes. Without these labels, the cost of the drugs will not be reimbursed.

The level of reimbursement for medicines varies from nothing up to 100% if you have obtained an exemption certificate proving that the drugs are essential to your well-being.

The chemist may advertise and/or ask if you wish to operate the **tiers payant** system. This means that you only pay one third of the cost of the drugs which is nominally at your charge, with the balance being reimbursable via the *Sécurité Sociale*. Some chemists are already equipped for this system with *Carte Vitale* card readers. For the majority, for the time being, you will be required to send in the completed *feuille de soin* for the records of the *Sécurité Sociale*. This option is only open to salaried employees within the French social security system, and not to self-employed workers.

Finding the medicines that you need

Most medicines are available in France, but may be marketed under a different name to the one you know. It is very worthwhile checking this with your regular pharmacy, or even the drug company, before moving to France. Another good idea is to take the packaging listing the ingredients with you, so that the doctor can check this against a similar product in the 'Bible' he or she always consults before prescribing.

Over-the-counter drugs are available in more or less the same way as in the UK. Chemists will advise you as to cost and value of the products you require. Paracetamol and aspirin are both known under the same names.

In 1999 the Health Ministry introduced a 'right of substitution' allowing pharmacists to propose (but not impose) generic copies of the medicines prescribed. These medicines must contain all the same compounds and properties as the brand-named medicines marked on your prescription. If you accept these cheaper medicines (the average saving is 30%), then the actual medicine handed over the counter to you will be noted in writing on the original prescription beside the first-named medicine.

Parapharmacies
There are chains of 'parapharmacies' covering Paris and the suburbs. These pharmacies are not allowed to sell medicines or prescription drugs. However, they do offer a wide range of homeopathic products, skin creams, etc. Some chemists also maintain a parapharmaceutical department.

Weekend and evening pharmacies
The pharmacies at 84, ave des Champs-Élysées and at Place de Clichy are open 24 hours a day, seven days a week. Other pharmacies take it in turn to stay open on Sundays and bank holidays. Details of pharmacies open late and at weekends are normally displayed in pharmacy windows.

Obtaining exemption certificates
If you have a disability or disease which requires regular and/or expensive medication, you may be eligible for an exemption certificate (**pris en charge**). Normally this will cover 100% of all fees associated with treatment, including medicines.

You will need to speak to your general practitioner or hospital specialist to arrange this. It is not an easy process, and can take a long time. There is a list of 30 diseases recognised as automatically offering exemption, and the minimum length of period for treatment is now considered to be six months.

The availability of such help can also vary from area to area, according to the local health authority budget. You will certainly need thorough medical documentation, a recommendation from a French doctor, and will be summoned to 'demonstrate' your disability or disease by a local health authority doctor (**médecin conseil**). Exemptions are also sometimes granted for a limited period after an accident and during the convalescence period.

Renewals of exemption certificates are always undertaken as case-by-case studies. With the *Carte Vitale* system, you should theoretically be reviewed automatically; but it would be as well to keep a close eye on the end-date of your exemption, and to make sure that your doctors have sent all the necessary documentation to your local *caisse* and *médecin conseil* at least three months before the expiry date of your exemption period.

REIMBURSEMENT

Once you have a complete **feuille de soin**, fill in the personal details, including social security number and means of payment (direct debit or cheque), and send it to your local *caisse* where your file (*dossier*) is held. Keep a copy of each *feuille de soin* sent. After several weeks, you will be reimbursed if all the paperwork is in order, and will receive a statement of how much you have been reimbursed for each expense. When the *Carte Vitale* system is totally in place, this procedure will be automatic, but the end is not yet in sight.

The DSS form E111, available from British post offices, will provide British citizens with emergency healthcare cover for up to three months from the date of issue. However, the level of cover is limited to emergencies. Reimbursement can take place in either France or the UK. Private health insurance will provide a fuller cover for a visit of several months.

ADDITIONAL HEALTH INSURANCE

The remaining part of your expenditure on treatment or medicines can be reimbursed by joining a **mutuelle**, which is the standard French private health scheme. If you are in paid employment, you will almost always find that you are automatically included in such a scheme. Contributions are deducted each month along with regular social security contributions, and will be indicated on your pay-slip.

Almost every trade and profession has its own **mutuelle**, and it is very worthwhile belonging to such a scheme. Benefits can also include extra sick pay, a 'top up' to retirement pensions, and the ability to use private clinics. In principle, *mutuelles* will cover the remaining costs incurred. They will also cover some dental and eye-care costs.

Some *mutuelles* offer the possibility to link your reimbursements from the *Sécu* directly to the reimbursement system offered by your *mutuelle*. For further details of this kind of service, you will need to make enquiries with your own *mutuelle*.

Students are required by law to join one of the special student *mutuelles*. See Chapter 5 for further details.

HOSPITAL TREATMENT

Every large town has at least one **hôpital conventionné** which acts as the local general hospital, and includes the casualty unit (**urgences**). You have a free choice as to whether to enter a public hospital or a private clinic. However, there are certain differences as regards reimbursement for the cost of your healthcare.

Private hospital treatment will only be reimbursed by the *Sécurité Sociale* at the same rate as treatment in a *hôpital conventionné*. If you choose a private clinic, you will be given a form which must be validated by your local health authority centre, where your file is held. Once this has been validated, you hand this back to the clinic at your admission.

Your local *caisse d'assurance maladie* will settle the largest part of your hospital bill (80%) if you are in a public hospital. Remember that private clinics will charge more for their services, and that you will only be reimbursed on the basis of a stay in a public hospital. The outstanding 20% (or more for private treatment) is at your cost. If you need hospital treatment this is the moment that you will most appreciate financially the benefits of a **mutuelle**.

In all cases you will be asked to pay the **forfait journalier** (about 70FF), which is basically a 'board and lodging' fee. You will normally also be offered the chance to hire your own telephone, and sometimes also a TV. Rooms are normally shared, except for those cases which require isolation.

There are numerous situations where your entire medical bill (i.e. not just the usual 80%), except the *forfait journalier*, will be paid entirely for you by your local *caisse*. For instance:

- important surgery

- if you are in hospital more than 31 days

- delivery of a baby (for 12 days) – when you are not obliged to pay the *forfait journalier*

- if your admission is due to a work accident – once again, the forfait journalier is not charged

- if you are receiving invalidity payments or benefit due to a work accident

- if you are suffering from a serious illness which requires expensive medical care (as recognised by your local *caisse*).

You may also find that certain minor operations and clinical tests will take place during the course of one day, in which case you will be assigned a bed and admitted only for the day (**hôpital du jour**).

DENTAL CARE AND EYE CARE

The same rules apply for visits to the **dentiste** or the **opthalmologiste** (optician) as apply to visiting a general practitioner. The optician will simply provide the prescription for your glasses or contact lenses, and you must then go to one of the many specialist shops in order to choose your frames or lenses. Treatment by **conventionné** dentists is reimbursed at the same levels as doctors' fees in the same category.

POINTS TO REMEMBER

1. It is very important to check if the medical practitioners and services you use – doctor, dentist, optician, hospital, physiotherapist, etc. – are **conventionné**. There is nothing to stop you using private medicine, but you must be able to bear the cost.

2. About 20% of doctors are **non-conventionné**. Their fees are reimbursed much less by the **Sécurité Sociale** and **mutuelles**. Practitioners who are **coventionné à honoraires libres** charge variable prices. The *Sécurité Sociale* will reimburse at their *conventionné* fixed rate, and the *mutuelle* normally covers the rest of the cost. For instance, if your *non-conventionné* doctor or doctor *à honoraires libres* charges you 160FF for a consultation, the *Sécu* will reimburse 70% of 115FF, not 70% of 160FF.

3. Make sure that all practitioners complete a **feuille de soin** and return this to you after each consultation. also make sure that pharmacists similarly complete their part of the *feuille*, and attach the **vignettes** from the medicine boxes. Even where your *Carte Vitale* is accepted and used, you will still need to make a paper claim for reimbursement as confirmation of your request.

HEALTH IN THE WORKPLACE

The French commitment to healthcare includes the company doctor (**médecin de travail**). You will be expected to undergo a medical examination by this doctor, paid for by the firm:

- when you join the company
- regularly once a year thereafter
- after a prolonged absence due to illness
- after pregnancy leave.

You also have the right to ask to see this doctor on request, and you may also be obliged to see the doctor at the request of your company. These doctors also carry out 'spot-checks' on your working conditions.

Smoking in the office

In 1992 a new law banned smoking in public areas (e.g. cafés and restaurants) and in open work areas and shared offices, except in designated areas. Smoking is extremely popular in France, and this law is often brazenly flouted. In other companies, it is strictly applied. If you find yourself in a smoking environment and you object, you will need to speak to your company's human resource division first of all to try to reach an amicable resolution to the problem. If this has no effect, it may be appropriate to speak to your *médecin de travail*.

Sick leave and sick pay

Under French law, absence due to illness during the first year of your contract is not paid leave. Application of this law is, however, often at the discretion of the firm.

If you are obliged to take time off work due to illness, ask the doctor for a sick note (**arrêt de travail**). You should complete and sign this paper, and send one copy to your employer, two copies to the *Sécurité Sociale*, and keep one copy for yourself.

The note will specify the length of absence permitted, and will also designate the hours in which you may go out to buy provisions, etc. This is from 10h00-12h00 in the morning and from 16h00-18h00 in the afternoon. If you intend to recuperate from your sickness elsewhere than your home, then you must have the prior agreement of your local *caisse*. If you are admitted to a hospital, you must also include a copy of the **bulletin d'entrée** given to you when you are admitted. **You must send off this note to your employer and your** *caisse* **within 48 hours.**

Be warned – the *Sécurité Sociale* regularly undertake random investigations to see if you are obeying the terms of the note. If you are not there when the inspector calls, the *Sécurité Sociale* can and will refuse to reimburse the firm for part of your salary during your absence. You could also face disciplinary proceedings. You are obliged to provide all details regarding the place where you can be visited during your *arrêt de travail*. This includes providing entry codes to your building.

Your employer will continue to pay you during your absence, but will recover part of the cost from your *caisse d'assurance maladie*. Your entitlement depends upon having completed a certain number of hours of work. If your inability to work lasts less than six months, your eligibility will depend upon your having worked 200 hours in the last three months. If your inability is more serious and requires a longer period off work, eligibility for sick pay requires you to have worked at least 12 months, with at least 200 hours work in the last three months.

Accidents in the workplace

If you have an accident at work or travelling to work, you should inform your employer within 24 hours. You must then ensure that the following steps are taken:

- **By your employer** – your employer must declare the accident at your own *caisse* within 48 hours; give you a form certifying the accident, *réf.* 6201, which will exempt you from paying medical fees in advance; and send an *attestation de salaire* to your *caisse* if you are signed off work due to the accident.

- **By your doctor** – the doctor who treats you should issue a medical certificate (*réf.* 6909) indicating your state of health and the consequences of the accident; send sheets 1 and 2 within 24 hours to your local *caisse*, and give you sheets 3 and 4 of the declaration.

- **By you** – send sheet 4 (*certificat d'arrêt de travail*) to your employer; and take sheet 3 of the medical certificate to every subsequent doctor's appointment.

Sick pay is subject to income tax, and basically you will receive half your normal daily pay. Maternity pay or monies paid as a result of a work accident are not subject to income tax. Payments are made every 14 days.

FAMILY MATTERS

Pregnancy healthcare

If you are a British citizen and pregnant at the time of moving to France, you should speak to your doctor and local health authority to find out what steps you need to take to ensure your health and benefit entitlements. You may need to obtain the form E112. To apply for this, write to: The Department of Health International Relations, Room 512, Richmond House, 79 Whitehall, London SW1A 2NS.

You must declare your pregnancy before the end of the third month to your *caisse d'assurance maladie*, and to the *caisse d'allocations familiales* (family benefit centre). To do this you must hand in the **Premier examen médical parental** form duly signed by your doctor. You will receive a **carnet de maternité** which contains vouchers allowing you to receive the services to which you are entitled.

The services to which you are entitled free of charge are:

- pre-natal and post-natal examinations

- eight pre-natal sessions to help you prepare for the delivery

- 12 days of free hospital treatment in a **conventionné** hospital or clinic or one which is '**agré**' (approved)

- from the first day of the sixth month of pregnancy, re-imbursement by the *caisse* at 100% of all medical expenses whether related to the pregnancy or not (except certain types of drugs).

These rights are limited by the number of hours worked and the amount of money you or your husband or partner has paid over the preceeding months. You will have to pay as usual for all the services you receive, but will receive reimbursement at 100%. To do so you need to stick your vouchers to the *feuille de soin* each time that you send in a claim for reimbursement.

The current cost is 1000FF for a delivery by a midwife (**sage-femme**). Extra costs are incurred for a night-time delivery, and for Sundays and bank holidays. All these costs are reimbursed at 100%.

Maternity leave pay

Once again, the number of hours and level of contributions made is one of the deciding factors in whether you receive paid maternity leave. You must also have been enrolled in the *Sécurité Sociale* for at least ten months by the expected date of delivery of your baby.

To obtain maternity pay, you must send the **attestation de salaire** (salary certificate) signed by your employer to the *caisse d'assurance maladie* as soon as you begin your maternity leave. You must then send a similar form to the *caisse* at the end of your maternity leave. The pay is calculated on the basis of your salary for three months before you stopped work, and works out at 84% of your daily wage. At the end of your maternity leave, you must also send a certificate from your employer to your local *caisse* stating that you have returned to work.

If you are already receiving Maternity Allowance when you leave the UK, you may be able to persuade your British social security office to carry on providing that benefit.

Maternity leave

For a first or second child, the normal leave period is six weeks before delivery and ten weeks afterwards. From the third child onwards, it is eight weeks before delivery and eighteen weeks afterwards. For twins, it is 12 weeks before delivery and 22 weeks afterwards; and for triplets (or more!) it is 24 weeks before delivery and 22 weeks afterwards. In the case of premature delivery, the total leave period is not reduced. In cases of medical necessity, a doctor may prescribe an extra two weeks.

Registering the birth

You **MUST** register the birth of your new child **within three working days** – i.e. if your child is born on a Thursday, you have until the following Tuesday at the latest. Otherwise, you cannot register your child's birth without making an application to the courts. The registration should take place at the *mairie* of the place where your child was born, and the following documents are required:

- the **déclaration de naissance** completed by the hospital, doctor, or midwife (*sage-femme*)

- a piece of official identity (driving licence, *carte de séjour*) for the person registering the birth

- the mother's **carnet de maternité** (see above)

- the **livret de famille** if you have one (you will only have this if you were married in France)

- your passports (if you and your spouse have separate passports).

You should also register your child's birth at your own Embassy to ensure the nationality rights of the child for the future. Contact the consular services to find out how to do this.

Once you have registered the birth, you need to send a copy of the birth certificate (**extrait de certificat de naissance**) or the **livret de famille** to your local *caisse*. You should also add one of your 100% exemption vouchers. The *caisse* will send you a guide for medical 'surveillance' of your child up until his/her sixth birthday. You will also receive vouchers corresponding to the obligatory examinations which must be undertaken. These should be taken to the examining doctor on each occasion together with the **carnet de santé** (personal health note book) of the child.

Maintaining foreign citizenship rights

The information below is taken from the American Embassy in Paris and the Paris-based magazine *Living in France*, www.parisfranceguide.com. Regulations change frequently, and it is important that you check with your own embassy as to the requirements for the correct registration of the nationality status of your children.

US citizens

Registration is by appointment only at the American Embassy (01 43 12 46 71). You will need to request a registration pack which must be completed before the appointment and bring the originals or certified copies of the following documents, and also your child:

- French birth certificate, **extrait de l'acte de naissance intégral**.

- evidence of parent(s) US citizenship (e.g. passport, naturalisation certificate)

- Parents marriage certificate and **livret de famille** if the wedding took place in France

- if either of the parents has been previously married either the decree of dissolution or divorce, or the death certificate of the previous spouse

- two recent passport sized photographs of the child for his/her passport

- fees in cash or traveller's cheques – check the exact amount required when you make your appointment

If the child has only one parent with US citizenship, the parent must have lived in the US for at least five years, two of which over the age of 14.

Australian citizens
A child born in France with two Australian parents has automatic Australian citizenship. Registration should occur either at birth or upon demand of a passport. Children with only one Australian parent need to apply to the immigration department of the Australian Embassy.

British citizens
British parents are not obliged to register their new-born children at the Embassy. A child may have a British passport providing at least one parent is British, and both parents agree in writing. Remember that all British citizens of no matter what age are now required to have their own passport, and children may no longer be registered on their parents' passports.

Canadian citizens
Any child born with at least one parent who is a Canadian citizen is entitled to Canadian citizenship. Certificates of Canadian citizenship can be obtained at the Paris Embassy.

Support groups for English-speaking mothers
There are two principal support groups for English-speaking mothers in and around Paris:

1. MESSAGE (Tel. 01 42 37 28 37 or 01 48 04 74 61, e-mail: messageparis@wfi.fr) – a network of English-speaking mothers and future mothers in and around Paris offering meetings and activities for mothers and children, specialising in early parenting.

2. The Junior Service League of Paris (JSLP) (Tel. 01 52 23 84 00) – a wide-ranging women's social welfare network and group including health and child welfare and training courses for child-minders.

Child benefit and family allowance

The current levels of family allowance are 679FF per month for two children, 1548FF for three children, 2418FF for four children, and 870FF per child for five or more children. The amount is increased for children over 10 years old by 191FF, and by 339FF for children over 15 years old. To apply for these benefits, you need to register at your local **Centre d'Allocations Familiales (CAF)**. Details of state assistance to which you may be entitled as a French resident can be found on the CAF website www.caf.fr (Tel. 08210 010 010). The *Mairie de Paris* also runs an information line on family benefits, family/work conflicts, etc. – **Allô Social**: Tel. 01 40 27 98 00

In January 1998, the Socialist government provoked outrage by introducing means testing for **allocation familiale**. This takes into account the salaries of both parents if they are working. Further details are available from your local centre.

A number of other benefits are available from the CAF under certain conditions for parents who are forced to give up work to look after children:

- **L'allocation de présence parentale** – Valid initially for four months and for up to a total of one year, available to parents to care for sick, handicapped or disabled children.

- **L'allocation parentale d'éducation** – Valid if you have given up your employment to look after your child up to the age of three years.

- **L'AFEAMA (aide à la famille pour l'emploi d'une assistante maternelle agréée)** – The level of aid offered depends on the total family income. The level of support is reduced from the age of three years, when the child could enter state school.

One parent benefit and child benefit from the British authorities normally cease if you move abroad permanently. However, if you or your child stay in the UK, you can receive these benefits. Any UK insurance contributions you have paid *may* help in persuading the French authorities to pay you the French *allocations*. More information is available from:

- The Child Benefit Centre, Washington, Newcastle upon Tyne, NE88 1BR

- The Family Credit Unit, Customer Service Manager, Room A106B, Government Buildings, Warbreck House, Blackpool FY2 0YF.

SEXUALLY TRANSMITTED DISEASE

Your nearest hospital will be able to put you in touch with services and clinics for sexually transmitted disease. Information in English on HIV and AIDS related issues is available from FACTS (see Figure 2 at the end of this chapter). For free AIDS information ring the SIDA Info Service on 0800 840 800 (24 hours a day, seven days a week).

HELP WITH DISABILITY

There are numerous support groups in France to help disabled or handicapped people and those who care for them. Your doctor should be able to direct you towards the appropriate association. You should also apply to the **Bureau de l'Aide Sociale** of your local *mairie* for a disabled person's card which will entitle you to certain discounts and assistance.

If you are receiving Severe Disablement Allowance in the UK and you want to go to France, you must contact The Pensions & Overseas Benefits Directorate, Department of Social Security, Tyneview Park, Whitley Road, Benton, Newcastle upon Tyne NE98 1BA. The decision as to whether you continue to receive this allowance will depend upon your age, how disabled you are and how long you have lived in the UK.

If you are receiving any form of disability/working allowance or carer's allowance, and you move to France, you will not be able to continue receiving British support. Visiting France may also affect your UK allowance. Contact your local benefits authority to see what help they can offer in transferring your rights gained by British National Insurance contributions to the appropriate French authorities.

The Paris branch of the British association Toc H organises regular meetings for elderly residents (Tel. 01 48 76 45 86). The American Aid Society (Tel. 01 43 12 48 07) also helps elderly, sick and disabled American residents.

Other services of interest for those with disabilities who are living in France include the following:

- **The English Language Library for the Blind** (35, rue Lemercier, 75017 Paris. Tel. 01 42 93 47 57, Tuesday-Thursday (09h00-17h00) supplies a wide variety of recorded books on cassette in return for an annual subscription.

- France Telecom provide a range of products called '**Arc-en-Ciel**' (rainbow) which are designed to facilitate communication for the disabled. These include telephones with flashing lights, and a system known as the **boîtier dialogue** which allows communication via Minitel for the hard-of-hearing or speech-impaired at an increased speed. Ask at France Telecom agencies for details.

- The RATP provides details of RER and Métro stations and bus lines with easy access for passengers with disabilities. More details can be found on their website www.ratp.fr.

- The French national railways service, SNCF, offer a variety of travel discounts and arrangements for disabled travellers. These include first class travel at second class prices. In some cases the accompanying person will be entitled to travel free. To qualify for these advantages, apply at the *bureau de l'aide sociale* of your local *mairie* for the appropriate card. Similar offers may be offered by other travel companies, so do check.

- FAVA (Tel. 01 42 45 17 91) is the Franco-American Volunteers Association for the mentally disabled, providing programmes for children and adults.

SERVICES FOR ENGLISH-SPEAKING PATIENTS

Many French doctors do speak some English. But unless you are reasonably fluent in French and familiar with medical terms, you

SAMU (ambulance service)	15
Police	17
Sapeurs-Pompiers (fire brigade and ambulance service)	18
(Pay services)	
SOS Doctors in Paris in Dept. 78	01 47 07 77 77
SOS Doctors in suburbs in Dept. 78	01 39 58 58 58
SOS Doctors in suburbs in Dept. 92	01 46 03 77 44
Free drug information service	0800 23 13 13
Free child-abuse helpline	0800 05 41 41
Free helpline for the homeless	0800 306 306
Free AIDS information service in French	0800 840 840
SOS Help. English-language telephone crisis line. Every day 15h00-23h00.	01 47 23 80 80
FACTS Helpline. English-language helpline for AIDS and HIV information and support groups. Monday, Wednesday and Friday 18h00-22h00.	01 44 93 16 69

Fig. 2.   Emergency telephone numbers in France.

could experience difficulties, especially if the illness or problem is serious. Help can be found at the following places:

- English-language consulates have lists of English-speaking doctors.

- Private health insurance companies and travellers' associations (e.g. American Express, Automobile Association) often have help-packs they can provide to their customers before they leave their home country.

- The American Hospital in Paris, 63, boulevard Victor-Hugo, 92202 Neuilly-sur-Seine Cedex. Tel. 01 46 41 25 25. Emergency Service number 01 47 47 70 15, Patient Access Department 01 46 41 27 27. The prices at the American Hospital in Paris make it as exclusive as the area it is to be found in. It may be accessible to you via your *mutuelle*, but otherwise do not count on receiving much reimbursement from the *Sécu* for access to this hospital.

- The Hertford-British Hospital in Paris, 3, rue Barbé, 92300 Levallois-Perret. Tel. 01 46 39 22 26 or 01 46 39 22 22 for emergencies, Fax 01 46 39 22 26. A full range of treatment available in a small modern hospital within the French social security system with English and English-speaking staff. Strong maternity unit but many other services also.

- The Paris English-language group of Alcoholics Anonymous can be contacted on Tel. 01 46 34 59 65.

- A cancer support group is based at the American Hospital and can be contacted on Tel. 01 46 41 25 25.

- FACTS is the English-language support group for people who are HIV-positive and people with AIDS. Tel. 01 44 93 16 32.

- SPRINT (Tel. 02 33 21 48 16 or 01 34 86 93 41) is an association of English-speaking therapists for children with special needs.

5

Enrolling for Education

The French state educational system is in an on-going period of reflection and potential change at the time of writing. Generally academic levels are very high, and teachers and pupils alike are expected to show a serious commitment to their work. The current Education Minister, Jack Lang, is seeking to convince the militant teachers unions that change is required in the schools sector, with more emphasis on arts and modern languages rather than the traditional French school subjects.

Crisis over educational funding are affecting certain regions of France faster than they can be resolved, and strikes – by teachers, students and even pupils – are quite common. Education was one of the major priorities to emerge from the Paris mayoral campaign in 2000/2001, and the city council is now spear-heading a renovation plan for the more dilapidated schools, as well as seeking to open new schools to meet Parisian needs. For students in Paris, the most pressing need is to re-house the dispossessed students of the Jussieu site, which will be partially achieved when the building works in the 13th arrondissement are completed in the next couple of years.

THE ACADEMIC YEAR

France very much beats to the rhythm of the academic year. This begins in mid-September with **la rentrée scolaire**, and ends in late June. A mid-term break occurs around All Saints Day (**Toussaint**) at the beginning of November, followed by a two week break for Christmas and New Year.

There is then another mid-term break in February, and two weeks for Easter holidays (not necessarily linked to the date of Easter itself). Holiday dates vary from region to region.

THE SCHOOL DAY

In state schools, children attend school from 08h30 to 11h30, and then from 13h30 to 16h30 from Monday to Saturday, with Wednesday and Saturday afternoons free. Variations occur according to the level of education of your child: Wednesdays are completely free for smaller children, whilst Saturday mornings and Wednesdays are obligatory for older children at **lycée**. Some private schools have adopted the more simple five-day week, as have some experimental **collèges**.

ELEMENTARY EDUCATION (age 2 to 6)

School is not compulsory in France for children until they are six years old. Nonetheless, 93% of three-year-old children in France are enrolled in the voluntary **écoles maternelles**. The current Schools Minister, Ségolène Royal, wants to introduce education for two year olds.

Enrolling your child

Enrolment takes place at your local *mairie*, at the published dates (normally around March), and can be performed as soon as the child reaches the age of two years. At enrolment, you will be informed of the school catchment area you fall into. It is possible to choose another school if you wish by following a typically long procedure. Documents needed to enrol your child are:

- the **livret de famille** (if you were married in France) or a **fiche d'état civil** of the child

- a proof of residence (**justificatif de domicile**) e.g. electricity bill with your name on

- the **carnet de santé** of your child, proving s/he has received all necessary relevant vaccinations.

Once you have received the enrolment certificate (**certificat d' inscription**) from the *mairie*, you need to make an appointment straight away with your school director. Children are accepted on a 'first come, first served' basis, with priority for older children. Schooling for children under three years old depends on the availability of places.

The classes offered in the **école maternelle** are roughly equivalent to early learning in the UK for French Year One; the UK Reception Class in Year Two; and the UK Year One in the French Year Three (for five- to six-year-old children). For US children classes equate to nursery schools for French Years 1 and 2, and Kindergarten for French Year Three.

PRIMARY EDUCATION (age 6 to 11)

When your child begins their compulsory education at the age of six, they will enter into the **11ème classe**. Your child then moves through classes in descending numerical order, finishing in the **Première Classe** and then **Terminale** (equivalent to Upper Sixth in the UK and 12th Grade in the USA) at the age of 18, when they will normally take the **baccalauréat** examination, which is equivalent to A-levels.

If your child is already enrolled at an **école maternelle**, s/he will automatically be enrolled at your local school. Enrolments must take place no later than the June preceding your child's entry into the school at the **école élémentaire**. For popular schools, the sooner you apply the better your chances are. The same processes must be gone through if you wish to choose a school in a different sector. If your child is not already enrolled, you must follow the process outlined above.

In the **écoles élémentaires**, (for 6- to 11-year-olds) the course of study may change according to the area you live in. Children are taught to read and write, along with basic maths and a few less academic subjects. As they grow older, they are rigorously taught the grammatic rules of the French language, including spelling and the use of tenses.

A great deal of time is spent learning poetry, which is considered good practice for the child's memory. 'Sciences of observation' will take up about an hour a week depending on the teacher. Most schools now spend a few hours a week on English, arts and crafts, an extra sport, and a computer class. A lot depends on the human and other resources available in a school as to what is offered. A current government project encourages the use of the Internet in schools and teaching.

Physical education (PE) usually includes two hours per week of general fitness classes, and at some time or other, all schoolchildren learn how to swim.

SECONDARY EDUCATION (age 11 to 15)

From the **6ème** to the **3ème** (11- to 15-year-olds), your children will attend a **collège**. Similar procedures exist for enrolling your child in a *collège* as for other state schools. If you choose a *collège* outside of your district, your choice requires further justification than at earlier stages. Acceptance depends upon, amongst other factors, the availability of places in the *collège* chosen.

At *collège*, pupils have a different teacher for each subject, and classes generally last about 50 minutes. Maths and French are still the most important subjects, and are really still considered as the keys to a child's success. History and geography are taught as one subject, and physics and natural sciences are each attributed equal importance.

When a pupil enters *collège* in the **6ème**, s/he chooses a foreign language to study – usually English or German. In the **4ème** there is the choice of an optional course, usually Latin or Greek. Other subjects include crafts, hand drawing, music and PE.

Repeating a year
When a pupil reaches the end of an academic year when they change from one cycle to another – at the end of the **6ème** or **3ème** – the **conseil de classe** ('class board') composed of the teachers concerned decides if the pupil is ready to move on to the next class. If they think not, then they can recommend the pupil to repeat a year (known as **redoublement**).

If you disagree with the decision, you must act swiftly to lodge your complaint (within three days). You will need to see the school director to request an explanation for the decision. However, if you are still not in agreement with the decision, you can force the issue to another 'commission' including other parents, at which you will be allowed to speak briefly. However, the decision here is final once it is taken.

Planning for the future
In February of the 3ème, families are requested to fill in a form indicating the proposed career orientation they wish their child to take. Final applications and decisions are taken in May of the **3ème**, with input from the school. At the end of the **3ème** (aged 14 to 15), pupils take a 'global' examination known as the **brevet**.

The results of this examination, together with the annual report, are used to decide upon the future education of the pupil.

However, it is not an entry examination to *lycée*, but simply a knowledge test for the end of this section of the child's education.

The choices made at this stage affect the type of *lycée* to which your child will next progress, and the sort of qualifications they will leave school with. The choice of *lycées* are:

- **générale et technologique**

- **professionnelle.**

The final decision is taken by a small commission, which informs parents at about the end of June which kind of *lycée* their child has been recommended for. More than 25% of pupils currently choose to orientate themselves towards professional life by opting for either a **brevet d'études professionnelles (BEP)** or a **certificat d'aptitude professionnelle (CAP)**, both of which are two-year courses at *lycées professionnelles*. Normally this will lead to an entry into working life almost immediately after leaving school.

THE FINAL SCHOOL YEARS (age 15 to 18)

The final school years are **Seconde, Première and Terminale**. The latter is when the final **baccalauréat (bac)** examination is taken. For these final years, your child will be educated at a **lycée**. It is here that final choices will be taken which affect the kind of **bac** for which your child will prepare, and consequently, the kind of higher education they will normally continue with.

Seconde

More than 60% of pupils currently enter the *Seconde* in the general/technology classes. This leaves scope for taking final decisions over which type of **bac** to study for. Only those seeking careers in music or dance, or a technical qualification (**Brevet de Technologie BT**) have specifically orientated courses. Those preparing either the BEP or CAP (see above) can study a further two years to take a **bac professionnel** before finishing their studies.

Première and Terminale

The choice must now be made which of the variety of **bacs** your child will study for. The general **bac** leaves the option open for entry into higher education. Other choices will be required if the pupil wishes to pursue a vocational course at university. The courses attended in these final years will depend on the option chosen. There are seven compulsory subjects, plus PE and two optional subjects.

At the end of the **Première**, there are written and oral French tests for **bac** candidates. The marks from these are included in the overall success or failure of the candidate. The final examinations are taken in the summer of the **Terminale**, and results are published very shortly afterwards in the end of June or beginning of July.

For those who fail the first time, it is possible to re-take the **bac**. As it is the key to any form of success in France, as well as entry to higher education, it is highly advisable to do so!

EDUCATION IN ENGLISH

The opportunity for a child to be educated at a French school can be excellent for their future prospects, ensuring that they will be bilingual in the future. However, it may also prove frightening and daunting for a child whose command of French is not sufficient. You must also consider the effect upon their education if you will only be living in France short-term, and will be returning to your native country and education system.

The options open to you are:

1. Boarding school in the UK or the US – this may not even be an option, depending upon your financial situation, your company's willingness to pay fees, and your and your child's attitude to boarding school.

2. Private international schools in France – the same financial criteria may affect your decision, as may accessibility to any such schools.

3. French schools with international sections – these are schools within the state system which normally charge a small fee for schooling in English. These schools work towards the *Option Internationale* of the **bac**, and teaching is by native English speakers.

4. French schools that offer high-level English programmes – extra-hours of education in English from native English speakers.

5. French schools with European sections – these will normally offer some extra education in English, but not necessarily given by a native English speaker.

The American School of Paris (Tel. 01 41 12 82 82, Fax 01 41 06 23 90, www.asparis.org) and British Schools of Paris (Tel. 01 34 80 45 90, Fax 01 39 76 12 69, www.ecis.org/bsp), private schools in the suburbs, each respectively follow the national curricula of their 'home' countries. Bus services from central Paris stops transport pupils each day to the schools.

The international sections of **lycées** probably offer the best option for those who want their children to benefit from an Anglo-French education at a very reasonable cost. Currently there are about eight British sections in France, and about six American sections. The general rule (which varies between sections) is about four hours per week of English language and literature, and two hours a week of geography and history. The Lycée International at St Germain-en-Laye is considered to be the best *lycée* in this section (Tel. 01 34 51 62 64, Fax 01 34 51 39 36, e-mail: adm@lycee-international.net).

Within Paris itself, bilingual private education up to six years old is offered at the Montessori Schools (Tel. 01 45 55 13 27, Fax 01 45 51 25 12, www.montessori-paris.com based at the American Church on quai d'Orsay, the Lennen Bilingual school (up to 12 years old) in the 7th arrondissement (Tel. 01 47 05 66 55), the International School of Paris in the 16th arrondissement (from 3 to 18 years old) (Tel. 01 42 24 09 54, Fax 01 45 27 15 93, www.isparis.edu); and the École Active Bilingue, a group of schools for all ages to be found in the 8th and 16th arrondissements (Tel. 01 45 63 47 00, Fax 01 45 63 62 23, www.eab.fr).

The international option of the **bac** is very highly regarded, and roughly equivalent to S-Levels within the British education system. It is therefore a good option for those seeking university entry not only in France, but in other countries too.

More information about native English education in France is available from **The English-Language Schools Association France (ELSA-France)**, e-mail: AssociationSis@wanadoo.fr, website address: www.assoc.wanadoo.fr/association.sis. This website has full information on all schools in the Paris region offering English-language education in all categories (state, private, exclusively English speaking and part English speaking). ELSA has strong links with the Section Internationale at the Collège et Lycée de Sèvres, rue Lecoq, 92310 Sèvres (Tel. 01 45 23 96 35).

If you are a Franco-British family in which English is not the principal language, but you want your children to remain bilingual, the British Council in de rue Constantine (next to Les Invalides) operates an English Young Learners Centre with 1,000 students aged from 5 to 18 (www.britcoun.org/france).

EDUCATIONAL BENEFITS

- **L'aide à la scolarité** This is available for children at *collège*. It is means tested, and limited to those who are already receiving another form of family or housing benefit, or benefit for a disabled adult.

- **L'allocation de la rentrée scolaire** This is available for children between 6 and 18 years old, under the same conditions as above. Each child will automatically be awarded the benefit. The limit of joint income permitted to obtain this benefit rises with the number of children that you have.

Both benefits are administered by the *caisse d'allocations familiales*.

HIGHER EDUCATION

Since 1987, France's student population has grown dramatically. However, there has been no similar growth in funding or facilities. Students tend to go to the university nearest to their homes, partly to keep down costs by continuing to live at home. Naturally Paris draws a huge student population of not only locals but 'foreigners' in all senses of the word, from other parts of France and from other parts of the world, drawn to the city's academically excellent institutions.

The only entrance requirement is normally a pass at *bac*. As a result, there is generally high competition to enrol on the course of your choice at the university of your choice. The university year runs from October until June.

The French degree structure

- **Years 1 and 2 – DEUG (Diplôme d'Études Universitaires Générales)** This is the core curriculum course which must be passed (and many fail) before continuing with further study.

- **Year 3 – Licence** This can be passed in most subjects. It is roughly equivalent to a BA or BSc.

- **Year 4 – Maîtrise** Roughly equivalent to an MA.

- **Year 5 – DEA (Diplôme d'Études Approfondies)** A preparatory year for a doctorate.

- The **Doctorate** is the final stage. There is now a limit of four years for completion of the doctoral thesis.

If there is any doubt over the level of your degree, a **lettre d'équivalence** can be requested from the *Ministère de l'Enseignement et de la Recherche*, equating your degree to a French degree level.

Student resident permits

Some colleges and university departments have agreements with the residence permit authorities of the *Préfecture de Paris* allowing you to submit your application directly to the college administration. In this case, they will pilot you through the formalities of application and you will only have to go to the *Préfecture* to collect your *carte* once it is ready. This applies to students of all nationalities.

If you undertake the process yourself, remember to take copies of everything with you as well as the originals. Details can be found on the website of the *Préfecture de Paris*, www.prefecture-police-paris.fr, including a page in English on student applications from EU students. Students from other countries unfortunately have to make do with information in French. But the main points are laid out below.

Students from the European Union
Cartes de séjour are issued at the *Préfecture de Police* on Île de la Cité, as for other European Union nationals. You need to take with you:

☐ a valid passport or ID card, with photocopies of the pages mentioning the identity and validity of the document

☐ a proof of the studies you are undertaking – either a student card, or an **attestation** (certificate) from the college at which you are enrolled for your main course

☐ a proof of residence in Paris – either an EDF bill or your rental agreement or your residence insurance policy, or a signed certificate of housing from your landlord (normally accompanied by a photocopy of your landlord's ID and a copy of his/her last EDF bill)

☐ proof of sufficient financial resources, normally deemed to be 70% of the French state allowance for students (currently 2800FF/month)

☐ proof of insurance cover for illness and pregnancy (see also below) – originals and copies. The E111 is acceptable

☐ three black and white passport size photographs.

Students from other countries
American students require an entry visa before arrival in France. In addition to the basic requirements for Americans applying for a **visa de long séjour** (see Chapter 2), students will also require a letter of admission (**attestation de pré-inscription**) when applying for the first time to a French university, or other similar evidence of enrolment. Academic credentials may be checked by the French consular services in the USA where you apply for your visa. Nationals of other countries should check with their nearest French Consular office for formalities which they need to complete.

You must apply for your *carte de séjour* within 30 days of entering France. *Cartes de séjour* are issued at the **Centre de réception des ressortissants étrangers, 13, rue Miollis, 75015 Paris**, open Monday-Thursday 08h45-16h30, Fridays 08h45-16h00, M° Cambronne or Ségur. You should bring the following documents:

☐ The original of your valid passport plus copies of the pages indicating the marital status of the applicant, the date limit of the passport, and the visa allowing entry into France.

☐ Originals plus copies of degree certificates, exam results, etc., to prove the seriousness of your application; and the **certificat**

d'immatriculation, d'inscription, or **pré-inscription** for your course at your college or faculty. For higher education establishments which do not fit into the university category, check with your college administrators for the documentation required.

☐ Originals plus copies of proof of residence (see above). If you are staying in a hostel or student residence, you will need a recent signed attestation from the director and also a recent bill.

☐ Proof of financial resources as above. If you are receiving a grant, you will need a statement on letter-headed paper from the grant-making authority stating the duration of the grant, the amount granted, and what studies you are undertaking. If you are receiving funds from abroad, you need to take as much evidence as possible of monthly payments. If you are being financed by a third party in France, you need to supply a certificate and personal and financial documents relating to your sponsor (enquire for further details).

☐ Original plus copies of your proof of social security cover – either your social security card or an attestation stating that you have signed up to the student **régime** of the Sécu; or a personal insurance programme either approved by URSSAF, the social security agency, or stating that you have complete cover for illness, accidents and pregnancy.

Student welfare

Students have their own *régime* in the Sécurité Sociale, for those between 20 and 28 years old. Students from the UK will need the Form E111 when coming to study in France. Upon arrival they will then need to contact the **Direction des Régimes Spéciaux** of their local university **caisse d'assurance maladie**.

You must join the student social security *régime* if you are over 20 and under 28, and/or you are a foreign student; have no rights deriving from a parent, or from your own paid employment; and you are enrolled in an establishment deemed to fall under the student social security *régime*. The annual cost of belonging to the scheme is currently 1100FF from 1 October to 30 September. Students who receive a French government grant are exempt from the social security fee.

There are also two student **mutuelles** (complementary health insurance schemes) available, from which you should choose one to join: either **La Mutuelle des Étudiants** (137 bd St Michel, 75005 Paris. Tel. 0810 600 601, www.lmde.fr); or **La SMEREP** (54, bd St Michel, 75005 Paris. Tel. 01 56 65 36 34, www.smerep.fr).

Housing and other benefits are means-tested on the basis of the income of the student's parents. All students are eligible for limited housing benefit. However, a distinction is made between those who depend solely on their parents for financial support, and those who work their way through their studies. In fact, those who work are worse off in terms of benefits.

Two of the most important places that you will need to find are the **CROUS (Centre Régional des Oeuvres Universitaires et Scolaires)**, 39 avenue Georges-Bernanos, 75005 Paris. Tel. 01 40 51 37 10), and the **CIDJ (Centre d'Information et de Documentation Jeunesse)**, 101 quai Branly, 75015 Paris, beside the Eiffel Tower (Tel. 01 44 49 12 00).

The CROUS will issue your student card, which will allow you a wide variety of discounts (e.g. travel, museum entrance, etc.). The CROUS acts to some extent as a student union would in a British university, in terms of the welfare and general information services it offers. The CIDJ has a job centre, travel agency and bookshop and a reference library on social security rights, etc.

The Grandes Écoles

The Grandes Écoles are the élite higher education institutions (some of which are private), which consistently produce the leaders of French commerce, industry, politics, and society in general.

Competition for entry is obviously fierce and very selective. Being a foreigner will probably not help your case, unless you have already attended a top-level university in your own country. However, if you do succeed in graduating from one of these schools, a successful professional life and a very useful set of future contacts will be almost assured.

English-speaking universities in France

The American University of Paris (www.aup.edu)

- **US Admissions Office,** 60 East 42nd Street, Suite 1463, New York 10017 Tel. 212 983 1414, Fax 212 983 04 44, e-mail: usoffice@aup.edu

- **International Admissions Office,** 6 rue du Colonel Combes, 75007 Paris. Tel. 01 40 62 07 20, Fax 01 47 05 34 32, e-mail: admissions@aup.edu

- **Continuing Education and Summer Programmes,** 102, rue St Dominique, 75007 Paris. Tel. 01 40 62 06 14, Fax 01 40 62 07 17, e-mail:ce@aup.edu or summer@aup.edu

The American University of Paris (AUP) is a private university based in central Paris in the 7th arrondissement, near to the American Church Community Centre. The AUP offers under-graduate courses in a wide variety of subjects, summer programmes and continuing education which will help you develop skills for the Parisian (and other) job markets (e.g. web design, screen-writing, accounting). All courses are taught in English. The AUP also offers help with accommodation for its students. Candidates may join the university for either the fall or spring semesters. The AUP also offers distance learning courses.

The British Institute of Paris (www.bip.lon.ac.uk)
The British Institute (Tel. 01 44 11 73 73, Fax 01 45 50 31 55), housed in the same building as the British Council (the cultural affairs department of the British Embassy, www.britcoun.org/france), is situated at 11 rue de Constantine, overlooking Les Invalides. The Institute is an integral part of the University of London, and offers a BA Honours degree course in French studies, the only British university department offering the chance to learn French in France. The Institute also works extensively with French nationals to develop their language skills, and offers continuing education courses such as translation. The British Council Library of 20,000 books is also open to the public (upon payment of an annual subscription fee), and includes a reference library, fiction and non-fiction, and a large video collection for hire. The British Council regularly organises work-shops and seminars with visiting authors and academics.

The Cité Universitaire Internationale de Paris
19, boulevard Jourdan, 75014 Paris. Reception: Tel. 01 44 16 65 54, admission office: Tel. 01 44 16 64 41, student welcome centre: Tel. 01 44 16 64 68. The extensive residential campus on the southern edge of Paris with its own sports ground and RER station is a popular choice for students. Thirty-seven nations have

their own College or Maison. The College Franco-Britannique, 9b, boulevard Jourdan, Tel. 01 44 16 24 00, admits over 200 students of at least 3rd year university level from all over the world, with 50% of the rooms reserved for British students.

The Open University (www.open.ac.uk)
The British distance-learning university, the Open University, has now been operating in France for several years, and has held two degree conferral ceremonies in Paris. All courses are taught in English using proven methods, and cover a wide range of subjects. The obligatory summer schools are also held in France. For further information, write to Rosemary Pearson, 51 rue de Villiers, 92200 Neuilly sur Seine. Tel. 01 47 58 53 73, Fax 01 47 58 55 25.

Other degree courses in Paris

There are an increasing number of **MBA** courses being taught from Paris bases with joint teaching programmes linked to US universities and business schools. These courses are almost all taught at least partially in English. Details of the courses and schools available will be found in most English-language magazines in Paris. The most renowned French business school is **INSEAD** (Tel. 01 60 72 42 42) near Fontainebleau, now ranked amongst the world's leading schools.

   Parsons School of Design in central Paris (Tel. 01 45 77 39 66, www.parsons-paris.pair.com) offers full-time, part-time and evening classes and Bachelor of Fine Arts degrees in fashion design, illustration, computer graphics, etc.

LEARNING THE LANGUAGE

Private language schools and teachers abound in Paris. The quality and value for money that you will receive from these institutions and individuals varies enormously, and you should try to seek local guidance from expatriate groups and colleagues. Sign up early to ensure your place at your preferred school and course. You will normally have to do a brief test to establish just how much or how little you know. After that you will be 'streamed' into the appropriate class.

   Your local **syndicat d'initiative** should be able to provide a list of language schools in your area. Many universities now offer language courses for foreigners. Foreign university students will also normally find that French tuition is included on their time-table. Try looking in *France-USA Contacts* and *The Free Voice* if you are having difficulty finding schools to choose from.

   The best-known language schools for foreigners are the follow-ing:

- **Alliance Française,** 101 bd Raspail, 75006 Paris. M° Rennes Tel.   01   45   44   38   28,   Fax   01   45   44   89   42, www.alliancefrancaise.fr – the flag-ship of a worldwide network of deservedly renowned French language schools.

- **Institut Catholique**, 21 rue d'Assas, 75006 Paris. M° Rennes Tel. 01 44 39 52 68, Fax 01 55 39 52 09, www.icp.fr, e-mail: ilfcp.fr (language school offices in the neighbouring building at 12 rue Casette) – the renowned private Catholic University in central Paris (open to people of all and no faiths) has a major centre for French language teaching to foreigners.

- **La Sorbonne**, Cours de Civilisation et de la Langue Française, 47 rue des Ecoles, 75005 Paris. M° St-Michel Tel. 01 40 46 22 11, Fax 01 40 46 32 99 – offers courses and diplomas at all levels, including business French.

Learning other languages in Paris

If you are already proficient in French, or you have a taste for languages, you may want to try learning another foreign language whilst you are in Paris. Most embassies will be able to put you in contact with their cultural centres in Paris (if they have one), who may offer language courses.

- **The Goethe Institute** 11 avenue d'Iéna, 75116 Paris. M° Iéna Tel. 01 44 43 92 30, Fax 01 44 43 92 40, www.goethe.de/fr/par – the German Cultural Centre offering courses at all levels.

- **Instituto Cervantès** 7 rue Quentin Bauchart, 75008 Paris. M° George V, Alma-Marceau Tel. 01 40 70 92 92, Fax 01 47 07 27 49 – the new Spanish cultural centre in Paris.

- **Local** *mairies* also organise evening classes in foreign languages at very low prices. Whilst you may have the dis-advantage of large classes, if you want to establish a basic grasp of a language, this could be a good cost-effective way to achieve your end.

Cultural learning opportunities

WICE (The Womens Institute of Continuing Education), 20 bd Montparnasse, 75015 Paris. Tel. 01 45 66 75 50, Fax 01 40 65 96 53 www.wice-paris.org M° Duroc.

Based on the Left Bank near Montparnasse, WICE offers everything from art history to creative writing classes and cultural tours of the great Parisian museums and French châteaux. WICE also offers TEFL English-language teaching qualification required to make a successful entry to the job market as an English teacher. Despite the name, the clientele is not exclusively feminine, although women account for about 90% of the 1,000 members from 25 different countries.

Cookery courses

Cookery classes in the capital of cuisine are not cheap (in fact they are anything but that), but your stay in Paris is a once-in-a-lifetime opportunity to learn unique skills.

- **The Ritz-Escoffier School**, 15 place Vendôme, 75041 Paris Cedex 01. Tel. 01 43 16 71 70/71/72, Fax 01 43 16 36 68/69, e-mail: resa@ritzparis.com, or in New York via The Leading Hotels of the World, 99 Park Avenue, New York 10016. Tel. 212 838 3110, Fax 212 758 7367, e-mail: hrihotel@idt.net. Learn to bake products to make your mouth water at the legendary Paris hotel with prices which will bring tears to your eyes . . .

- **Le Cordon Bleu**, 8 rue Léon Dulhomme, 75015 Paris. Tel. 01 53 68 22 50, Fax 01 48 56 03 96, www.cordonbleu.net – one of the most renowned French cookery schools, with five different 'schools' and a nine-mouth diploma which will enable you to rustle up a little something your loved one will not choke on when s/he sees how much the classes cost.

- **École Princesse ERE 2001**, 18 avenue de la Motte-Picquet, 75007 Paris. Tel. 01 45 51 36 34, Fax 01 43 47 38 68. Who better than one of the leading members of the French aristocracy, the Princesse Marie-Blanche de Broglie, to teach you how to dismiss your famished family with a royal wave of the hand and a simple, 'Let them eat cake'? After all, her ancestors were hanging around when Marie-Antoinette dropped her classic one-liner. The school offers courses in English, French and Spanish.

6

Deciding Where to Live

Deciding where to live in Paris will involve balancing professional, and perhaps family and educational obligations with personal preferences. Deciding what sort of accommodation to live in, whether to buy or rent, and which area of the city to select, are personal choices which will be shaped by your circumstances and future plans. Think carefully about the following points when you decide where to live:

- **Size** Do you prefer to have a larger home in a less popular but cheaper area, or a smaller home in a more central and/or expensive area?

- **Facilities** Which facilities do you want to be nearest? Shops, schools, entertainment, your workplace?

- **Transport** What public transport facilities are there nearby? Do you need parking space?

- **Safety** How safe is the area you have chosen? Is it really as safe – or as dangerous – as you have been told?

If you have the opportunity it is a good idea to briefly visit the **quartier** (district) where you are considering living. Bear in mind the points above, be observant when you visit the **quartier**, and decide on your priorities before taking a decision. Moving can be expensive, time-consuming and unsettling.

LOCAL CONSIDERATIONS

Each arrondissement has its own mayor and local council, and state-run services from education to taxation are operated on the basis of sub-divisions of the arrondissements. This can have varying degrees of importance at different stages of your Parisian life. For instance:

- Your chances of finding a place in a municipal crèche for your child. The number of places available varies greatly from arrondissement to arrondissement.

- Your children will be assigned to state schools according to the arrondissement you live in, and the sub-divisions are crucial when it comes to entering your child into one of the élite Parisian **lycées**, or being faced with sending them to one of their much poorer 'cousins'.

- Your local housing tax (**taxe d'habitation**) will vary according to not only the size of your apartment or house, but also to its last official listed valuation by the local authorities, which will take into account average market prices per square metre at the time of the valuation. However, in the suburbs surrounding Paris in particular, the presence of large businesses or factories can have a very beneficial effect for local residents in terms of their *taxe d'habitation*. For instance, Boulogne-Billancourt on the western edge of Paris' city centre, ideally placed and offering good quality housing, has a substantially lower *taxe d'habitation* than neighbouring **communes** because the French car company Renault has its historic headquarters in the *commune*.

- Certain arrondissements and towns have generally better social security centres (including their attendant family support centres) than other more central or poorer areas. There is no hard-and-fast rule, and you will only find this out by discreet enquiries amongst friends and acquaintances.

- Local authorities rival each other on the quality of services they offer to their residents. Mainly this is part of the party political game, but the results of a sustained programme over a number of years to restore a certain *quartier* or maintain a general standard of living across the arrondissement can make a considerable difference.

- In March 2001, Parisians elected their new municipal council (composed of councillors and mayors from all twenty arrondissements) and their new mayor. For almost a quarter of a century Paris has been a right-wing stronghold, and for many years the arrondissements which returned Socialist local mayors were deprived of central city funds in petty political vendettas. However, the change in the political wind since

March 2001 will set in motion a levelling of the differences between the arrondissements on many scores such as municipal crèches.

2001 is the start of a new municipal cycle. When you do narrow your choices down, it is worth taking a trip to the local *mairie* to find out what is planned in the area in the near future. If it is planned to close the school and move it a kilometre away, or to cut a new Métro line under your street, or to build a block of new flats on the site opposite, you may want to think again.

FINAL CONSIDERATIONS

As you begin your home search, there are three basic rules to remember, as in any major city:

1. Furnished rented accommodation is generally more expensive than unfurnished accommodation.

2. The suburbs are generally less expensive than the city centre, although everything depends on location.

3. Weigh up a larger home in a more distant location against increased travelling time and monthly cost, as well as perhaps inferior amenities – although that calculation can work in both directions.

7

Living in the City – La Rive Droite

Some 67.5% of Parisians live in the 14 arrondissements of the Right Bank, stretching from the luxurious west to the up-and-coming east via the colourful and sometimes difficult northern arrondissements, and including the historic and fashionable heart of Paris.

Couched between the two green lungs of Paris, the Bois de Boulogne and the Bois de Vincennes, the heart is composed of the ancient royal and noble districts which are still renowned for luxury shopping and art galleries, fine apartments and vibrant nightlife. Stretching out to the west along the former rural playground of the Champs-Élysées is the most important business district in France (leading out to the second most important in La Défense). To the north, the former villages of Batignolles, la Butte Montmartre, Belleville, les Buttes-Chaumont, Ménilmontant and Charonne still mix working-class communities with trendy artistic revolutionaries.

THE 1ST ARRONDISSEMENT

According to one local resident interviewed by *Le Figaro* (10 February 2001), 'The real problem with the [1st] arrondissement is that it is an arrondissement which runs length-wise, a cut-through, with few residents, monopolised in the west by a rich population – French and foreign – [whilst] in the east, near the Forum, it is much more working-class', echoing the sentiments of the Socialist local mayoral candidate a few weeks before in *L'Express* magazine (11 January 2001), 'The two quartiers do not mix with one another.'

The reasons for the geographical layout and social divides are mainly historical in this busy and elegant area in the heart of Paris. Unlike the majority of central Parisian arrondissements which complain of lack of open green spaces, the 1st is dominated by the **Jardin des Tuileries**, all that remains of the missing third royal palace which once filled this area. The original palace and

114

fortress was the **Louvre**, and the oldest exposed sections of the great palace can be found now underground in the newest addition, the **Carrousel du Louvre**. The Sun King Louis XIV left his mark on the Cour Carrée even though he removed the court to Versailles, and it was Napoléon and his successors who added the great long wings running down to the Tuileries – with the final pharaonic flourish of the pyramids added by François Mitterrand. Just next door stands the **Palais-Royal**, originally built for the powerful Cardinal Richelieu and later ceded to the crown. The tranquil gardens of what is now the French Ministry of Culture were once the scenes of revolutionary ferment when this was the residence of the Orléans branch of the royal family in the years leading up to 1789. The end result was the final demise of the lost palace of the Tuileries which stood at the end of the gardens, razed to the ground by the mob in 1870 after the fall of Napoléon III. Now all that rests of the historic palace where Louis XVI and Marie-Antoinette were imprisoned by the mob are the two museums perched on the terrace, the **Orangerie** with its unique collection of Monet paintings, and Napoléon III's tennis court the **Jeu de Paume**, now a contemporary art museum.

Linking the right bank and fortress of the Louvre to the Île de la Cité and the Cathedral of Notre-Dame and royal palace on the island (now the Palais de Justice, with just the Sainte-Chapelle as a reminder of bygone days), is Paris' oldest bridge, confusingly named the **Pont Neuf** – old French for the New Bridge. The medieval city grew up behind the Louvre, and the maze of tiny streets beside the *Samaritaine* department store is a reminder of this medieval heritage. The royal churches were St-Germain L'Auxerrois, and the majestic St-Eustache beyond the great market district of **Les Halles** at the eastern end of the arrondissement.

Les Halles was a vast covered market, and the rival of the old Covent Garden for London. Like its British counterpart, the market activities were exiled to a distant suburb, and the markets were flattened before Paris' biggest hole was bored to build the subterranean **Forum des Halles** shopping and entertainment centre, with gardens at ground level. Beside the market district, a commercial district grew up in what is now the area known at **Châtelet**, where the street names mark what were the principal activities of each street.

The wealth of the merchants and nobles drawn to this area led to the expansion west towards the city limits along the **rue St**

Honoré of fine 17th and 18th century town-houses, now converted into offices, shops and apartments. The luxurious and exclusive **Place Vendôme**, home to the Ritz and most of the world's leading jewellers, is a showpiece of the wealth of this area both today and yesterday.

The polarity of the 1st arrondissement is indeed very remarkable, with the haute-couture fashion industry concentrated at the western end, and luxury shops at the *Trois Quartiers* shopping centre, in addition to many trendy interior design shops. Even though prices are more affordable in the area around Palais-Royal, with its flower-filled gardens and border of covered galleries, this area remains one of the most expensive in Paris for good accommodation. In addition, there is a dearth of ordinary shops where you can simply buy your groceries and life's little necessities. The overall effect has been an exodus of 30% of the population in the last 25 years. Paradoxically, as for the 4th arrondissement, there is a high level of childcare and education opportunities which under other circumstances would draw families to the area.

With a bottle-neck medieval street plan and 18th century streets designed for horse-drawn traffic, and the great rue de Rivoli and main Paris thoroughfare on the river-banks (**quais**) of the Seine, the area also suffers from the traffic and pollution problems common to all the central arrondissements. The Forum des Halles drains into its RER station (the busiest such station in Europe) the outlying suburbs, many of which are much less than pleasant. Les Halles is a highly nocturnal quartier, of Irish pubs and restaurants, and the night-buses (**noctambus**) leave and arrive at the Place du Châtelet. But the result of this activity is that Les Halles is an unsafe area at night, and the gardens of the Forum are a favoured hang-out for drug dealers and addicts.

Yet, with its impressive number of theatres (notably the **Comédie-Française** and the **Théâtre du Châtelet**), concerts, museums and monuments, the 1st arrondissement is the cultural as well as geographical heart of Paris. The Les Halles redevelopment has breathed new life into an old quartier, and brought the most fashionable swimming pool and multi-screen cinema complex to the heart of the city. No matter where you live in it, the 1st arrondissement does not offer you a quiet life, but it certainly does offer you a good one if you have the means to support it.

THE 2ND ARRONDISSEMENT

Covering only one square kilometre and with about 20,000 in-habitants, the smallest arrondissement of Paris is a rich collection of contrasting communities, which ensures that the most densely populated arrondissement is anything but a 'ghetto' of one group or another. Nestling between the Grands Boulevards to the north, the gracious 1st arrondissement and the gardens of Les Halles to the south, and the Marais to the east, the area contains elements of all its neighbours, as well as a tangle of calmer streets in the centre around the old Bibliothèque Nationale.

The western half of the arrondissement, beginning almost at La Madeleine and stretching to the rue du Quatre-Septembre, is one of the most prestigious commercial districts of Paris. The **rue de la Paix** leading from the Place Vendôme to the Place de l'Opéra has for generations been associated with the world's leading jewellers, whilst the **avenue de l'Opéra** is the headquarters of Paris' travel industry. Also to be found in this area is one of Paris' main banking districts. Just around the corner in rue Daunou is Harry's Bar, the most famous American bar in Paris. Apartments in this area are scarcer than elsewhere in the 2nd, and essentially this is luxury living at commensurate prices. Between the boulevard des Italiens and the rue du Quatre-Septembre is a business area, leading down to the Paris Stock Exchange at Place de la **Bourse**. For opera fans, the 2nd is almost paradise, with the great Opéra-Garnier at one corner (now mainly used for ballet) and the independent but renowned Opéra-Comique at place Boïeldieu a few minutes up the road.

Beneath the Bourse area and the rue du Louvre, lies an area of elegant apartments and shops centred around the old **Bibliothèque Nationale**. Just beyond, the Place des Petits-Pères and the grand **Place des Victoires** next door all announce the proximity of the Palais-Royal. The Place des Victoires, a 17th century gem, is also the gateway to the fashion designer district which is firmly established in the 2nd arrondissement. Between the rue Montmartre and the Boulevard de Sébastopol, the most sought-after section of the 2nd can be found in the restored pedestrian district centred on the thriving **Montorgueil** market. The influence of the fashion industry is heavily felt on this street, which often seems to be one long fashion show. Trend-setters of all styles have moved in here, and there is also a large gay community in the area. Rents are high, and families are unlikely to find value for their money in this area.

The Grands Boulevards lining the north of the arrondissement are filled with shops and theatres, and feeding off these are the charming and characteristic covered shopping galleries, the **passages**. The Grands Boulevards were originally conceived as places of amusement and promenades, but the proximity of music halls soon attracted some of the less desirable forms of entertainment industry in the 19th century. Wandering through the **passage des Panoramas** at dusk in winter, when the great lamps are half-lit to produce a gas-light effect and the galleries are emptying, allows you to catch something of the *demi-monde* atmosphere that once lingered over the area. Today, the Grands Boulevards live up to their original intent even if they are less elegant than before and attract the masses each weekend. The night clubs here are amongst the most popular in Paris. **Le Rex** cinema near the eastern end of the arrondissement is one of the great 1930s picture palaces and cinemas of Paris, attracting large crowds, especially for the children's matinées at the weekends. Underneath, one of Paris' consistently coolest clubs keeps the old nocturnal spirit alive. Beyond the Rex is the unsavoury Strasbourg-St-Denis. Take care here especially at night.

This northern area of the arrondissement contains the **populaire** element of the 2nd, even though apartment prices do not really vary much. Directly above the Montorgueil *quartier* is **Sentier** also now known as 'Silicon Sentier'. Traditionally a bastion of sweat-shop clothing factories in the extensive attics of dilapidated 18th century buildings, the area has become the centre of the **nouvelle économie**, internet start-up companies, drawn to cheap rents and the close proximity of the Bourse with its high-speed internet access. The clothes industry remains and the two dynamic industries happily co-habit in this crowded area of Paris. The streets surrounding **rue St-Denis** are increasingly becoming an anomaly. On the one hand, the rue St-Denis is one of the sleaziest streets in Paris, certainly at the upper end. On the other hand, lack of space and the attraction of 'like to like' has drawn more reputable 'fashion victims' than those of Sentier to move into the area and renovate the apartments. However, do take care in the St-Denis area.

A lack of local amenities and open spaces is off-set by the fact that transport is so easy in this area that you can soon get to a park or a pool. The biggest problems that the 2nd arrondissement

faces are property prices, with high prices across the arrondissement; traffic and parking in the crowded narrow streets which
nonetheless provide much of the charm of the area; and crime.
The 2nd suffers from being couched between the Forum des
Halles at one end and Strasbourg-St-Denis at the other, both
known for drug-dealing and racketeering of all kinds. Add the
prostitutes on the rue St-Denis, and you have a lot of problems for
such a small area.

The 2nd arrondissement provides a fast-pace vibrant heart
to Paris. It is probably not the best adapted area for families,
although it has a very socially mixed environment and young
families are said to be moving back to the area. Perhaps their
return and the area's enduring popularity is proof of the greatest
claim to fame of the 2nd – combining fashion, finance and fine
housing in such a small area, demonstrating that in the heart of
Paris 'small can be beautiful'.

THE 3RD ARRONDISSEMENT

In comparison to its larger richer neighbour and *quartier* partner,
the 4th arrondissement, the northern half of the Marais which
forms the 3rd arrondissement seems to be a poorer deal. You can
almost imagine 'the mother of the Marais' saying that her other
daughter got the talents and the looks, and that the 3rd arrondissement is such a difficult child. But given the history of this part of
Paris, it is almost unsurprising that the area is like no other.

The history is written in street names and in stone in this
popular part of Paris, with the rue du Temple, rue des Archives
and rue Vieille du Temple providing the principal arteries from
the river bank to the Place de La République, passing via the
Square du Temple, all revealing that this was the site of the Paris
headquarters of the mysterious Order of the Knights Templar.

In the 17th and 18th centuries, noble and merchant families
had extended the mansion building campaigns further north into
the area that is now the 3rd, such that the southern parts
of the arrondissement contain some of the finest examples of
architecture in the Marais. The **Musée Carnavalet** (the excellent
Museum of the History of Paris) became the home of Madame de
Sévigné, and the princely de Rohan family installed themselves in
the magnificent palace that now houses the **Archives Nationales**
(open to the public). The Hôtel de Saint-Aignan (the brand new

Museum of Jewish Life and Culture) has been restored from rubble and ruin to its 18th century splendour, and all of these attest to the golden era of the 3rd arrondissement.

Despite being small, the 3rd arrondissement falls into roughly five different sectors. The south-west corner is centred on the **quartier de l'Horloge**, a gloomy modern development. In this area you will pay less to live on one of the busy main thoroughfares which criss-cross the arrondissement than on one of the grid of smaller narrow side-streets crossing this section, which contain ancient oak-beamed apartments built around spacious courtyards originally planned for horses and carriages. At the junction of the rue de Turbigo and rue Beaubourg is **Arts-et-Métiers** Métro station, and the heart of a popular district – close to the centre, but close also to the shops of rue de Bretagne and République. The area takes its name from the renowned engineering institute housed in an ancient abbey which dominates the district.

Leading down from Arts-et-Métiers, along the **rue du Temple** in particular, is what was Paris' first Chinatown in the 1920s. The street is still dominated by Chinese and Arab wholesalers and a small 'rag-trade' have also made their home in the northern part of the arrondissement, and sturdily resist all attempts to move them. The result is a breath of more working-class air in the otherwise rarefied Marais atmosphere, but at the cost of traffic congestion. To the east of the **rue des Archives** is probably the most pleasant part of the 3rd, leading across to the boulevard du Temple, the boulevard des Filles du Calvaire, and the boulevard Beaumarchais. Running from the rue du Temple in this direction is the **rue de Bretagne** market street, and the whole area is a comfortable relaxed mix between Marais style and good practical living, with an interesting selection of apartments in the rue Charlot and the streets surrounding the rue de Turenne. The sector from the rue **Vieille du Temple** along the rue des Francs-Bourgeois is one of the chicest parts of the 3rd, with the **Musée Picasso** and other cultural centres behind the busy commercial street and centred around the tranquil rue du Parc-Royal.

What then makes the 3rd 'a difficult child'? Although the area has a very cosmopolitan feel to it, with Arab, Chinese, and Jewish communities, a large gay community drawn into the Marais orbit, and a rich influential community of stars and business people, the communities do not all seem to appreciate each other – or more to the point the last group are not always very keen on the others. In addition, social priority housing is virtually non-existent, adding to the social imbalance in the area. Crime has also soared (up 18%) in the area over the last year – probably more an indicator of the success of the area and its population than anything else.

Property prices in the 3rd are amongst the highest in Paris, with *Le Figaro* (10 February 2001) quoting a reported 26% increase in the last year. The result is that the 3rd is experiencing the same population drift from young families to rich, childless households as the 4th arrondissement. Finally, if property prices were not enough to ward off potential young families from the area, the waiting list for a place in a municipal crèche in the 3rd has over 300 applicants. Endless traffic jams, the lack of green open spaces and a lack of local supermarkets all detract from the area's charm. Yet in spite of all these problems that local activists love to hate, the 3rd, with its oak-beamed, character-filled apartments, remains one of the most attractive areas of Paris, especially for young couples or single people, who enjoy the mixture of populations which makes for variety and the spice of life.

THE 4TH ARRONDISSEMENT

The 4th is most often referred to under its *quartier* name, the Marais, even though that name also applies to the 3rd arrondissement next door. The Marais, originally the marshlands bordering the river-bank and the original Parisian settlements on the Île de la Cité which also falls within the 4th arrondissement, was a popular area of settlement from the earliest days of Parisian urban expansion. The splendid 18th century high-ceilinged mansions beside earlier medieval and Renaissance buildings attest to a long residential tradition on this site. The Île St-Louis behind the Île de la Cité was in fact a speculative 17th century property development on a mud-flat, which explains the homogeneous date of many of the fine structures. As you will see when you wander around the streets of the tiny island, St-Louis quickly became the favoured residence of courtiers and artists, and to some large extend it remains the favoured residence of similar groups today.

So much which represents Paris – the cathedral of Notre-Dame, the Centre Pompidou, the City Hall (**Hôtel de Ville**) itself – all falls within the 4th arrondissement, that it is sometimes difficult to remember that the area has a life of its own. Yet the 4th remains one of the most enduringly popular areas of the city in which to live, with a number of different 'mini-*quartiers*' making up the urban puzzle. On the eastern edge, bordering on the 1st arrondissement and Les Halles and spreading into the 3rd arrondissement, is Paris answer to London's Soho, the gay village centred on **rue des Archives, rue St-Croix de la Bretonnerie**, and **rue Vieille du Temple**. Lively and bustling, open almost all hours in many cases, the bars, restaurants, shops, and cafés have completely transformed the quartier. Gallery owners and designers are keen to move in, as the **branché** (trendy) heterosexual population follow the gay lead into the Marais.

Check-by-jowl with this community lives happily one of the city's most well-known Jewish communities, now centred on the **rue des Rosiers** and its tributaries. The result of a successful and lively co-existence of these two areas is that on Sundays, the area is packed with shoppers visiting the interior design shops and clothes shops of the rue des Francs-Bourgeois leading down to the third area of the 4th arrondissement, the aristocratic village St-Paul. In this section of the Marais, centred on the beautiful **Place des Vosges** (an arcaded garden-filled former royal square), the apartments in the restored noble palaces are expensive. From beyond the Place des Vosges to Bastille, and between the rues St-Antoine and de Rivoli (one and the same but with a name-change at St-Paul), and the river bank, apartments are still expensive but a little more affordable.

The islands do both offer accommodation, even if the Île de la Cité is principally the administrative headquarters for Paris, with the cathedral, the **Préfecture** (police headquarters), the **Palais de Justice** (Supreme Court of Paris), and all their attendant buildings, plus one of Paris' oldest hospitals, the Hôtel-Dieu, renowned as an eye hospital. The Île St-Louis has beautiful 17th century apartments, but does betray its origins when the Seine rises and occasionally floods. Residents complain at such times that they find their expensive wine collections floating around their flooded cellars, and parking is impossible on the island. However, the views are unique from the island, and if any other enticement was required, it is also home to the world-renowned Berthillon ice-cream shops.

The 4th almost overflows with cultural and creative life (note the recently-restored **Marché des Blanc-Manteaux** exhibition area), and with the rue de Rivoli running straight through the middle of the arrondissement, the area certainly does not lack for shops either. The Bazar de l'Hôtel de Ville (BHV) manages to meet most requirements, and in the small streets behind you will find everything associated with the diverse communities which inhabit the 4th. The main market street is on the **rue Rambuteau**, although supermarkets are pretty scarce in this part of town.

Statistically the 4th has a high level of crime, but for much the same reason as the figures for other tourist centres such as Montmartre, with the figures exaggerated by pick-pocketing and handbag snatching concentrated in the 4th around the Place Beaubourg. Parking is notoriously difficult in the Marais at any time, but especially at the weekends and in the evenings. But probably the main problem with the 4th arrondissement is that its property prices are amongst the highest in Paris. The cultural richness of the area, its geographical location, the quality of the apartments on offer and the general desirability of the area, and a wealthy gay community all combine to make the 4th arrondissement an expensive choice.

Ironically however, the 4th is one of the arrondissements with the highest number of crèche places and the smallest school class sizes in Paris, and local initiatives aim to develop facilities for children and young families. The dichotomy arises from a right-wing mayoral majority elected last time concentrating on their 'family and tradition' programme whilst ignoring the fact that there are decreasing numbers of clients for the services they propose. As it stands, the 4th arrondissement is a highly desirable place to live – central, varied and fun, with a large stock of excellent apartments and good schools, including the renowned **Lycée Charlemagne**. But with high property prices, the 4th remains a residential area limited to those with the appropriate means to survive.

THE 8TH ARRONDISSEMENT

When the medieval city of Paris could no longer offer the nobles the space, distraction and peace that they required for their town houses, they breached the city walls into the surrounding fields – the so-called 'Elysian Fields' of **Champs-Élysées** – towards the outlying villages and hamlets. The palaces on the **Faubourg St-Honoré** pursued the path of the rue St-Honoré, and the American, British and Japanese embassies and the presidential Élysée Palace are the most magnificent examples of the new prestige of this area of villas and upmarket entertainment. The great **Place de la Concorde**, with the matching splendours of the

Hôtel Crillon and the Navy Ministry, attested to the glory of the Sun King's descendants – until the day that the revolting locals placed a large, precise, scientific and efficient head-chopping device patented by Dr Guillotine in the middle of the place and experimented on the royal family, the court, and then each other.

In some respects, little has changed today (although the guillotine has been replaced by the obelisk, twin sister of Cleopatra's Needle in London). The area remains extremely fashionable, and one of the great centres of nightlife, not to mention of course shopping. The Faubourg is *the* fashion house address in Paris, whilst the Champs-Élysées generates approximately 3.8 billion Francs of business a year. After a lengthy restoration, nightlife returned in force to the Champs not only with a number of the most famous nightclubs on the avenue itself, but in streets such as **rue Marbeuf** leading down to the fashion house headquarters on ultra-chic avenue George V and its luxury hotels. This area, bordered by the 16th arrondissement at avenue Marceau, the riverbank, and the **Grand et Petit Palais** exhibition complex, is one of the most expensive areas of Paris in terms of accommodation – as chic as the 16th but more lively because of the luxury shopping and nightlife. Slicing across this area is the **avenue Montaigne**, another luxury fashion paradise, leading down to the **Théâtre des Champs-Élysées** with its excellent repertoire, and the **Place de l'Alma** with its views across the Seine to the Eiffel Tower.

Whilst the southern side of the Champs-Élysées has become the headquarters of luxury living, the north side including the continuation of the Faubourg St-Honoré is an area of galleries and offices. This is the real residential 8th, up to the northern border on the boulevards de Courcelles and des Batignolles. In the rue Daru, the **Russian Orthodox cathedral** (features in the film of *Doctor Zhivago*) is packed at the Orthodox Easter. In the neighbouring streets surrounding the small but eternally popular **Parc de Monceau**, famed for its 18th century follies and children's playground, apartments overlooking the park are highly sought-after. The areas around both **St-Augustin** and **Villiers** have the sort of shops which make you feel that you are living in the real world rather than peering out of an expensive shop window. But the descent towards the **Madeleine** returns you to luxury shopping.

The north-eastern quarter of the 8th offers the most affordable residential accommodation in the **quartier d'Europe**, centred on the place of the same name behind the **Gare St-Lazare**. Unusually for areas surrounding major train stations, this is a calm and bourgeois grid of streets bearing the names of major European cities. The area is popular for its solid well-built apartments and proximity to both central Paris and the more lively 18th arrondissement. Traditionally this area attracts young professional families.

With some of the best museums in Paris, such as the **Jacquemart-André**, the best night clubs from the extravagant Queen to the exclusive Monkey Club or Manray, and more fashion houses than anyone can shop at in a single day, the 8th is bursting with attractions. Add to this solid, grand apartments and a fast track to Normandy and the coast from St-Lazare, and the 8th appears to be an excellent choice for slick city living. The downside is a lack of amenities such as parks and sports facilities, and scarcity of schools. A large part of the arrondissement also lacks regular food stores or reasonably priced high-street stores.

THE 9TH ARRONDISSEMENT

Stretching from the ultra-chic of **La Madeleine** to the hippy chic of **Pigalle**, the 9th is a sought-after arrondissement of Paris, offering something for everyone and drawing everyone into its midst. It is a shopper's paradise yet still replete with offices and company headquarters.

Consequently, the 9th is packed daily with a huge number of suburban commuters, using either public or private transport. One of the principal complaints of its inhabitants is the level of traffic using the main thoroughfares on the boulevards, the rue Lafayette and the rue de Châteaudun. The arrondissement also suffers from a lack of open spaces and waterways, with neither the Seine nor the canals passing through the arrondissement. This is not, therefore, an area for claustrophobes.

What then makes it so enticing? First, it is precisely the centrality and accessibility of the 9th that is one of its attractions. Small wonder that young bankers like to live in the quaint streets of the '*village St-Georges*' centred on the **Place St-Georges**, the **rue des Martyrs** and **rue Notre Dame-de Lorette**, and the **Place Gustave-Toudoze**. The apartments are large and well-built, having first been constructed by the bankers' 19th century predecessors, who placed the principal banking district around the **Opéra-Garnier** at the southern limit of the 9th.

The neighbouring **rue des Martyrs** is a bustling market street, and this area of Paris has drawn many showbusiness and fashion celebrities as neighbours to the bankers and young middle-classes in a truly village atmosphere. The proximity to Pigalle and a young wealthy local community has also led an increasing number of trendy clothing and interior design shops to open in the streets between the rue des Martyrs and the place Gustave-Toudoze. The **avenue Trudaine** at the top of the rue des Martyrs is a spacious tree-lined street more reminiscent of the 7th arrondissement, quite simply offering the best of both worlds.

The fact that the area is favoured by many showbiz celebrities is hardly surprising given the number of theatres in the area. Surprisingly, however, cinemas are limited to the edge of the arrondissement, near to Opéra or at the Place de Clichy in the 18th. The area has always had a reputation as an artist's quartier. Their haunts and those of their peers and successors can be found behind the wedding-cake extravaganza of **La Trinité**, in the *quartier* known as the '*Nouvelle Athènes*' – the New Athens of the 18th century intellectual élite. The Museum of the Romantic Life (**Musée de la Vie Romantique**) in the quiet rue Chaptal is dedicated to George Sand, where she received her lover Chopin. The nearby charming **Place Adolphe Max** seems a million miles from the Place de Clichy and the Moulin-Rouge, both a couple of minutes away.

The extremities of the 9th bring you to calmer more bourgeois areas. To the west is part of the *quartier d'Europe*, shared with the 8th arrondissement, behind the Gare St-Lazare. The eastern limits of the arrondissement bring you to the area around **Cadet** and the square de Montholon. Bordering on the 10th and only minutes away from the Gare du Nord, this area too has a bourgeois calm about it. However, the recent RATP construction works have caused a famous foundations collapse, notably in the rue Papillon, as attempts to open up the **quartier** took a literal and unexpected turn.

The 9th arrondissement is bounded north and south by boulevards – to the north the boulevards de Rochechouart and de Clichy, with music and sex industries vying for shop space beneath artists' *ateliers* converted to sought-after loft apartments facing north to the Sacré-Coeur. To the south, the Grands Boulevards offer a non-stop parade of shopping and entertainment. The boulevards between La Madeleine and the Opéra offer the chicest shopping, whilst the great Parisian department stores of Galeries Lafayette and Printemps are on boulevard Haussmann.

Cinemas are concentrated on boulevard des Italiens, whilst the boulevards Montmartre and Poissonnière still play home to many theatres and night clubs, which make this a frantic part of Paris at the weekends. In the rue du Faubourg Montmartre, beside the now-forlorn Palace music hall, a significant Jewish community is based in the streets between the boulevards, the rue de Provence, and the Folies-Bergères. In contrast, the quiet rue de Drouot is the headquarters of the main Paris auction houses and stamp-collectors. Weaving their way between the two streets and the boulevards, a series of covered shopping galleries or *passages* offer an enticing view of 19th century Paris.

Perhaps the greatest advantage of the 9th is that to go out and enjoy yourself, you need never be very far from home. The world of entertainment and all the major shops are at your door-step, whilst you have the chance to live in generally spacious apart-ments in either neat and calm or a livelier more haphazard village atmosphere.

THE 10TH ARRONDISSEMENT

It took me almost ten years to finally become reconciled to the 10th arrondissement of Paris. In fact it was not until a fine January Sunday afternoon in 2001. Up until then, my view of the 10th was mainly limited to visits to the Gares de l'Est and du Nord, and occasional peripheral views of this arrondissement, as I willed the taxi driver to get me out of this part of town as quickly as possible. And yet I now find myself being drawn back again and again by the charm of what really is an up-and-coming *quartier*, which mixes almost sublime romanticism with the ridiculously squalid.

For all the efforts and improvements that have been made, squalor does remain an overriding problem in this arrondisse-ment, with an extremely high immigrant population, legal and otherwise; a renowned crime problem which cannot and should not be ignored when considering living in this area; and a fair number of less salubrious 'low-lifes' who tend to congregate around the major railway stations.

What then draws me back to the 10th? Most important is the **Canal St-Martin**, running through the 10th from Stalingrad to République where it disappears from view underground to

Bastille. It has been beautifully restored, and the various bridges criss-crossing the river lead on both sides to a fine selection of shops, which mark the complete regeneration of this very industrial waterway – especially the wonderful Pont de la Granges des Belles (best viewed by walking down from Stalingrad along the quai de Valmy).

But the 10th has much more to offer than simply the canal. On the southern side stand the two magnificent triumphal arches of Louis XIV, the Porte St-Martin and the Porte St-Denis, both newly restored. You should take care here, especially at St-Denis, which is at the heart of one of the most infamous drug-dealing districts in Paris, Strasbourg St-Denis. Beside the **Gare de l'Est** stands the derelict 18th century convent-turned-hospital Villemin. Empty and abandoned since 1968, it is now finally being converted to a cultural centre and artists' residence. The gardens just behind it are already open to the public, offering a rare haven of green open space. Just across from the Gare de l'Est and the Villemin Hospital stands the medieval gem of the Église St-Laurent.

In terms of shopping opportunities, the high immigrant population has left its mark on the arrondissement. The **Passage Brady** off Faubourg St-Denis is the well-known capital of Indian cooking in Paris – a little Bombay seemingly frozen in time since the 1950s. The Marché St-Quentin on boulevard Magenta offers a choice of fresh produce in a 19th century covered market. For some strange reason, the rue de Paradis has always been the mecca of fine porcelain and crystal glassware buyers in Paris. Trendy restaurants and cafés are creeping along the canal and the Grands Boulevards to the south, although cheap Kurd cafés still abound.

There is little doubt that things are only going to get better in the 10th arrondissement (cynics would say, given that in certain areas they could not have got any worse . . .), and it is one of the few central Paris arrondissements still to offer the opportunity to purchase real lofts in Paris in former warehouses. New transport plans will further increase the attraction of the area, as will continued urban renewal feeding out from the canal. Advertising companies and internet 'start-ups' are moving in beside the fashion houses, beside the immigrant sandwich shops and cheap clothing stores of what is already being called Paris' answer to Soho. Even the great railway tracks may soon disappear beneath 'hanging' gardens, although fans of industrial design and the authentic *populaire* nature of the arrondissement are opposed to this. The plans to cover the back of the Gares de l'Est and du Nord, along with similar plans to cover stretches of Paris' ring road, the **périphérique**, are potentially some of the most exciting urban renovation projects of the first decade of the 21st century.

THE 11TH ARRONDISSEMENT

The 11th is an area of Parisian paradox, both highly successful in many respects and yet failing in others. This is best seen in its population figures, for the most densely populated arrondissement of Paris also has the highest rate of population decline. The population of the 11th is a rich social mix from the traditional bourgeoisie to the new Parisian 'Bobos' of eastern Paris and also a high number of low-income immigrants.

In the north-eastern corner of the 11th, bordered by the **rue du Faubourg du Temple**, the boulevard de Belleville, the boulevard Jules Ferry and the rue Jean Pierre Timbaud, you will find the concentration of the poorer north African immigrant communities. Previously the whole *quartier* north-west of the avenue de la République was a working-class district of workshops and workers' homes and communities.

But the explosion of activity on the **rue Oberkampf**, now one of the trendiest in Paris, has spread into the surrounding streets and even up to the Métro stations at Ménilmontant or Belleville, where the Cannibal Café proudly marks the limit of the 'Oberkampf effect'. On the rue Oberkampf itself, cafés and bars are to be found in converted shops which have kept their original shopfronts and used the original names and are now thronged in the evenings. Around this street property prices have rocketed as 'internauts' and artists vie for space in the new Abbesses. Locals fear the loss of the working-class feel to the area, and this is what everybody is desperately craving even if they prefer the look to the reality as they convert and upgrade their homes.

A large swathe of the 11th from the upper end of avenue de la République to boulevard Voltaire and down to Nation is deeply residential and frankly not very exciting territory. There are plenty of apartments on offer, but the real excitement in the 11th is in the south-west corner, with the exception of rue Oberkampf.

Bordered by the **boulevard Beaumarchais** (and the Marais) and the **rue du Faubourg St Antoine**, and with the pivotal point of the place de la Bastille, this area offers a mix of excellent apartments, the best transport links and some of the finest nightlife from opera to bars to nightclubs. The western boundary boulevards running from République are chic addresses with solid ancient buildings and good apartments. In the **rue Amelot** just behind there is a good mix of styles also, and a fine selection of shops and bars. The garden-filled **boulevard Richard Lenoir**, covering the lower section of the Canal St-Martin, is home to the local market, considered one of the best in Paris.

The rues **Popincourt** and **Sedaine** have become one of the last battlegrounds in the 11th between the newer and older styles of population. Noticeably less well-maintained, but with good apartments available nonetheless, the area has been subject to a recent Chinese immigrant innovation of wholesalers. Prices may remain low in the area if parking is not a priority for you.

From the **rue de la Roquette** to the rue du Faubourg St-Antoine and bordered by the rue Faidherbe is 'the golden triangle' of the 11th – the ultimate in trendy living. Nightlife is centred on the Faubourg, the restored **rue de Lappe**, and the lower end of the **rue de Charonne**, all of which also house designer clothes shops. The **rue Keller** with its bars, galleries, shops and the Paris Lesbian and Gay Centre never lacks for imaginative street theatre.

In some respects both the short **rue de la Forge Royale** and the rue Keller (with a school opposite the Paris Lesbian and Gay Centre) best represents the paradox of the 11th. At the quieter end leading off rue Basfroi stands the solemn St Marguerite church, last resting place of the never-crowned Louis XVII. Around about the streets seem run-down, even menacing at times. At the other end of the street, side by side, stand the trendy nightspots *Le Casbah* and *Le Réservoir*, reserved for the **'BCBG' (bon chic bon genre)** middle-to-upper-class youth, surrounded by a clutch of trendy shops and galleries. Beyond the rue Faidherbe, the rue du Faubourg St-Antoine slips rapidly into suburban dullness and a seemingly never-ending path to the Place de la Nation.

THE 12TH ARRONDISSEMENT

In March 2001, the political battle of Paris was fought and lost by the former right-wing RPR majority who had in one shape or form ruled Paris for over a century in the 12th arrondissement. Spreading from the **Bastille**, which symbolises an earlier political revolution, to the **Bois de Vincennes**, the 12th is the great success story of Parisian urban regeneration. It has the highest level of population growth of all the arrondissements, and with its forest, parks, promenades and cycle tracks, the Seine waterfront and the Canal St-Martin yacht harbour, it is not difficult to understand why the area is now so popular.

The area has undergone several vast renovation projects since the 1970s when it was a dreary industrial backwater covered by railway tracks, most notable for its exits to the south via the Gare de Lyon or the forest in the east. The construction of the great **Opéra** house at Bastille was the signal for the renovation of the area directly adjacent, and around the **rue de Charenton**, the **avenue Ledru-Rollin** and along the south side of the **rue du Faubourg St-Antoine** is one of the trendiest districts of Paris, buzzing with designer shops, bars and people, and shared with the neighbouring 11th arrondissement. The exclusive **Port de l'Arsenal** on the edge of the Place de la Bastille adds a mini-St Tropez feeling to the whole area, with yachts and pleasure boats bobbing about at the entrance/exit to the Canal St-Martin. And just to round off the area, the formerly dull **quai de la Rapeé** is now also acquiring a selection of nightlife similar to the restored banks of the 13th opposite.

At **Faidherbe-Chaligny**, the rue du Faubourg St-Antoine seems to calm down into more tranquil and picturesque residential calm, before filtering out into the dull residential mass of the area around **Nation. Picpus** is a distinctly upper-class area, with good schools nearby. Nearby avenue de Saint-Mandé leads into the neighbouring town, a chic suburb nestling between Paris and its eastern forest.

Forming a natural barrier between the 'old' 12th and the 'new' is the **Viaduc des Arts**, running along the **avenue Daumesnil** from just behind the Opéra to the park at Reuilly. The abandoned railway viaduct has now been converted into a selection of superb design shops for both interiors and clothing, and just for good measure you will also find a sprinkling of trendy cafés from which to watch the passing roller-bladers on the broad pavements.

The **Gare de Lyon** still dominates its own *quartier*, with the inimitable Train Bleu restaurant in the station forming a romantic railway meeting point. Between the station and the river is the area which has caused the most excitement in recent years, following on from the massive construction of the Finance Ministry at Bercy in the 1980s and the great Palais Omnisport, home to indoor concerts and international sporting events.

The smaller disused **Bercy** station and its attendant areas have been almost completely razed, redesigned and reconstructed to provide a highly sought-after series of apartment complexes over-looking the beautifully designed **Parc de Bercy** at the **Cour St-Émilion**, which is ideal for children. Beside the park the former wine stores for the produce from the south have been converted into a shopping mall, finished off with a massive multi-screen cinema complex. Unfortunately the architects got so carried away that they forgot to plan a school or any local shops, but this is apparently to be resolved in the near future. In any case, it has not stopped property prices soaring in this new development which symbolises the new wealth of Paris.

At the far end of the avenue Daumesnil before it disappears into the Bois stands the **Porte Dorée**, a relaxed area with direct access to one of the large boating lakes in the Bois, and the popular Pelouse de Reuilly, where each year the great Paris fun-fair the *Foire du Trône* takes place. Beside the lake you will also find the Paris Zoo, considered to be the best in France. New plans to bring the Parisian tramway to this part of the 12th (in about 2007) and to redevelop the areas between the *périphérique* and the inner parallel boulevards (**boulevards des maréchaux**) should further develop the amenities of this area.

With all of this so close at hand, it is not hard to see the attraction of the 12th for young families. Property prices have risen steeply in the area, but the 12th has successfully renewed its population to attract the kind of young families who can afford the higher prices; young professionals looking for spouses in the bars of Bastille, or those who found them looking for a place to raise their children. The urban addition now seems to be that the Bastille + Bercy + Bois = Bobo, and the 12th is the tribal home-land *par excellence* of this new breed.

THE 16TH ARRONDISSEMENT

The rich tree-lined western edge of Paris, equivalent to London's Kensington in population and style, provides the other, western, 'lung' to the city, bordering on both the *périphérique* and the **Bois de Boulogne**. Centred on the three ancient villages of Auteuil, Chaillot, and Passy, and stretching out to the Porte de Saint-Cloud and down to the Seine, the arrondissement encompasses everything west of the 'new town' and villas which grew up in the **Champs-Élysées** beyond the royal palace in the Tuileries Gardens, and is now the most *huppé* (ultra-chic) area of Paris.

The 16th is a solidly rich, upper-class, and family-orientated residential area beyond the offices of the avenues **Kléber, Marceau** and **Victor Hugo**, the shops of the **rue de Passy**, and the headquarters of Radio France, and the Organisation for Economic Cooperation and Development (OECD) With its grand avenues and discreet leafy *villas* (private streets), the area is popular with film stars, diplomats, the richer expatriate community and an increasing number of young families. The result is that demand far out-strips supply for places in municipal crèches. Given the wealth of many of the residents, the lack of crèche places proves less of a problem here than in other areas, as the number of au pairs and domestic staff is higher. However, for young single people, living in the 16th can be a lonley experience if you don't have the means to enjoy it.

The gilded youth of the 16th, who often are the scions of French noble families or captains of industry, will more often than not be educated at the same schools as their parents, such as the excellent **Lycée de Janson de Sailly** in the rue de la Pompe, where generations of the same family have been educated and inter-married, before themselves settling in the leafy streets nearby. The local Mayor is right when he says that the family is the principal value of the arrondissement but he is also talking with his tongue in his cheek.

Locally, *la jeunesse dorée* of the 16th can be found hanging out in the '*M'as-tu vu?*' ('Did you see me?') havens of La Gare at Porte de la Muette (the former railway station converted into a bar-restaurant) or Le Duplex, handily situated at the end of Millionaire's Row on avenue Foch.

Strolling through the streets of the 16th, it is not difficult to see what the residents are seeking to preserve for themselves and those whose incomes allow them to join the merry throng. From the **Place du Trocadéro** with its unrivalled views across to the Eiffel Tower, a stroll up the avenue Georges Mandel and a few detours on the left-hand side below rue de la Pompe brings you to the exclusive *villas* which would be incentive enough to make anyone want to move in; small leafy mews-style streets and some of the most desirable property in Paris. From rue de la Pompe down to rue de Passy, and around Place de Mexico and rue de Longchamp, you are in closest proximity to the local shops. **Auteuil** has retained a sweet village-like atmosphere around the

Métro stations and church. But the further west you go, the duller the area becomes, with plenty of property at elevated prices for the sought-after 75016 postcode, but less of the attractions. The apartments along the Seine have the advantage of the views towards the Eiffel Tower, if you are lucky, or the disadvantage of views of the high-rise 15th arrondissement coupled with one of Paris' principal highways along the river bank.

In terms of facilities, the 16th does offer immediate access to the magnificent **Bois de Boulogne** (the equivalent of Hyde Park or Central Park for Paris), the **Parc des Princes** football and rugby stadium (with the accompanying upsides and downsides), a large municipal swimming pool, a racing course of its own at Porte d'Auteuil, and the Longchamp racing course and *Roland Garros* tennis club all on its door-step across the arrondissement border. It also offers Paris' botanical gardens, the **Serres d'Auteuil**, and museums of note, such as Balzac's former home; the Musée Guimet of oriental art; the Museum of Modern Art on avenue du Président Wilson (with its terrace café looking on to the river); the Fashion Museum; and the Musée Marmottan with its world-renowned collection of Impressionist paintings.

But not everything in the 16th garden is rosy. Public transport is sparsely distributed over this large arrondissement, which has the highest number of cars per household in Paris, a reflection of both necessity and wealth. Taxis are not always willing to take passengers to the 16th at night because they will not be able to find a return fare from the deadly calm residential streets. Surprisingly the 16th also had until recently the unhappy reputation of the highest number of prostitutes in Paris, and the avenue Foch by night still has a collection of partner-swappers. Most of the problems were or are concentrated around Porte Dauphine and the Bois, parts of which were closed at night as a result, and parts of which are still closed following the disastrous storms at the beginning of 1999. Whilst the 16th appears to be squeaky-clean, there is an uneasy sub-culture which can be annoying for local residents but also dangerous because of kerb-crawlers.

Despite this, the 16th is indisputably one of the best areas of the city. But like marriage which forms its bedrock, it is not to be entered into lightly, irreverently, or inadvisedly. It is an expensive, conservative and potentially socially cold climate into which to move if you are not prepared for it, or already in some way 'a member of the club'.

THE 17TH ARRONDISSEMENT

Covering a large expanse of north-west Paris beyond the original city walls, the 17th contains three distinct geographical sectors and populations between the *périphérique* and the city centre. To the west, the area between the **Place de l'Étoile** and **Villiers** and from the **Parc de Monceau** to **Porte Maillot** is the *haut-17ème*, a *'quartier huppé'* as sought-after as the 16th arrondissement and Neuilly next door. The commercial vibrancy of the upper end of the **avenue Wagram** and the village-like streets around the **Place des Ternes** and the avenues Mac Mahon and Carnot soon gives way further down the avenue Wagram and along boulevard de Courcelles and in the streets beside the park to grand mansion apartments and residential calm. The reputed bustling market in **rue Poncelet** echoes to the clack of well-shod ladies stealing surreptitiously into the Central European patisserie Stübli for a slice of one of their exquisite cakes.

Between Monceau and the noisy but elegant Place du Général Catroux, the 17th starts to liven up as you hit rue Legendre and **rue de Lévis**, which provides another excellent market street leading up to Villiers. In the streets leading off **rue de Prony**, there is an eclectic mix of architecture, apartments, ateliers and offices. If the lower end of the rue Legendre still bears all the hallmarks of the bourgeois population, the middle section leads you into bohemian **Batignolles**, originally a working-class district around the open railway tracks leading down from Pont Cardinet to the Gare St-Lazare, centred on the pretty little square des Batignolles and its church.

In the 17th, social standing was always literally defined by being on 'the wrong (or the right) side of the tracks'. Even before the Batignolles revival, the Marché Bio on the boulevard des Batignolles on Saturdays was drawing an ecologically-minded crowd to the 17th. But now Batignolles is an area of hot property, as it booms and flourishes unexpectedly into a 'Bobo' paradise, centred on the **rues des Dames, des Batignolles** (with its ugly Mairie), and **rue Biot**. The clientele at l'Endroit in front of the church has enough self-confident Parisian attitude to rival Abbesses, Ménilmontant or Oberkampf, with the same draw of (potential) lofts, large apartments and a down-at-heel and rich-in-pocket creativity in a village atmosphere. Property prices have risen steeply in this part of Paris, which was lacklustre and dull until only a few years ago, and which still is more residential than many of the *quartiers* it is often compared to.

A planned suspended garden over the railway tracks will lead up to the northern extremity of the 17th, the new development under the direction of top French urbanist Christian de Potzamparc at the **Porte d' Asnières** on the disused (and detoxified) SNCF lands beside the exterior boulevard Berthier. This will provide a controlled socially mixed area of new apartments around a central garden and beside renovated school and community facilities, as well as a hotel, to complete the renovation of the central section of the 17th.

Beyond Batignolles lies what property agents like to call the *village des Épinettes*, a poorer area with a large immigrant population bordering on the **avenue de Clichy** up to the **Porte de Clichy**. Property prices here are lower, but so is the general standard of living. However, one of the advantages of the eastern edge of the 17th is the proximity to the cinemas at **Place de Clichy**, both the multi-screen complex and the art cinemas, which host small cinema festivals, and a number of art and drama schools. Access to the industrial areas north of Paris is also easy either via public or private transport.

Both the boulevards de Courcelles and des Batignolles and the avenue de Clichy are major thoroughfares leading to the suburbs, and the 17th suffers from a drive-through syndrome. Critics also complain about the lack of cultural amenities, open spaces, schools and waterways. Traffic and parking is a major problem, and ironically for the *quartier* known for its ecological market on boulevard des Batignolles, it has a scarcity of bicycle lanes in comparison to the rest of Paris. But many locals seem content with their lot, and are attracted by the quality of residential life in an easily accessible area. The lack of crèches seems to be due more to a lackadaisical local mayor than a lack of children, and certain *lycées* such as those of the rue Cardinet are sought-after educational establishments. Overall, the negative points seem to be accepted with a shrug of the shoulders by laid-back locals, happy in their varied but balanced communities.

THE 18TH ARRONDISSEMENT

'Why are they all so worked up about the 18th', asked the Paris entertainment and lifestyle guide *Zurban* in a banner headline in

December 2000. Those of us who live here and have done for a number of years know the reasons why we love to live where we do, and we have no shortage of would-be neighbours when apartments fall free in the trendy bohemian hill-village around the old village centre of Abbesses, rolling down from the Sacré-Coeur to the southern border on the boulevard de Clichy and the Place Pigalle, or to the quieter upmarket lower slopes around the Mairie.

Ostensibly, the 18th has little going for it. In a monumental survey in January 2001, the 18th was ranked 19th out of the 20 arrondissements in a survey of the best places to live in Paris by *L'Express* magazine. The cheapest price per square metre for purchasing property in an arrondissement is cancelled out by the highest rate of unemployed residents and the densest population per square kilometre in Paris. Add to this one of the worst crime rates linked to the numbers of tourists plus a virulent drugs trade in a highly volatile area, some of the worst living conditions, a serious lack of schools, and a sizeable chunk of the *périphérique* as a northern barrier from the unsalubrious neighbouring *département* Seine-St-Denis (93) and by now you must be thinking that I am clinically insane to recommend the area to you.

. . . And yet – Parisians and the literati and glitterati cannot get enough of Montmartre. It all began with a small village on a hill overlooking Paris, the site of the execution of the first Parisian Christian martyrs. Later came the nuns – the Abbesses – and then came the windmills, the farms and the vineyards. The earlier nuns lost their heads in the revolution, the windmills stayed, and the area gradually became transformed into a retreat for revolutionaries, exiles, workers, painters and their whores. By the time that the penniless Picasso moved in, urban expansion had already joined the hill-top of the city below. Montmartre became home to the music halls and a timeless symbol of *la vie parisienne*.

Today, above and beyond the sex shops of the boulevard de Clichy from Place Pigalle to Place Blanche, you will find one of the most vibrant and cosmopolitan communities in Paris. The bars and shops of the **rue des Abbesses** are a rag-bag of new and established designers and their muses side-by-side with traditional shops, trendy bars, and a thriving market on the **rue Lepic**, where Dior launched the New Look in post-war Paris to the howls of the mob. South-facing apartments are bathed in sunlight on fine days, and the higher you are, the better your view is likely to be, with Paris laid out at your feet. Small houses can still be found in the richest and the poorer areas, from the villa Léandre in **avenue Junot** to the villa Poissonnière in the rue de la Goutte d'Or, or the cité du Midi off the boulevard de Clichy. The old farmhouses are still there, but are now ultra-chic apartments. The avenue Junot is now almost wall-to-wall with French TV and film personalities. Two old windmills recall the past, as does the tiny vineyard which is the excuse for the annual Montmartre Wine Festival, complete with traditional wine confraternity, village parade, wine, women and song. Practically any excuse is a good excuse for a party in Montmartre, even a wine that nobody can drink.

In the **rue des Martyrs**, two transvestite revues are amongst the favourite venues for French tourists to the capital for the quality of their shows. The Divan du Monde and the Élysées-Montmartre regularly host some of the best Paris club nights and more popular concerts, and together with La Cigale on boulevard Rochechouart, and La Loco and the Moulin-Rouge at the **Place Blanche**, ensure that Montmartre remains one of the principal areas of nightlife in Paris.

The area between the cemetery and the Mairie is a calmer bourgeois enclave centred on the **rue Caulaincourt** and the **rue Lamarck**, with solid apartments and leafy avenues. The area around the Mairie has proved popular with young families, but beyond the atmosphere changes rapidly to become much more *populaire*. However, with plenty of cheap property and good transport links across the city, the areas beyond the Mairie and the cemetery are popular choices for first-time buyers.

There is a distinct division betwen 'the dark side of the hill' – the poor northern areas beyond the cemetery from **Marx Dormoy** to the *périphérique* and **La Chapelle**; and the immigrant *quartiers* of the **Goutte d'Or, Barbès**, and **Château-Rouge** – and the 'designer darlings' playground of Abbesses, where the worst you can really expect is to be jostled by an inattentive advertising executive or musician glued to their mobile phone. Plans are now well advanced for a renovation of the *quartier* around Barbès, best known for the giant Tati store where you can buy a wedding dress for 500FF. In many respects, this project represents both the hopes and the fears of the local population.

Barbès is one of the least-safe Métro stations in Paris, best avoided after dark and on Saturday afternoons when the area explodes with activity outside Tati. On the boulevard Barbès itself, a large derelict ruin behind Tati, opposite the notorious rue de la Goutte d'Or is the centre of a renovation project which is hoped will transform this down-and-out area into an up-and-coming neighbourhood.

THE 19TH ARRONDISSEMENT

The squalid conjunction of the 10th, 18th and 19th arrondissements behind the Gares du Nord and de l'Est along boulevard de la Chapelle has for a long time been one of the eye-sores of Paris. But in the same way that urbanists and local communities and their politicians have planned to change these areas in the 10th and 18th, so their counterparts in the 19th are now following suit. In many ways, the 19th is a mirror-image of the 18th in almost a butterfly pattern. The area where the 18th ends and the 19th begins forms the central body, a ghetto of essentially North African immigrant poverty. The centre of the 19th is also to be found around a chic and charming hill-village, with less animation but a beautiful park, the **Buttes-Chaumont**. The 19th is fringed beyond its Buttes by further poorer areas, with a spectacular preponderance of high-rise concrete *cités* in the 19th, which has already had more than one bite at the urban regeneration apple with the restoration of the canals and the renovation at **La Villette**.

The Canal St-Martin continues gently north from the 10th into the 19th with the quay-sides neatly cleaned and scrubbed to make pleasant Sunday afternoon strolling territory. But the cafés and shops of the lower section have not spread north, nor yet the converted loft apartments. The result is that the canal still cuts its way through an urban priority area rather than a renovated *quartier*, despite the nearby cultural mecca of La Villette.

La Villette itself is a definite success. Arriving by Métro gives you the worst impression possible – you feel like you are arriving in an underground car park. But save your judgements until you reach the other side of the **Cité des Sciences et de l'Industrie**, with the giant **Géode** and its non-stop Zen music, fountains and lawns. Inside the Cité, huge *médiathèques* for students and for children, and a succession of free permanent exhibitions and pay-entry changing exhibitions illustrate in English and French scientific themes, from biology to electricity. In the Géode, a giant 360° cinema, a changing selection of nature films are shown. Outside, vast lawns and a number of playgrounds make this a popular area for young families. Of note is the fact that this is one of the rare areas in Paris where the French suspend their belief that walking or sitting on grass will kill you, or you will kill it. Suspended walkways allow you to continue your walk along the canal and to view the scenes below. Across the canal is the **Cité de la Musique**, and the Grande Halle exhibition centre. Music festivals and the summer open-air cinema complete the official culture complex, while the aptly named Cabaret Sauvage nearby is an increasingly popular alternative night-club venue.

Beyond the Bassin de la Villette, behind the old customs house at **Place Stalingrad**, lies the 'other' 19th. When Haussmann banished the working clases to the north of Paris as he rebuilt an imperial capital for Napoléon III, the population shifted to live beside the quarries at the **Buttes-Chaumont**. The remnants of the village of **Belleville** can be found not only on the rue de Belleville itself, but much more interestingly in the area from **Botzaris** Métro station up to the Place de Rhin et Danube. Examples of the houses originally built for the workers can be found in the grid of *villas* between the rue de Bellevue and the rue de la Mouzaia, whilst those in the *villas* between the rues de la Liberté and de l'Égalité, and the rue Miguel Hidalgo, were the homes of the foremen and bosses. Clinging to the side of the hill and with leafy gardens and high walls protecting them, these are now some of the most sought-after addresses in Paris – real town-houses, with real gardens, a rarity for Paris. Better, still, they are beside a favourite Parisian park, created by Haussmann on the side of the quarries. Skirting around the park are broad boulevards of fine apartments, but even these with their park-side views do not rival the charm of the original villas.

To some extent the 19th arrondissement is a little bit of Parisian history repeating itself: always working class, beyond the main city, and socially mixed, with surprise benefits compensating for an industrial use and dormitory-town effect. The 19th century quarry workers have been replaced by one of the most religiously and culturally mixed communities in Paris, with Arabs, Jews and Orthodox Christians all being prominent in the area. On one side of the rue de Bellevue, the former workers' cottages are now less sought-after but still lucrative villas; on the other side of the street, the destroyed village square at the **Place des Fêtes** is surrounded by high-rise horrors similar to those of the 13th. Whilst the 19th century workers were compensated with the Buttes-Chaumont park, their 20th century successors were given the Parc de la Villette complex. The *cités* accentuate the sense of insecurity, but the flip-side of the coin is a beautiful ordered calm but a lack of real *quartier* life, although it is undoubtedly better to stay east of the canal and nearer to the park. The suburban sentiment is reinforced by the fact that the area is principally served by a looping Métro branch line and three parallel lines cutting through to the city limits. But the 19th does offer a strong mix of styles, which makes it accommodating to single people or couples of all styles.

THE 20TH ARRONDISSEMENT

Present-day chroniclers of Paris repeatedly have difficulty finding something worthwhile to say about the 20th and final arrondissement of Paris. Originally a conglomerate of annexed villages – **Belleville, Charonne** and **Ménilmontant** – saturated by urban expansion and explusion when Haussmann remodelled Paris, the area has in recent years been the subject of endless articles proclaiming the arrival of another example of the 'Oberkampf effect'.

Like the neighbouring 19th the 20th was the land of the excluded and most significantly of the famous Parisian dead. The arrondissement is dominated by the renowned **Père Lachaise** cemetery, last resting place of everyone from Oscar Wilde to Jim Morrison to Yves Montand, with many earlier names of note.

From Belleville to Ménilmontant along the boulevard you will be certain of finding almost any type of food and of hearing almost any language other than French. The area has strong Arab and Jewish communities living side by side, and the rue de Belleville is the high street of the local Chinatown. A few bars have opened up in the lower end of the **rue des Panoyeaux**, but generally this livelier side of the 20th is dominated and animated by the immigrant communities. Ironically, in this most unparisian part of Paris, that most Parisian of popular amusements the *guinguettes* (music halls) were originally found. Amongst the favourite creations of these *guinguettes* was the fictional character of Milord Arsouille, the eccentric English aristocrat living in 19th century Paris and later immortalised by Belleville's most famous local girl, Edith Piaf.

Behind the Père Lachaise cemetery is the area that 'trendologues' like to pin their hopes on for an urban revival. A handful of charming streets surrounding the medieval village church of St-Germain de Charonne, its cemetery, and the upper end of the **rue St-Blaise** (avoid the lower part beyond Place des Grés) are rare remainders of the villages that once formed this part of Paris. A few yards away stands what was the end of a lost line of transport (one thing the 20th sorely lacks), the **Petite Ceinture**, which surfaces in odd places around the edge of Paris as overgrown, disused and generally attractive railway lines. The old terminus is now the ultra-trendy Café de la Flèche d'Or, but it is an isolated beacon in this part of Paris. The secret of the café's success can be found a few minutes walk away at the Porte de Bagnolet, in the highly sought-after Bobo paradise of streets such as the rue Paul Strass. Verdant gardens surrounding well-built town houses makes this a little corner of the countryside in the midst of the urban jungle.

Elsewhere in the 20th, other tiny isolated pockets of interesting buildings have survived, but with the exception of the solid bourgeois buildings around the **Place Gambetta** or the modern apartment blocks along the rue des Pyrénées, the area is most known for the social-priority tower blocks which cover the area like blisters. Some 15% of the total Parisian housing in this category is to be found in the 20th arrondissement. The middle-range accommodation to be found bordering the 11th at Nation is not as high quality as in the 11th and 12th, but it is generally better quality than elsewhere in the 20th except around Gambetta.

You may well find good value for money in terms of property surface area, but the overall quality of life is definitely lower here than elsewhere. What you will find, however, is a large selection of accommodation, and especially more recent buildings, to choose from. Given the hilly landscape (the rue de Ménilmontant is not to be walked *up* by the faint-hearted!), a well-chosen apartment at the right level here can offer you a view of the whole of Paris at your feet, even if you might lack all the facilities.

8

Living in the City – La Rive Gauche

The Left Bank of Paris, the Rive Gauche, has for more than a century inspired visions of languid intellectuals, artists and students, all associated with the seats of learning and the residential areas around them. But the Rive Gauche also has Paris' most famous monument, the Eiffel Tower, some of the finest museums, and the heart of government with the Assemblée Nationale and the Sénat. It consists of six of the arrondissements of Paris – three large, three small – including the largest populations, ranging from the immigrant communities of the 13th to the fashion victims of St-Germain to the respectable bourgeoisie of the 15th.

THE 5TH ARRONDISSEMENT

In many respects the 5th arrondissement is the political and historical alpha and omega of Paris. The arrondissement contains two of the most important Roman sites of the ancient settlement of Lutèce: the Roman baths beneath the **Hôtel de Cluny** at the crossroads of the boulevards St-Germain and St-Michel, and the amphitheatre (**arènes**), one of the largest known structures of this kind, built in the 1st century AD and abandoned after the first destruction of Lutèce at the end of the 3rd century. When the urban population withdrew to the safer Île de la Cité and the city spread on the northern bank, the students of the medieval University of Paris, **La Sorbonne**, moved in and the 5th acquired its romantic nickname as the **Quartier Latin**, referring to the fact that university teaching was in Latin. Today about 100,000 students invade the 5th each day in term-time.

Ever since, the 5th has been the heart of French-learning, from the exclusive and sought-after **Lycée Henri IV** and **Lycée Louis le Grand**, to the Sorbonne, to the specialised faculties and business schools such as the famous **Polytéchnique**, all of which have produced many of France's leaders. The huge complex at **Jussieu** has swelled the student numbers in recent years. Other parts of the decentralised Paris University are also to be found further down at Censier-Daubenton.

As if to confirm that this is where great French citizens are made, the great dome of the **Panthéon** on the Place Ste Geneviève is the state mausoleum for those deemed good and great by the French state. It was originally planned by Louis XV to rival St Peter's in Rome (and best viewed from the rue Soufflot), but the interior is large and lifeless. Of much greater beauty and interest is the tiny church next door, **St-Étienne du Mont**, where the 7th century monarchs of France are heaped one upon another beneath the shrine of St Geneviève, in a perfect Renaissance church (which holds the remains of Descartes). The exquisite **St-Séverin** church with its open cloister is a popular concert venue in the Latin Quarter, whilst the newly-restored **Val de Grâce** church is a stunning example of 17th century Baroque.

Appropriately enough, the eastern edge of the 5th is dominated by the great Parisian monuments to Islam, with the **Mosquée de Paris** and the **Institute du Monde Arabe**. The former is a real oasis of Arab elegance, and the latter is a major cultural centre, mounting exhibitions of international importance and calibre and other cultural events. Behind the mosque, science and religion rub shoulders with the **Jardin des Plantes** (botanical gardens), offering a variety of exhibition areas, gardens, giant greenhouses and even a miniature zoo.

The southern edge of the 5th is luxurious calm slipping into the 14th and 13th arrondissements, and is most known for the **Closerie des Lilas** restaurant beloved of the 'Lost Generation' of Montparnasse literati and present-day politicians. Excitable youth meanwhile diverts itself in the **quartier Contrescarpe** around the **rue Mouffetard** and the **rue du Cardinal Lemoine**; or in the cheap Greek restaurants of the Latin Quarter near the Seine; or at the cinemas of the noisy **Place St-Michel.**

As if all of this were not enough to make people talk about the 5th, it has attained a much less pleasant notoriety in the last six years; for this is 'Tiberiland', the chosen fiefdom of Jean and Xavière Tiberi, the corrupt husband-and-wife team of politicians who were ousted in the 2001 elections as Mayor and Mayoress of Paris. The quality of life in the 5th arrondissement is now reckoned to be amongst the highest in Paris, as well it should be: in 1999 the average spend per Parisian across Paris was 763FF, whilst in the 5th it amounted to 2,765FF. Discreet donations 'to the cause' and the personal intercession of Xavière for donors and voters in search of housing or a place in a municipal crèche for their children (not difficult, as the 5th has the highest number of crèches in Paris, strangely enough) have characterised the couple's style. In spite of all this, or more properly because of it, Tiberi was re-elected in the 5th arrondissement with a firm majority.

With so many churches, schools and a large botanical garden, you might be wondering if there is anywhere to live in this part of Paris. The answer is that it contains some of the most enchanting hidden corners of the capital, but naturally the prices are high. Add to the charm of the area its superb situation on the banks of the Seine at the centre of the city and its over-large slice of municipal funding for crèches and general amenities, and you will understand the attractions of the 5th.

Whilst the Latin Quarter and Quartier Contrescarpe offer the charm of hilly streets with a mix of medieval, baroque and rococo buildings, the lower part of the 5th near Val de Grâce beside the **Jardin du Luxembourg** and the Jardin des Plantes probably offers the more pleasant lifestyle, away from the carousing of students and tourists. However, the most sought-after addresses are those in the catchment areas of the state-run *lycées* Louis le Grand and Henri IV beside the Panthéon. Many parents are even willing to rent a small studio in this area in order to be able to join the geographical allocation list for these schools, such is the reputation of the two establishments. Yet no matter where you live in the 5th, if you make your home here, you will know that you are living in one of the best neighbourhoods in Paris.

THE 6TH ARRONDISSEMENT

The fields (*prés*) to the west of the Latin Quarter were turned over to the monks who built there, on the site of a Roman temple, Paris' first Christian church, at the centre of a great abbey dedicated to the popular Burgundian bishop St Germain. Ironically, the old village of **St-Germain-des-Prés** which grew up in the shadow of the abbey is now one of the most expensive areas of Paris and the new 'must have' address for the Parisian fashion houses – in an area founded on the principles of poverty and sack-cloth.

Stretching from the river bank opposite the Louvre to Montparnasse and bordered by the 5th and 7th arrondissements, the 6th is now one of the most expensive and desirable areas of Paris as the jewel in the Parisian crown. Wandering through its streets it is not hard to see why. It has the highest number of cinemas, bookshops and theatres in Paris, some of the best shops, the most famous cafés and bars, art galleries, and one of the greatest and best parks. In addition, it has two excellent markets, one of which has a public swimming pool in the basement. Finally, just to add to the injustice of it all, it contains Parisian educational institutions, from the Fine Arts School on the banks of the Seine (**École des Beaux-Arts**) to the privately-funded Catholic University (**Institut Catholique**) or the Alliance Française language school. And the icing on the cake is that all of this is to be found in an enchanting network of medieval streets with beautifully preserved buildings dating back several centuries.

The best approach on foot is from the river, across the pedestrian **Pont des Arts** with its wonderful vista onto the **Institut de France**, where the language is defined and French culture studied. Once across the bridge, slip through one of the side-passages of the Institut, and you will find yourself in a garden at the top of the **rue de Seine**, an exquisite street of art galleries and cafés where the art students from the Beaux-Arts mingle with the gallery owners. During the day the place to be seen is at La Palette with its Art Nouveau interior, and the terrace is also packed on warm evenings. Around the corner in rue Mazarine is Conran's Paris restaurant-lounge bar in a former music hall, L'Alcazar, where the *tout-Paris* comes to dine, be 'hip an' cool', and see and be seen.

The **rue de Buci**, which intersects with the rue de Seine, is a lively market street supplying neighbourhood needs before being transformed into the narrow but charming **rue St-André-des-Arts**, with its cinemas and shops leading up to the Place St-Michel and the passage cutting through to the cinema and student sprawl of **Place de l'Odéon**, and the great national theatre just behind. If you carry on up through the tiny streets parallel to rue Jacob, you will arrive at the Place St-Germain-des-Prés, with the great church and the now dominant fashion houses. Next to the church you will also find the eateries of the St Germain set, the Cafés de Flore and Les Deux Magots, and the Brasserie Lipp opposite.

Tucked behind the boulevard is the other great church of the 6th **St-Sulpice**, which dominates its own *quartier* of little streets full of bookshops, designers and restaurants leading up to

Mabillon Métro. This area has a strong student population, and is often lively. Just beyond St-Sulpice lies the great **Jardin du Luxembourg**, containing the French upper house, the Sénat, and the museum attached to it. This was the former palace of Marie de Medici, who when she was not killing Protestants or consulting her astrologers to decide who to poison next, built herself a magnificent palace and art collection. The gardens are one of the traditional favoured haunts of Parisians, providing a lung for this over-crowded corner of Paris, with fountains, tennis courts and a children's puppet theatre at the quieter end of the park leading to the Paris Observatory.

To the west of the park lies a quieter, more habitable and very attractive area. To explore it at its best, take the **rue du Cherche Midi** from the Place de la Croix-Rouge and keep walking. This street is pure St-Germain, a mix of clothes shops and interior designers, trendy little cafés further on, and innovative little twists in every shop window. In the rue Jean Ferrandi, a small group of warehouses have been converted into loft apartments with vines strung between. By now you are pushing towards Montparnasse, and you are in an area always preferred by the English-language communities. Hence it is no surprise to find the excellent Children's English Learning Centre in **rue de Fleurus**, handily situated next door to the Alliance Française and its language courses.

Cutting across this whole sector, from ultra-chic Sèvres-Babylone to more relaxed Montparnasse, is the **boulevard Raspail**. Right from its beginnings next-door in the 7th arrondissement.

Traffic is one of the major problems of the 6th, with major arteries curving their way through medieval streets, clogged with badly-parked cars. The other major problems of the 6th are both symbolic and symptomatic. The young people who live there are often single or childless couples, and young families are less common than elsewhere on the Left Bank. For despite a high number of crèches and excellent schools, the urban drift is away from the 6th, with its staggering house prices.

THE 7TH ARRONDISSEMENT

The last of the 'poor little rich' arrondissements nestling on the left bank of the Seine, the 7th is the most aristocratic arrondissement in Paris. Part of this allure comes from the uniformity of architectural styles in the lush avenues built for and still inhabited by the French aristocracy, and part from the enormous concentration of power in the *quartier*, with the Assemblée Nationale and the embassies and government ministries all located here. But even if the outward appearance is one of ordered calm – far too calm, for many people's liking – the 7th remains an area of paradox.

On the one hand, this right-wing bastion of family values has unsurprisingly the highest number of *familles nombreuses* (three or more children) in Paris. Yet the arrondissement has the highest level of urban drift away from the centre, having lost 8.5% of its population between 1989 and 1999. It occasionally has the appearance of a *quartier populaire* when the concerts, exhibitions and rallies on the **Champ de Mars** at the **Tour Eiffel** are taken into consideration, and fine weather transforms the lawns in front of **Les Invalides** into an impromptu park and sports ground. But it remains one of the most exclusive areas of Paris, with many of the gardens are behind high walls in private hands, including those of the Church, which owns vast tracts of land in the 7th. For those same embassies and ministries which are so well-guarded that you always feel safe in the 7th are surrounded by van loads of police for a reason – because they are the target of demonstrations and marches. So the silver-lined 7th is not without some clouds to spoil the view occasionally.

And then, local activists would like you to know, the 7th has its own *quartier difficile*, although everything is relative. The real heart of the 7th the **Gros Gaillou** district lies between the **avenues Bosquet** and **de la Motte-Picquet** and the **rue St-Dominique** up to **Les Invalides**, with the cheerful market street on **rue Cler** where ladies who lunch buy provisions for their friends and families. This is the one area which breaks out of the general mould to demonstrate signs of individuality and local colour, and is an area popular with English-speaking expatriates, many of whom wander down from the **American Church** and community centre at 65, quai d'Orsay. This area is not in any way dangerous, and is a real joy to shop or live in; but it does have a distinctly different feel to the areas all around.

To the west, the 3,000 residents overlooking the Champ de Mars need not be pitied too much for ring-side views of the best concerts and the annual fireworks displays for Bastille Day. The avenues on either side of the Champ de Mars represent the height of exclusive luxury. The École Militaire provides a natural dam at the end of the Champ, with UNESCO directly behind, creating an area around avenue de Breteuil where you could hear a pin drop in the streets much of the time.

Les Invalides was founded by Louis XIV as a home for his old soldiers and today houses the national army museum as well as Napoléon's tomb beneath the golden cupola. It remains an extremely popular tourist site, whilst the lawns in front are busy in summer as Parisians stretch out in the sun or play football or softball, and the area takes on a festive feel to match the weather. On the rue de Constantine overlooking the lawns you will find the British and Canadian cultural institutes, which together with the American Church nearby make the 7th a likely venue to meet other English-speakers. Directly next door to Les Invalides you will find the Musée Rodin, dedicated to the sculptor's work displayed in the mansion and its park.

On the river bank beside Les Invalides you will find the Ministry of Foreign Affairs, then the residence of the President of the **Assemblée Nationale** (the Speaker), then the Assemblée itself. This eastern flank of the 7th, with its concentration of ministries and the Prime Minister's residence at the **Hôtel Matignon**, is the Westminster of Paris, and other embassies are found here in the magnificent 18th century mansions of the **rue de Grenelle**. Each year in September the **Journées de Patrimoine** (also known as the **Portes-Ouvertes**) allow visitors to cross these hallowed thresholds free of charge for a weekend, but queues for the finest palaces are very long.

On the river bank above, the **Musée d'Orsay** is one of Paris' finest museums. Housed in the converted railway station of the Gare d'Orsay, it contains a stunning collection of Impressionist art, and hosts major exhibitions. The Quai Voltaire (where Rudolf Nureyev lived and died) has some of the allure of the neighbouring 6th, and continues along the rue des Saints-Pères leading down to the **rue du Bac** and the boulevard Raspail. This boulevard, together with the lower stretches of the boulevard St-Germain itself, has now been effectively annexed by the fashion houses in the neighbouring district.

The great Parisian department store **Le Bon Marché** dominates the eastern edge of the 7th, with the disputed **Hôpital Laënnec** (about to be redeveloped) just behind it. Beside Le Bon Marché and its **Grande Épicérie** sits the popular shrine of the Miraculous Medal, which also explains the heavy concentration of convents and religious orders in this corner of Paris. Pushing north from Le

Bon Marché you are in the heart of St-Germain. The tiny square **Chaise Recamier** with its luxury apartments overhanging the square and the neighbouring Éspace Électre, home to the EDF's art foundation in a beautifully converted power-station, perhaps best marks the point at which the verdant 7th merges effortlessly into the innovative 6th arrondissement.

Like the neighbouring 6th arrondissement, the 7th and its municipal leaders are perplexed by the urban drift away from the area and the need to 'maintain standards', with house prices in this area providing a natural filter on those who can afford to join the happy and decreasing few. The lack of cinemas and bars in the area is a serious handicap to drawing a younger population to the 7th, although both Gros Caillou and the St-Germain side are *'plutôt sympa'* (quite pleasant) and represent the human face of the 7th. Perhaps the real danger of the 6th is the ivory-tower effect which overcame the first aristocratic builders and inhabitants of the area, who were so overwhelmed with their walled-in splendour and beauty that they became cut off from reality. *L'Express* said of the 7th in its Parisian survey in January 2001, 'It's not the end of the earth, but it is elsewhere.'

THE 13TH ARRONDISSEMENT

Covering a large expanse of south-east Paris from the Seine behind Notre-Dame to the city limits, the 13th is the fifth largest arrondissement in terms of population (171,000 people in 1999), the same size as the city of Lille. Originally an area of rural cultivation on the edge of the city, centred on the **Butte aux Cailles** and its windmills (rather like the Butte Montmartre in the north), the 13th was scarred for decades by the traces of the industries which for centuries had used it as a convenient base and dumping-ground. By the late 20th century, the river banks were home to derelict warehouses alongside the open railway tracks leading to the **Gare d'Austerlitz** similar to those behind the Gares de l'Est and du Nord; and the 13th is chiefly known for the jungle of concrete towers built in the 1970s to house the influx of Chinese immigrants, amongst others.

However – like other former forlorn and industrial districts of Paris, the industrial and urban scars are beginning to heal and new life is returning to an area dominated by one of the largest projects of urban reconstruction in Paris. The 13th is building its hopes for the future not on restoration but on innovation. The ZAC Paris project (planned completion date 2006) along the river bank is divided into three zones, with plans to cover the railway tracks with a 26 hectare concrete roof, 100m wide and 2.6km long. The new Bibliothèque Nationale François Mitterrand on the river bank is to be the centre-piece of a new zone of offices and social-priority and private housing, cultural centres including the Cité de l'Image with 14 screens due to be opened in 2002, and the new Paris-VII university due to be opened in 2003. The new Météore Métro line 14 and a link to the RER line C will complete the pattern in an area which suffers nonetheless from a lack of public transport. If this project succeeds, the 13th could become one of the most exciting areas of Paris within the next five years.

The arrival of the new Métro line is a matter of real importance in an area of Paris which has the air of being a dormitory town for Paris. One local politician said that the reason so many people choose to live in the 13th is because, 'it's near to'; the sub-text being that it is near to everywhere you would rather be than here, i.e. you sleep there, but shop, work or go out elsewhere. The 13th does possess a large number of parks and open spaces, especially on the southern border, and also boasts some of the best sports facilities in Paris. These include the tiled Art Deco masterpiece swimming pool at Place Verlaine. But one of the real problems of the 13th as a place to live has been its inability to establish its own *esprit du quartier* or particular style.

There are, however, notable exceptions to this rule. The north of the 13th, bordering on the 5th, contains an elegant area around the **avenue des Gobelins** and the former royal tapestry factory. The Gobelins tapestry factory is the major museum in the arrondissement, housed in a 17th century complex which can be visited by appointment. The large and charmless **Place d'Italie**, with concrete towers peering down upon it, is nonetheless a major cinema centre and the home to the wildly popular roller-blade rallies across Paris. Just nearby is the old village centre of **La Butte aux Cailles**, a much calmer but still charming example of the old Parisian hill villages epitomised by Montmartre. Small houses with creeping ivy-covered façades and gardens in narrow twisting streets create a small oasis of calm. Whilst the other main avenues and the rue de Tolbiac remain long lifeless thoroughfares, situated beside them are small pockets of houses similar to La Butte aux Cailles, cheek-by-jowl with the ever-present towers. Town-houses such as these are a rarity in Paris, and are only to be found in the outlying arrondissements such as the 13th, the 18th, the 19th and the 20th. Signs of new life are already appearing along the river, with the trendy 'Batofar' **péniche** (barge) nightclub and restaurant, and a colony of artists (the highest registered number of any Parisian arrondissement) and gallery-owners moving in around the **rue Louise-Weiss**. But, above all, the 13th is known as one of Paris' two '**Chinatowns**', with some 30,000 or so Asian immigrant families settled in the areas around avenue de Choisy and avenue d'Italie. The traditional Chinese New Year Festival in the 13th, complete with dancing dragons and parades, draws thousands of people each year.

THE 14TH ARRONDISSEMENT

Fans of the 14th, stretching from Montparnasse to the southern *périphérique*, often say that it is one of the best kept secrets in Paris, or the symbol of the art of discretion, as *L'Express* described the area in January 2001. The fact that it does manage to keep this secret so well is perhaps the final victory of many such French victories that this area has known and commemorates. The choice of Alésia as a name for a Métro station, and the long rue Vercingétorix beside the railway tracks at Montparnasse commemorate the first great Gallic victory over foreign invaders. The avenue du Général Leclerc from the Porte d'Orléans commemorates the most recent French hero to have led his troops and their American allies into liberated Paris on the 8th May 1945, earning Leclerc the right to almost as many streets named after him as de Gaulle.

For Americans in Paris particularly, the 14th is associated with the northern corner of the arrondissement forming part of the Montparnasse *quartier*, with its mythical mix of writers and painters who moved down-town from the higher views and rents of Montmartre in the 1920s. The bars and cabarets are still there, and like any self-respecting artist's quarter, the local Montparnasse cemetery has its fair share of writers and performers, from Jean-Paul Sartre and his muse Simone de Beauvoir, to the modern French singer-songwriter Serge Gainsbourg. But the Montparnasse of the artists is only one small corner of the 14th, and most of the artists left a long time ago.

The 14th is now a heavily residential district, even if a few theatres and bars keep the old flame burning, and residential calm now reigns in the area. In the north of the arrondissement, bordering on the 5th (and with the same effect as in the neighbouring 13th arrondissement), lies the Paris **Obsérvatoire**, founded in the 17th century. In the rue Cassini directly in front of the Observatory stand a row of excellent Art Nouveau artists' studios from the beginning of the 20th century. On the Boulevard St-Jacques can be found one of the original 18th century palaces which was moved stone by stone from the former rural playground on the Champs-Élysées, and which is home to the Société des Gens de Lettres et du Theâtre, a distinguished writers' and actors' club. On the opposite side of the road is one of the 14th's many hospitals; and on the broad sweeping boulevard Arago where artists used to have their ateliers, the reason for the cheap property on this otherwise attractive boulevard becomes clear: a club with a very strict door policy and solid gloomy dark brick walls, the Prison de la Santé, with its 'celebrity' cells for France's corrupt politicians. Here in a geographical microcosm then, you have the 14th – the learned, the talented, the medics, the famous and the infamous, side by side in calm, discreet surroundings.

Population-wise, the 14th traditionally draws young people starting out in their professional life, without the means to live in more central Paris, and attracted by the security and calm of the area and the reasonable property prices. There is certainly no shortage of housing in this area, and perhaps even too much of the same sort of apartments: drab high-rise blocks of municipally-owned social priority housing (*cités*) which reflect the working-class origins of the 14th during the Universal Exhibitions at the end of the 19th and beginning of the 20th centuries. The rue Vercingétorix with its open spaces is the most recent attempt at this old formula. It leads down from the Place de Catalogne, with its expensive modern apartments for the middle and upper classes who generally live in the northern half of the arrondissement near to the best transport connections. Public transport does go out to the further reaches of the 14th, but it is more sparingly distributed along the interior boulevards and on the two Métro lines and one RER line piercing the residential mass. What then makes for the best-kept secret in Paris?

Before the restructuring of the Paris hospital sector began under Alain Juppé in the mid-1900s, the 14th was most well-known for its seven hospitals, six of which are still operational at the time of writing, including the psychiatric Hôpital St-Anne (be careful if anybody suggests that you should try a stay there – it is common parlance for suggesting that you must be mad). Now that Broussais has been closed down in the already saturated social-priority housing area beyond Plaisance, new uses are having to be found for the vast site, which will inevitably include housing nontheless.

Under current plans, the 14th should be the site both of a *périphérique* cover-over with a new garden and sports grounds on top of the concrete, and of one of the earliest stretches of the new Paris tramway system. It also benefits from a string of parks and sports stadiums between the boulevards Brune and Jourdan, including the *Cité Internationale Universitaire de Paris*. This was founded in the 1920s to be a sort of university-level League of Nations, with each country building and maintaining their own House for higher education students from their country to come and study together in Paris. 'A city within the city' (just), it has its own sports grounds, theatre, church and even its own hospital up the road. The mock-Tudor style familiar to Americans creates a comfortable campus effect on the edge of the city, and the Cité is served by its own RER station. The Parc Montsouris opposite is a favourite with Parisians, offering everything that parks should in the popular imagination – greenery, a lake, a puppet theatre and restaurant. The streets around the park have fine apartments looking over the park, and the avenue René Coty provides a quick link back to the real hub of the 14th, the **Place Denfert-Rochereau**.

Denfert-Rochereau, with its RER station and the Orlybus for Paris' southern airport, leads out in all directions, to the commercial heart of the 14th on avenue du Général Leclerc and the cinemas at Alésia; to the market street **rue Daguerre** with its collection of renovated trendy cafés nearest to Denfert-Rochereau and a good selection of apartments above the shops and stalls below, running all the way to avenue du Maine. It is also the entrance to the 14th's very own and very particular underground system – the Catacombs of Paris.

Emerging from the catacombs (via narrow deep spiral staircases) brings you out opposite the kind of accommodation that many people associate with the 14th. The Passage Montbrun, or else villa Alésia, contain small houses and collections of artists' studios which have been converted into loft apartments.

THE 15TH ARRONDISSEMENT

Forming a neat south-western corner for Paris from the Eiffel Tower to the *périphérique* and the Portes de Sèvres and Versailles, this solidly residential monotone middle-class area in some respects feels like an anchor for Paris. The arrondissement with the highest population (230,000), but a dearth of cultural and transport facilities for such a large area is a bastion of family values – keeping Paris' feet on the ground in the face of the trendier individualist arrondissements to the east. The arrondissement provides a perfect synthesis between the 7th next door which hogs the local culture, the ultra-chic 16th across the river, and the well-to-do suburbs to the west.

It is difficult to identify real *quartiers* in the 15th, which has no real history or former villages but instead represents the urban expansion of Paris which started in the 1820s with the developments of Grenelle served by the 'new' church of **St-Jean-Baptiste-de-Grenelle**. On the eastern borders, the *haute-bourgeoisie* live comfortably between the avenue de Suffren, with its access onto the Champ de Mars, and the **boulevards de Grenelle** and **Garibaldi** with the Métro viaduct forming a natural barrier.

As might be expected from an area of planned dense housing, the 15th is peppered with small squares with public gardens and playgrounds. Municipal benefactors endowed these with bandstands and open-air stages such as the **Place Dupleix**, the **Place du Commerce** or the **Square St-Lambert**. Unfortunately, these bandstands now seem to stand well-preserved but forlorn in the parks where the children still play, although they have not gone unnoticed by artists in search of venues and audiences.

Ironically for an area that slumbers culturally, two of the best parks in the area offer a cultural world of their own, resulting from highly original conversions of the 15th's industrial past. At the entrance to the **Parc Georges Brassens**, on the southern city limits, two smiling copper cows stand aloft and guard the entrance to the site of the former Paris abbatoirs. The park is bordered by a school, and rather like the more recent Parc de Bercy in the 12th, this park has areas of cultivation especially conceived and reserved for local school-children. Along the rue Brancion side of the park in the former sheds reserved for condemned horses the Paris book market for new and second-hand books is now held every weekend. A small theatre in the park completes the cultural complex in the shadow of the vast looming *cités* on the outer boulevards.

In the far north of the 15th on the banks of the Seine lies the converted Citroën factory site now known as the **Parc André Citroën**. Surrounded by the state-owned TV stations France 2 and FR3 on one side and the privately-owned cable TV channel *Canal+* on the other, the futuristic centre-piece park feels more like a botanical garden than a place to relax, although it is undoubtedly beautiful. Eight giant greenhouses (including one dedicated to the vegetation of Australasia), colour-coded gardens and concrete canals and interspersed by controlled waterfalls and fountains give an impression of being in a latter-day Versailles. With so much creativity and wealth concentrated in one corner of the arrondissement, you might expect to find a lively neighbourhood nearby. Instead the rue Balard which runs beside the park is deathly quiet. Only the highly popular sports complex at **Aqua Boulevard** just beyond gives any indication of human life in this area.

On the river bank between this park and the Eiffel Tower is the **quartier Charles Michel**, a dull jungle of modern apartment blocks. Just behind lies the more animated and pleasant area centred on the **rue du Commerce**, a busy shopping street with a clutch of cafés and bars, most notably the three-storey café du Commerce at the far end nearest St-Jean-Baptiste-de-Grenelle and the rue des Entrepreneurs. This lively area, feeding off the **avenue de la Motte-Picquet**, is one of the most pleasant corners of the 15th. Around the Métro **Convention** a similar but lesser effect can also be seen, although how much that will last if the two threatened cinemas are closed remains to be seen.

The area around **Pasteur** is best known for the Institut Pasteur, a world-renowned medical research institute. Just nearby, the Hôpital Necker is France's principal paediatric hospital. Until recently the 15th was as well-endowed as the 14th with hospitals, but restructuring is threatening a number of closures including the Hôpital St-Michel. The hospitals have followed the urban tide to a new super-hospital on the western extremity, the **Hôpital Européen Georges Pompidou** beside the Parc André Citroën, which has opened to a cacophony of complaints.

The advantages of the 15th include its solid like-minded respectability, which is noticeable in the behaviour of polite and helpful local residents who are not frightened to go towards a stranger who is obviously a little lost. Apartments are everywhere, and the standard is always at least fair if not very high. There are enough local transport links and shops scattered across the arrondissement to survive comfortably, but nothing more than that. Even if the area is the bastion of family life, the number of young children is leading to problems in placing children in crèches and schools.

9

Living in the Suburbs

Parisian attitude comes in many forms. City dwellers who choose to live within the *périphérique* and the twenty arrondissements almost rejoice in cursing *banlieusards* (suburban-dwellers) when it comes to complaining about bad driving in the city at weekends or over-crowding at the entrances to favourite nightclubs or restaurants. In so doing, they neatly over-look the fact that some of greater Paris' best addresses are to be found cheek-by-jowl with some of Paris' worst addresses.

One of the greatest physical difficulties Paris faces is breaking down the barrier it set up in the 1960s and early 1970s with the construction of the *périphérique*. Urban planners took this necessity as an opportunity to build a modern wall around the city to keep out the immigrants that had been allowed into France to do the low status low-paid work which the French did not want. Nobody wants to live next to Europe's busiest ring-road, so this was also the obvious place to build high-rise towers to accommodate France's immigrant communities from the former African colonies. Two necessary but undesirable protective rings were thus placed one upon another, and today 985,000 people live within 800m of the ring-road around Paris.

Beyond this lies what is known as the **petite couronne**, the little crown, of inner Parisian suburbs (*banlieues*) the *départements* 92, 93 and 94, followed by the **grande couronne** of the outer and generally chic suburbs (77, 78, 91 and 95), which represent what many Parisians aspire to: individual houses, greenery, calm and space, within easy striking distance of the heart of the city. The twenty arrondissements of Paris make up the *département* 75, but the surrounding *départements* are each known by their own name and number. Some are surprisingly rural whilst others are characterised by concrete rather than cows. The difference between communes is quite marked, and even within communes, so take a good look at the area before deciding where to live.

THE WESTERN SUBURBS

Département 92 – Hauts-de-Seine

Curling around the western edge of Paris, the département des Hauts-de-Seine (literally the Upper Seine) has long been one of the most desirable parts of the Paris region. The greatest advantage of the Hauts-de-Seine is its proximity to Paris and La Défense, with a good transport system, whilst maintaining the advantages of calm, space, individual houses and verdant woods. It is also one of the two *départements* which have traditionally drawn strong English-speaking communities, attracted by the high-quality lifestyle, the business opportunities and easy access to the American and British schools.

Amongst the most sought-after areas are those which slip effortlessly into the Parisian city landscape beside the river and the Bois de Boulogne. **Neuilly-sur-Seine** (not to be confused with the very different Neuilly-Plaisance in the east) is one of *the* Parisian addresses. Served by the Métro line, a few minutes from the Arc de Triomphe in one direction and the business district of La Défense in the other, Neuilly exudes luxury living at every street corner. A mix of ancient and modern apartments and houses are home to some of the cream of French society who have spilled over from the 16th next-door. Neighbouring **Levallois-Perret** was originally a working-class district, but is now firmly in the upward spiral of gentrification which began quite some time ago. Both suburbs have good transport links, English-speaking hospitals, and rich populations. The living is easy, but definitely more down-beat than life in the city.

The avenue Charles de Gaulle leading up from Paris through Neuilly takes you straight to **La Défense**, the great business centre built on the site of a former defensive fort. A vast array of different towers representing company headquarters built over a vast shopping centre, La Défense only really lives during the daytime and mainly in the week. The shopping centre has, however, proved to be a huge draw, so Saturdays are also very lively. Apartments are being built all the time to create a local population instead of a commuter population, but the area still feels pretty lifeless and sometimes rather sinister after dark. The Métro, RER and local SNCF trains all serve La Défense, as does an extensive network of buses.

Downtown La Défense skulks under the name of **Nanterre**, the headquarters of the département. More industrial and definitely not as upbeat as La Défense, Nanterre is home to a major university. The Thêatre des Amandiers, the local theatre, was one of a number of theatres established in the suburbs 'to bring culture to the people' in one of President Mitterrand's grand initiatives. The theatre does offer some excellent productions, and occasionally these are in English.

If you are going to move near to La Défense, you would be much better advised to check out the towns of **Puteaux** and **Courbevoie** on either side of the business park, and perhaps **Asnières-sur-Seine**. Of the three, Courbevoie is probably the most pleasant, with an extremely attractive selection of houses near to the station off avenue Marceau and rue Barbès, and an ever-increasing selection of new apartments being constructed nearer to La Défense itself. Asnières, with its château and world-renowned Pets Cemetery, is a town 'on the up'. You should stick to the river-side areas, as further north and east the quality of life declines.

Puteaux and **Suresnes** offer views across western Paris with a good mix of apartments and houses, and is the gateway to a succession of highly desirable suburban towns to the west leading out to Versailles. **Rueil-Malmaison**, to the west of Suresnes and centred on the château of the Empress Joséphine, is another popular choice amongst young families. **St-Cloud** at the end of the Métro and also served by the SNCF, is home to the American School of Paris and also one of Paris' chic race-courses. All that remains of the former royal château where Napoléon III held court is the wonderful park overlooking Paris – a mini Bois de Boulogne. **Sèvres** is renowned for its porcelain factory and museum, whilst neighbouring **Ville d'Avray** was home to French politicians and artists who lived by the woods surrounding the lakes. All of these are very sought-after areas, as are the exclusive trio of **Garches, Vaucresson** and **Marne-la-Coquette**. Like their desirable counterparts across the forests leading to Versailles in the neighbouring département, the appeal of these communes is the small-town feel, abundant greenery and high-quality housing.

On the other side of the Bois de Boulogne from Neuilly lies **Boulogne-Billancourt**, a former industrial area and home to the Renault car company. Once again the gentle change from city to suburb makes this a very sought-after area, even if it lacks charm. There is a plentiful supply of apartments, and the presence of the giant Renault factories and headquarters has made the commune a kind of fiscal paradise in terms of local taxes, with Renault picking up the brunt of the town's budget. The historic heart of the car works is a large island in the Seine, now disused, and the subject of fierce debate as to redevelopment. One of France's leading entrepreneurs, François Pinault, intends housing his modern art collection there in a new museum, but there are also plans to build luxury apartments. Meanwhile locals are crying out for recreational facilities on the islands. The jury is still out on this development as on so many others in Paris at the moment.

The south-western corner of the Hauts-de-Seine across the river from Boulogne is home to two other areas of interest. **Issy-les Moulineaux** at the end of the Métro has traditionally been a workers' district and Communist stronghold for generations. The area is now experiencing the 'Levallois effect', and upward mobility is evident as young executive families move in. This is the spill-over in fact from neighbouring **Meudon**. The lower reaches might not seem attractive, but you are only minutes from the Meudon forest, which also houses the major British sporting club, the Standard Athletic Club. Neighbouring **Clamart** appears to be the poor relation in comparison, but it is worth taking a look at for cheaper prices.

The final two areas of note in the Hauts-de-Seine are **Chatenay-Malabry** and **Sceaux**. Chatenay-Malabry is a quiet and comfortable suburb, one of the favourite escapes of Parisians. The magnificent gardens in Sceaux rolling down to a grand canal, overlooked by a small 19th century château which houses the Museum of the Île de France, are the centre-piece of this bourgeois enclave.

Département 78 – Les Yvelines

Whilst the Hauts-de-Seine seems to cuddle up to Paris, the Yvelines département represents the real descent into rural living within commuting distance of Paris, separating 'them' (the rest of France) and 'us' (the Parisians).

The capital of the département is the royal mini-city of **Versailles**, which is as good a starting point as any from which to explore the area. The historic heart of the town around the great château (still the centre of local cultural life) is full of former ministries, embassies and noble mansions built to serve the court. Obviously this is the best and most sought-after *quartier* of the town and the liveliest. The Chantiers district may be less sought-after but the house prices are also noticeably different.

Versailles was originally a royal hunting lodge, and the forests of the Yvelines département are in fact littered with former royal hunting lodges which drew favour from Louis XIV. Many of these have now disappeared, but the park at **Marly-le-Roi** which surrounded one such overgrown hunting 'lodge' is still the principal attraction of this town. At the other end of the forest stands **St-Germain-en-Laye** where the exiled Stuart court settled at the end of the 17th century. The great château in the town centre is the starting point for a terrace overlooking Paris, leading down via restored formal gardens and lawns transformed into a public park, into the forest. The town is about 40 minutes from Paris on the RER, and like other former royal towns has its fair share of fine buildings in the centre. It also has the advantage of the International Lycée, one of the most renowned schools in France catering to foreign residents, with English and American sections amongst others.

On either side of the Forêt de Marly lie the two straggling villages of **L'Etang-la-Ville** and **St-Nom-la-Bréteche**. Both are popular with the English-speaking communities, but you are definitely lost here without a car.

West of Versailles, you will also find very rural territory, beginning with **St-Cyr-l'Ecole**, the former rural orphanage which was transformed into the élite military academy. To the south lies **Damperre, Chevreuse**, and the sought-after but isolated villages of the **Yvette** valley. If you do choose to look for a home in these areas, you should be wary of isolating yourself too much, especially in the early stages of your move to France. **Rambouillet** in the far west of the département is the centre of its own forest, and its château is one of the official presidential residences occasionally used for international conferences. Discretion and calm are the key words of this part of the world, although between Chevreuse and Versailles you will find a more industrial area stretching from **Trappes** and the new town of **St-Quentin-en-Yvelines** to **Viroflay** and **Vélizy** (with its large shopping centre) on the département borders.

Between Marly-le-Roi and the département border are the more developed but highly sought-after suburbs of **Louveciennes, La-Celle-St-Cloud** and **Bougival**. Across the river lies **Croissy-sur-Seine**, another Anglophone favourite, with the British School of Paris split between the Junior School in Bougival and the Senior School in Croissy-sur-Seine. The neighbouring towns of **Chatou, Le Vésinet, Le Pecq**, and **Montesson** complete the 'Golden Triangle' formed by St Germain-en-Laye, Marly-le-Roi and Le Vésinet. All have significant American and British presences.

Beyond the A14 autoroute you will find another extremely popular expatriate community base in **Maisons-Laffitte**, originally centred on the racecourse beside the impressive town-centre château, and stretching down to **Le Mesnil le Roi**. Maisons-Laffitte was first colonised by British workers constructing the first French railways in the mid-19th century, and a second wave of British immigrants arrived with the development of the stables and races. Maisons-Laffitte and Bougival have their own Cubs and Scouts, Brownies and Guide packs, in addition to being near to the British Schools, and there are thriving Anglican/Episcopalian churches in Maisons-Laffitte and Versailles.

The rest of the département is a mixture of small country villages and less interesting modern towns displaying clear signs of urban problems. Some of the older towns such as **Poissy** have attractive medieval centres, but others such as **Mantes-la-Jolie** fail to live up to promising first signs.

By the time that you reach Mantes – only 40 minutes by fast train from central Paris – you are on the doorstep of Normandy, and the grand collegiate church and medieval town centre may seem very appealing. But you should be careful here. Not only are the best areas away from the town centre, requiring a car once again to begin your journey, but the town also is home to one of the most troubled collections of *cités* around Paris, along with Chanteloup-le-Vignes further down the river. Before you choose where to live in Les Yvelines, you do need to check on where your transportation lines run through, as not everything in the département which forms Paris' garden is rosy.

THE NORTHERN SUBURBS

Département 95 – Val-d'Oise, Département 60 – Oise and Département 93 – Seine-St-Denis

There is a stark contrast between the western and northern suburbs of Paris, and both the Val-d'Oise and the neighbouring Seine-St-Denis are infamous for being the 'bad boys' of the suburban Parisian pack. However, the 'Neuf-Trois' and the 'Neuf-Cinq' as they have come to be known represent in microcosm the best, the worst and the most challenging aspects of Parisian and French contemporary society.

The best areas

As the rural sounding name might suggest, the Val-d'Oise has been subject to some of the worst effects of reckless urbanisation in recent decades. Moreover, it suffers from the domination of France's major international airport, Roissy-Charles de Gaulle. The result is a hard-core of problem areas bordering on the Seine-St-Denis, obscuring some extremely desirable regions in the northern wooded areas of **Montmorency, Taverny** and **L'Îsle Adam**.

These three communes and those beyond them represent 'the acceptable face' of the Val-d'Oise, a reverse situation to Neuilly-Levallois and Boulogne in Département 92 where the city and suburbs meet. For in the further communes of Département 95 the suburbs and the countryside merge effortlessly with the bourgeois calm of the equestrian village of **Chantilly** (60) centred on its great château and racecourse in the forest, and the noble and exclusive **Senlis** (60) on the furthest reaches of the Parisian shores in Département 60. You can dream of buying a house in Senlis, but do not count on it unless you marry into one of the local families who have lived there for generations. Chantilly, on the other hand, has long British links once again via the racecourse, and boasts a busy Anglican church and community centre, and English lessons for local Anglophone children run by a local association of English-speaking families (APARC, BP 60634, Chantilly Cedex. e-mail address: aparc@aol.com).

Nearer the centre of Paris, the other isolated area of note is **Enghien-les-Bains**, the sophisticated lakeside playground with its casino and racecourse. Like the other towns mentioned above, Enghien was a favoured retreat for Paris businessmen and stars. The result in all of these towns is an ample selection of fine 19th and early 20th century villas, side by side with more recent luxury developments.

Pontoise has been completely eclipsed by the new town on its outskirts, Cergy-Pontoise, a tough new town at the end of the RER line which should be avoided. But beyond to the north-west lies a large stretch of the Val-d'Oise département which really does not associate itself with Paris but is still in striking distance, a land of small tranquil country towns and villages pushing down towards the Norman border.

The northern suburbs
When you see the poverty of some of the northern suburbs which you should definitely avoid (Sarcelles, Gonnesse, Stains, Aubervilliers, Aulnay-sous-Bois, La Courneuve), it is difficult to imagine that Roissy was once a Roman rural retreat (as excavations have shown), and that the solitary medieval church in old Gonnesse was the centre of a rural community. These towns and others around about are now the 'badlands' of Paris, home to the *racaille* (hoodlums or yobs). They are mostly but not exclusively second and third generation immigrants from former African colonies, easily identified by the baseball cap and designer label sportswear 'uniform' they have created for themselves. The prevailing atmosphere is violent, drug-trafficking is rife, unemployment is endemic, and crime is for many a way of life.

You will not be able to avoid crossing these areas when you take public transport to and from the airport; or a train at the Gare du Nord or de l'Est; or a Métro which finishes up at Bobigny or La Courneuve but runs through central Paris and across to the other side. The sense of insecurity you will feel if you are confronted with this even once will help you understand why security is the number one priority on every political agenda.

The cultural revolution
It is hard to understand how the French state could have allowed one of the finest monuments of French Gothic architecture and one of the cradles of French history to become enveloped by a town known for squalor. But this is precisely what has happened to the **Basilique-St-Denis** (93), which was the coronation and the burial church of the French kings. The result is a magnificent and unique display of royal tombs and sculpture and soaring architecture best viewed on a sunny day when light floods the cathedral, home to a renowned annual music festival. Nearby the **Stade de France**, built for the last Football World Cup and destined to be one of France's Olympic stadiums in 2008 if their bid is successful, has been a centre-piece in seeking to reconstruct this part of Paris, which is also destined to host the next International Exhibition hosted by Paris in 2004. There is also talk of trying to renovate the nearby canal de l'Ourcq which runs down to La Villette on the northern edge of Paris.

Bobigny, the capital of Seine-St-Denis, has always been known as one of the main trouble-spots of this deeply troubled area. For this reason, it was one of the sites chosen for the suburban distribution of culture under François Mitterrand, and the **MC93** theatre now hosts major productions and visiting companies, including many in English. The town has also become the centre of the annual Banlieues Blues jazz festival, part of a cultural urban renewal which has really worked. The other component is the local rap music scene, and many of France's leading rappers hail from the high-rise blocks and low-living northern suburbs.

The cheapness of land and property in such an environment has led a number of major companies to relocate to Métro-served towns such as Pantin. At Aubervilliers, tempers are high over the arrival of a major hypermarket complex which could on the one hand bring jobs to the area, but on the other threaten local traders (although the majority of local street traders in this area are not the sort that the local authorities would necessarily approve of . . .).

The up-and-coming east
In the east of the Seine-St-Denis, the push across the *périphérique* has produced a number of more or less linked pockets or urban renewal. All of these feed off the 20th arrondissement, with 'Bobo' colonies in loft apartments and small houses in **Lilas** and the **Pré-St-Gervais** at the end of Métro lines. But the real success story has been **Montreuil** between the Métro stops Croix de Chavaux and Robespierre. The proximity to Vincennes in the neighbouring Département 94 has led many families to wander into Montreuil. Running off the lower end of the avenue Président Wilson and along the rue Carnot, you will find a great selection of houses in all shapes and sizes. The area is calm, but the living is good, and you are in close proximity to both central Paris and the Bois de Vincennes. **Rosny-sous-Bois** with its police headquarters is another growing favourite, and the neighbouring town of **Le Raincy** has also caught the 'Bobo' bug. Families will need to bear in mind the problems of schooling in these areas, but also the better living space on offer, when deciding whether to move here. You are still definitely in the working-class suburbs in the east of the département, but the contrast between the troublesome volatile central areas and the calmer east is re-markable.

THE EASTERN AND SOUTHERN SUBURBS

Département 94 – Val-de-Marne

The inner eastern suburbs of Paris are amongst the most sought-after for a number of reasons linked to the landscape of the Île de France. The département takes its name from Paris' second major river, the Marne, which joins the Seine at Charenton. The towns running along the borders of the **Bois de Vincennes** and within the loop of the **Marne** are amongst the most sought-after: **Charenton, St-Maurice, Maisons-Alfort, St-Maur, Joinville-le-Pont** and **Nogent-sur-Marne**. All of these towns have good transport links to Paris, and the Métro runs out to **Créteil**, the capital. Créteil itself is another modern mess from the 1960s and 1970s, but it does have a university and shopping centre, and is the basis for a number of festivals and experimental theatre and dance.

North of the Bois de Vincennes lie the two gems of the département, the adjoining towns of **Vincennes** and **St-Mandé**. The latter is the more chic of the two, and merges effortlessly into bourgeois Paris. Vincennes, on the other hand, rolls up and out into neighbouring Montreuil and **Fontenay-sous-Bois**. With its fortress and RER and Métro stop, Vincennes is in fact the better served of the two. Both give access to the immediate attractions of the Bois (the boating lakes, the château, the zoo and the Parc Floral children's area), making them highly desirable for family living.

The south-western corner of this small département is dominated by Paris' second major airport **Orly**, the displaced Paris food market of **Rungis** and the main Paris prison at **Fresnes**. Forming a thin barrier between these areas and the *périphérique* lie the southern tips of the Métro lines at **Villejuif** and **le Kremlin-Bicêtre**. As might be expected, these are the problematical areas of the département and you should avoid them.

Département 77 – Seine-et-Marne

When I first came to Paris in 1991, France was still in culture shock from the arrival of 'Mickey's Magic Kingdom' at **Marne-la-Vallée**. The French government had sold prime farming land at a rock-bottom price to establish a major theme park and new urban centre in the eastern Paris region, and the impact was staggering.

The first time I saw the site was in early 1992 when I was invited to act as an advisor on the care of the anticipated influx of English-speaking young workers at the park. I was driven out to the village of Chessy on a winter's evening across open fields along country roads, until suddenly the road surfaces became smooth and in the distance the great pink castle soared out of local fields. The impact was stunning. The contrast was further exaggerated when I arrived at the village hall to find wood smoke curling out of the chimneys, to listen to local community leaders expressing their consternation faced with an influx of foreigners who did not speak their language in an area which already had a housing shortage. The result was that apartment prices had rocketed to the same level as in central Paris! The fraught meeting with an urban planner demonstrated the exclusion of local people from the grand plans that others had taken on their behalf.

At that time, I did not believe that the **Val-d'Europe** scheme would ever come to fruition. Ten years on, the **EuroDisney** experience has worked for local people, but it remains an exceptional site which has had a profound impact on an otherwise rural area. But the effect has definitely been more positive, with urban damage limitation and many advantageous spin-offs, such as fast-tracks into Paris by road and rail, and TGV and Eurostar links to the EuroDisney site. Now that everything is in place, this is a good place to be especially for young families, even if local infrastructure is still being developed to support the new arrivals.

Beyond Marne-la-Vallée lies the beautiful medieval town of **Meaux**, the capital of Brie country, with its cathedral and walled medieval centre. The hour-long train journey into Paris may be a turn-off for some people, but you will still have a good quality of life here. The rest of the département is pretty much nothing but rural villages, and this is certainly not somewhere you would consider living without a car.

The southern half of the département is dominated by forests. In terms of urban patterns the south resembles the north, except that it is the more sought-after area of the département, especially towns such as **Lesigny**, or **Barbizon** where the British community in Paris used to send their young and invalids for breaths of fresh air. But the feature in the south of the département remains the former royal town of **Fontainebleau** in the heart of the forest. The vast château is a popular attraction, but the main pole of foreign resident interest in the area is the internationally renowned INSEAD business school.

An English-speaking church has been formed at Fontainebleau, and there is an English-speaking section at the Lycée offering education in English for children aged 6 – 18, with British examinations and preparation offered for American and British universities (Tel. 01 64 22 11 77). In the northern half of the département, as might be expected with the proximity to EuroDisney and to Paris, a private state-approved bilingual primary school for children aged 6–11 has been opened between Marne-la-Vallée and Meaux (Tel. 01 60 04 34 70, www.frINTsch.fr). It is possible that further expatriate community infrastructures will develop in this area in years to come, but essentially you must realise that if you do choose to make your home in Seine-et-Marne, you will be choosing immersion into French lifestyle.

Département 91 – Essone

Like its neighbours, the Essone département sprawls out into deep countryside to the south of Paris where forests, farms, villages and rural pursuits predominate rather than the hurly-burly of Parisian life. But the **Yvette** valley and its villages served by the RER line, are very popular areas for Parisians with a taste for country living. **Orsay**, with its university population, is another preferred spot on the north-western edge of the département and within easy reach of Paris.

On the eastern edge of the département the **Forêt de Sénart** provides a welcome green lung along the lower banks of the Seine, but the towns on the opposite bank such as Arpajon, Juivsy and Evry are modern urban expansions which face the same problems as some of the more well-known suburbs of the north. **Evry** does boast the most recent French cathedral but not much else to recommend it as a town. The Russian cemetery at **St-Geneviève-des-Bois** is the last resting place of Rudolf Nureyev.

Overall, the north-east of the département is the most in-dustrialised, although factory closures threaten to cause renewed problems in this sometimes troubled area. Probably the main attraction of the Essone département over its neighbours is that the RER cuts deeper into the southern countryside and forests, to Dourdan, Étampes and Malesherbes, than in other comparable areas. If you can stomach the long rides on branch lines of public transport this could offer you a chance to really enjoy country living and combine it with working in the city.

10

Renting Property in Paris

A survey in *L'Express* magazine (16 November 2000) showed that Paris property, including both private residential accommodation and public buildings, is still largely in private hands. Some 49.8% of Paris buildings belongs to **copropriétés** (collective ownerships), and 20.2% belong to individuals. This does not mean that all of these are potential landlords, as many are also owner-occupiers. About 17% of the Paris property market belongs to companies, including holding companies of banks and insurance companies.

Your experience of negotiating your way into a lease will depend largely upon whom you are dealing with a company or an individual. There is increasing alarm at the level of information being demanded of applicant tenants (see below). Even working for a big-name foreign corporation may not necessarily spare you from intrusive demands for a range of documents. This seems to be truer of rental agencies acting on behalf of landlords or companies than of the landlords themselves. The only advice that can be given in these scenarios is that you have to grin and bear it if you really want to break into the property market to rent an apartment in Paris.

FINDING THE ADVERTS

Obviously you can use estate agents (**agents immobiliers**) when you first arrive in Paris, but there will be a charge to pay for their services. As a foreigner in France, you may well find it easier to deal directly with landlords rather than use agencies. To find accommodation in Paris yourself, there are a number of journals, newspapers and noticeboards which will prove indispensable.

- *France-USA Contacts (FUSAC)* available free from a large number of outlets across Paris, from consulates to churches to bars and bookstores. Be careful, however, as some landlords and agencies not only bump up the market prices but also try to impose illegal payments on unwitting new foreign arrivals. Some ads can also be found in *The Free Voice*, available at the same locations, and occasionally in *Irish Eyes*.

- *Particulier à Particulier (PAP)* comes out every Thursday, available at all major newsagents and kiosks. The major way to find an apartment, although some agencies do masquerade behind the ads from the vast majority of independent land-lords. Be prepared for an early start every Thursday – you need to get the PAP around 07h30, mark up the ads which interest you, and call as soon as possible. Some are let before the paper even comes out, and landlords receive hundreds of calls from these advertisements. Long-running advertisements should make you wonder what exactly is being offered and what are the snags.

- *Le Figaro* **and** *Libération* (newspapers) – daily. Mainly agencies, with some independent landlords. You will find more same-day appointments (e.g. 12h00 today and tomorrow). The problem is of course that the first person who comes with the right profile for the landlord is normally the lucky new tenant. It is also worth checking *Le Parisien*.

- Noticeboards – The American Church (65 quai d'Orsay 75007, M° Invalides or Alma-Marceau) is one of the major housing (and employment) centres for expatriates. New advertise-ments go up every day at about 14h00. Have a pen and block of paper with you and prepare to join the scrum, then run for the nearest 'phone. Housing can be found in all sizes, forms and locations here. Some landlords do simply hang around and ask if you are looking for somewhere to live. It is also a good connection point for those looking to share. Advertisements have to be paid for. Less active but still useful free noticeboards can also be found at **St George's Church** 7 rue Auguste-Vacquerie, 75116 (M° Kléber, George V, Étoile) and **St Michael's Church** (5 rue D'Aguesseau, 75008, M° Concorde). You should also keep an eye out in **local neighbourhood shops** such as grocery stores, newsagents, bakers, dry cleaners, pharmacies, etc., where independent landlords often place advertisements.

UNDERSTANDING THE ADVERTS

Once you have started to locate the housing advertisements either independently or via agencies, you will need to understand the terminology used in property advertisements so that you can concentrate on looking for the style of home which suits you and your budget. The examples given below will help you understand the jargon, and save you much valuable time:

14e Studio meublé, salle d'eau. Près Montparnasse. 2.500F/mois + charges. Tél. après 20h00.

Furnished studio in the 14th arrondissement of Paris. Includes a 'bathroom' (probably) consisting of shower, washbasin and WC. Near to Montparnasse station. 2,500 Francs per month plus building charges. Telephone the following number after 8pm.

Comment: This is probably a very small studio flat of about 18–20m^2. Much important information is missing. When you telephone to enquire about such studios ask: the size of the flat; on which floor it is situated; if there is a lift; what are the kitchen facilities; what furnishings are provided; how much are the building charges (i.e. how much is the total rent). If there is no mention that it is furnished (**meublé**), then you must assume that there is no furniture at all. This may also be one or possibly two **chambres de bonne** (maid's rooms) knocked into one flat. These are small rooms in the attics of large residential buildings. Single *chambres de bonne* are often let to students, but you sometimes have to share a WC and shower with other residents on the corridor.

3e Beaubourg. Immeuble ancien rénové. Digicode, interphone. Studio 35m^2; neuf, aménagement standing. Séjour avec 2 fenêtres, poutres apparentes, cuisine équipée, salle de bains, wc, rangements. Libre 31/12 4.100/mois charges comprises.

(Unfurnished) studio measuring 35m^2 in the 3rd arrondissement of Paris, in the Beaubourg *quartier*, in an old building which has been restored with both key pad entry system and entryphone. Newly redecorated to a good level. Living room with two windows, exposed beams, equipped kitchen, bathroom, WC, and built-in cupboards. Available from 31st December. 4,100 Francs per month including building charges.

Comment: This is a much clearer advertisement. You still need to check about which floor the studio is on as it could well be 6th floor without a lift. Space is at a premium in French flats, so it is important to know that there are built-in cupboards. Other terms for these are **placards** and **penderies** (normally referring to small built-in wardrobes). Check what is included in the kitchen area.

15ᵉ Convention. Immeuble pierre de taille, 2 pièces, 41m², clair, exposé sud. Fenêtre dans chaque pièce. Calme. Au 4ᵉ sans ascenseur. Digicode. Entrée, salle de bains (baignoire), wc, branchement lave-linge, séjour, coin-cuisine, chambre.

(Unfurnished) two-room flat in the 15th arrondissement of Paris near Convention Métro. Two rooms totalling 41m². South facing with a window in each room. Quiet, situated on the 4th floor without a lift. Key pad entry system. Entrance hall/passage, bathroom (with bath), WC, outlet for a washing machine, sitting room with 'kitchen corner', and bedroom.

Comment: This is a classic one-bedroom flat. **Digicode** refers to the means of access to the building from the street. There may also be an entry-phone system as in the example above. The 'kitchen corner' is a classic feature of smaller flats. You will also see references to a **cuisine américaine**. This is a kitchen with a bar to separate it from the main room. **Pierre de taille** indicates that this is a good quality stone building, probably well-maintained.

CLAMART (92) Maison 4 pièces, 80m², sur terrain 272m². Cuisine aménagée, salle de douche, wc séparés. Près commerces, écoles et transports. Dans quartier résidentiel calme. Chauffage gaz.

Four-roomed house in Clamart in Département 92, 80m² of a total property site of 272m². Fitted kitchen, shower room, separate WC. Near to shops, schools and transport. In a quiet residential area. Gas heating.

Comment: The number of rooms (two or more) does not normally include the entrance hall, WC or bathroom. In this case, there will be a sitting room, at least two bedrooms and either a significant kitchen, a dining room or a third bedroom. The total property site probably includes a garden and parking space. It is a small house, but the advertiser is obviously seeking to attract a young couple with a small family. Note the facilities on offer.

Heating (**chauffage**) is either **individuel**, i.e. you control and pay for this yourself, or **collectif** in which case it is included in the building charges. However, in the latter case it is switched on and off at a defined date which may not always suit you. Air-conditioned residential property is almost unheard of.

Houses may have attics, but few if any flats will. However,

certain flats will include the use of an individual cellar (**cave**). You should check the security and state of the cellar before deciding whether to use it to store your belongings. Large flats may have a **chambre de bonne** attached several floors above, although many are now rented out separately.

Some flats may also have a parking space allocated to them. This will instantly increase the price of the flat, certainly in cities and large towns. Check whether the **parking** is in an attached car park, or a garage complex under the building. Parking spaces (also known as a **box**) can be separately rented if needed.

VIEWING PROPERTY

Select the properties which interest you, and call immediately to arrange to view them. If you are organised, you should be able to view several in one day, and so compare the properties more easily. In some cases the advertisements will simply announce a date, time and address to which you should come in order to visit. Expect to queue, and get there early.

Remember that when you go to view a property, you yourself are being viewed by the landlord as a prospective tenant. Competition is sharp for good homes, so you must be prepared.

- **Appear friendly and professional** – smile and dress smartly. Nobody wants a difficult tenant, and a landlord will want to feel sure that you can pay the rent.

- **Take proof of your spending power** – money talks loudly. Take along as many recent wage slips as you can, and also bank statements. They will almost certainly be asked for by the landlord. If you refuse to show them, it is very unlikely you will be accepted as a tenant.

- **Have your cheque book ready** to make a down payment on a rental if you and the landlord agree terms. However, **BE CAREFUL** to ask for a receipt from the landlord, and preferably your signed rental contract.

Questions the landlord will ask you

Expect to be asked at least one of the following questions by a prospective landlord:

1. If you are employed, '**Do you have a permanent contract**?' If you have just arrived, take along past pay slips, and an **attestation d'emploi** from your employer, stating that you have an indefinite contract, and your annual or monthly salary before tax.

2. If you are a student, '**Do you have a *carte d'étudiant***?' Renting to students is advantageous in one sense as there are tax benefits for landlords.

3. '**Are you sure that you can afford the rent**?' Officially your monthly salary after tax and social security deductions must be three times the total rent on your home. In practice, this is rarely the case. However it can be a sticking point, and with good reason. Do not over-stretch yourself financially.

4. '**What guarantees can you offer for the payment of the rent**?' Very frequently landlords will ask for **références sérieuses** and **garanties parentales**. This is a written undertaking either by your parents, or your firm in some cases, that if you default on the rent, they will settle any outstanding debts. It is not an undertaking to be made lightly, as the standard notice period for leaving a French rental arrangement is three months.

Rent guarantees
Students will almost certainly be asked for references and guarantors, but so too will young people who are in full-time employment (single or married). According to one newspaper article (*Libération*, 13 September 2000), rental agencies are now insisting on social security details, access to the previous three months' bank statements, and even court rulings regarding divorce settlements and loan repayment plans, in order to assess your financial capabilities to pay the rent. Foreigners have traditionally been singled out in the recent past for this kind of treatment on the grounds you may flee owing months of rent. Gentle negotiation and reassurance with an individual landlord can often resolve the problem.

Taking out a lease
Once you have chosen the property which interests you and been accepted for the tenancy, you will have to sign the lease (**contrat de location** or more properly the **bail**, pronounced 'bye'). This should usually be a standard grey and green form, including

mentions of the laws governing rental agreements. They can be obtained from Tissot, 19 rue Lagrange, 75005 Paris. The front and back will be filled in and signed by your landlord and yourself, and the inside pages will include the general terms of the agreement. Two identical copies of the contract are signed and completed, one for you and one for the landlord.

Beware of 'home-made' contracts which could lead to difficult situations should a problem arise. They will certainly not offer you the same legal protection and security of residence as the formal contracts. Some landlords may have had a separate contract prepared by a lawyer for larger properties. Read contracts carefully before signing them, and if necessary seek professional advice. **Do not panic and never lease a property without a contract (i.e. cash-in-hand).**

To conclude the contract, take along copies of your *carte de séjour* and passport, and your deposit (**caution**) for the flat. This sum is normally equivalent to two months' rent, but must be defined and mentioned in the contract. Normally the first month's rent is also paid in advance, making a total of three months' rent in advance.

The contract should include the name of the landlord; your name; the full address of your flat including the staircase, etc.; a description of the property; the length of the contract; the rent you are to pay, including building charges; when you are to pay it; and the amount of the **caution** you have paid for the property.

ÉTAT DES LIEUX

The contract is not completed until one final process has taken place, known as the **état des lieux**. This should happen **before** you move in, and is undertaken with the landlord (or representative), to establish the exact state of the property (e.g. cracks in the wall, broken windows, etc.).

Both of you keep a signed copy. Keep this safely in case your landlord later tries to make you pay for repairs which are not your fault. For furnished lets, you should also have an itemised inventory of the furnishings provided.

The *état des lieux* is the moment to try and negotiate minor changes in the presentation of the apartment before you move in. No landlord is going to agree to redecorate completely and re-equip an entire kitchen. Some will, however, agree that you need a cooker and that the damp patch in the bathroom must be dealt with before you can be said to be 'enjoying' the property. You are not obliged to forever hold your peace once you move in, but you can hopefully save yourself a lot of hassle by sorting things out in advance.

ADDITIONAL COSTS WHEN RENTING PROPERTY

In addition to the *caution* and first month's rent, you may also find yourself presented with a bill for the **frais** or **honoraires** as they are sometimes called. These will be the costs involved in preparing a contract, and undertaking the **état des lieux**. A landlord is within his or her rights to use a baliff (**huissier**) to undertake the *état des lieux*. All of these charges will be at the tenant's expense.

The other additional cost you may face will be the estate agent's fee if you have used their services. This is also normally equivalent to one month's rent. Remember to check this before you take advantage of their services and include it in your budget.

YOUR RESPONSIBILITIES AS A TENANT

The general conditions of the standard contract list 16 responsibilities! The most important are:

- To pay the agreed rent at the agreed time (normally the first day of each month).

- To use the premises in a safe and reasonable manner for the purposes for which they were intended. Also not to transform them for another 'purpose' e.g. offices.

- To take out a standard insurance policy against fire, water damage, etc.

- To obey the regulations governing the day-to-day running of the building and concerning the **parties communes** (e.g. lifts, corridors, etc.). These rules are agreed by all the owners (**copropriété**). These rules often concern petty obsessions about putting out the garbage in the correct manner or shutting the front door of the building. If you have a major problem because of a broken lift, for example contact your landlord directly and officially rather than taking illegal punitive action by withholding part of your rent.

- Not to sublet your property without prior written approval from your landlord.

- Day-to-day minor repairs are the responsibility of the tenant. Be careful to note that certain preventative maintenance e.g. an annual check-up for the boiler – are normally also the tenant's responsibility. This can prove to be important should you need to change the boiler (one of the landlord's responsibilities) later on.

- If you rent a furnished property (**meublé**) then you are obliged to ensure either that the furnishings stay in the apartment when you are living there, or that they are correctly and safely stored for return to the apartment when you leave. If you do decide to discreetly move one or two items of dubious taste out of your view and into your cellar, make sure the cellar is clean and safe and the items are well protected against pests such as wood lice or rodents. Otherwise, speak nicely to your landlord . . .

THE LANDLORD'S RESPONSIBILITIES

- Ensure that the property is clean, that all repairs have taken place, and that all appliances included under the contract are in working order when the tenant enters the property. The landlord is responsible for ensuring that the wiring is in order and that all plumbing is in full working order.

- Ensure that the tenant can 'peacefully enjoy' the use of the property. Should you find yourself with noisy neighbours or a problem elsewhere in the building, this will be important.

- Undertake major repairs which are not the responsibility of the tenant.

- Not to oppose improvements to the property which will not change the basic use and structure of the property. This means a tenant can redecorate an apartment, even against the wishes of the landlord. However, it is best to obtain agreement from the landlord otherwise you are obliged to restore the original decoration when you leave. A tenant is responsible for giving back exactly what they received.

- To send a receipt for the monthly rent as and when demanded, including for part-payments.

SHARING PROPERTY

Flat sharing on the Anglo-Saxon model (i.e. a large apartment or house shared by a number of people of similar financial means looking to benefit from combined spending power and personal companionship) is becoming increasingly popular in France, especially in the 'twenty-something' fledgling executive group.

In the case of a formal property share, for example two or more friends or an unmarried couple, it is best to arrange a separate formal lease between the landlord and each tenant in their own name dividing the rent between the tenants. Should one party leave, the others will not then be responsible for the rent of that person. For unmarried couples who have signed a PACS contract (which requires cohabitation as a prerequisite), in the case of the loss of one partner the surviving partner is protected from eviction.

It is also a good idea to put the electricity bill in the name of one tenant, and the telephone bill in the name of another. This provides each person with another proof of residence (**justifactif de domicile**), and helps to ensure each person's rights should a problem arise. In the case of an informal flat share (i.e. subletting a room in a flat or house without a written contract which is strictly illegal), you may be asked to pay a smaller **caution** (i.e. one month instead of two). But you should still **be sure to ask for a receipt from the person to whom you pay the** *caution*. Your rights in this situation are much less well-defined, so do be careful.

Think carefully before entering into a flat-share, and if you share a flat with a French person because you want to improve your French, remember they may also want to improve their English.

11

Buying Property in Paris

For many years, buying property especially in Paris was considered to be a sound investment. The property market rose steadily in value as banks and insurance companies bought heavily into the available residential market and added new buildings. At the same time, less and less residential space and more and more office space was being created in central Paris, leading to a housing crisis of which Parisians still complain.

Financial crises in the late 1980s through until the mid-1990s saw banks and insurance companies forced to liquidate their property assets, at the same time that a new law also threatened the institutional landlords with forced repossession of empty buildings to house the increasing number of homeless. The result was a rash of renovations and conversions by company landlords anxious to retain their properties.

At the end of the 20th century, property prices were spiralling higher and higher as the new 'BoBo' generation came to the fore and the fruits of a healthy economy allowed the French to start doing what they love talking about – buying and renovating property. A number of laws inciting the French to buy and lease property – either old or now – and massive tax incentives to help the French construction industry have also contributed to a new property boom.

As you will see from Figures 4 and 5 at the end of this chapter comparing prices in central and suburban Paris, prices have more or less stabilised within Paris over the last year. However, with the push towards the suburbs for large spaces, a better environment, and more and better schools, certain suburbs have seen a considerable rise in home prices, as much as 25 – 30% in some areas. As the French magazine *Challenges* said in March 2001, the French prefer to 'not only buy an environment to live in but also a manner of living'.

FINDING THE ADVERTS

As with the rental of property, using professional estate agencies implies a certain cost for the transaction. However, this can be weighed up against the protection of a professional contract with the agent, should anything go wrong.

About half of all property transactions in France are dealt with by estate agents (**agents immobiliers**). Estate agents cannot enter into negotiations unless they hold a **mandat de vente** (written power of attorney for sale) from the seller, or a **mandat de recherche** (written power of attorney to make a search) from you as the purchaser.

The seller usually has to pay the estate agent's commission, fixed by power of attorney, upon written completion of the transaction. Anything not referred to in the power of attorney cannot be charged by estate agents. They may fix the amount of commission they receive, but their scale of charges must be on open display. The commission must also represent a percentage of the purchase price. The price displayed for a property must include the commission. Many agents will be the sole agent for a property and so will have the **exclusivité** mentioned in the advertisement.

Both buyers and sellers eager to maximise their profit and minimise their costs can and do organise their own property sales. You are most likely to find direct advertisements from private home-owners in the *Le Figaro* (www.explorimmo.com), *Libération* (www.libération.fr) and *Particuliers à Particuliers* (www.pap.fr) (on Thursdays).

If you want to start your property search before even arriving in France, the development of websites now gives you easy access to visit the properties on offer at your leisure. The French magazine *Challenges* produced an exhaustive and excellent guide to the French property market in March 2001 which shortlisted the following websites as presenting the best value and interest for home-hunters:

www.123immo.com
www.century21.fr
www.explorimmo.com
www.fnaim.fr
www.homevillage.com
www.immo-by-tel.com
www.immostreet.com

www.minitelorama.com
www.nexdom.com
www.pap.fr
www.pro-a-part.com
www.se loger.com
www.smartimmo.com

Look at www.directgestion.com for a useful website for those people considering buying and renting out a property in France. It offers free advice from property business experts such as lawyers and architects. Go to www.batiweb.com for a website detailing a building industry contact and information for those considering building or renovating a new property.

UNDERSTANDING THE ADVERTISEMENTS

Advertisements for properties for sale use much of the same jargon and short-hand as those for rented property, already decrypted in the previous chapter. However, important extra information will also be included in sale advertisements, and you need to understand this before deciding if the property corresponds to your search. The real examples given below will help you understand some of the most important extra points:

CLAMART – Secteur pavillonnaire. Petite Résidence. Studio 30m²
– 330.000FF.
In Clamart (92). In the part of the town which contains small individual houses (**pavillons**). In a small modern apartment block (**résidence**). A studio of 30 square metres.
Comment: a pretty minimalist advertisement from an agency (often indicated simply by reference letters such as GEI, LF, etc. followed by a telephone number). The term **résidence** in this context normally applies to a modern apartment block without a **concierge**, but with a **digicode** (key pad entry system) at the front door and/or a second **interphone** (entryphone). There will probably be no more than ten apartments in this building, which may have a small garden in front or behind the building. **Pavillon** is a term used to describe small detached suburban houses.

Nation (5mn) 2P 34,5m² (loi Carrez) – 2ᵉ étg. Cuis. éqp., séjour, chambre, SdB, wc sép. Très clair. Parquet. Refait neuf. 690.000FF.

Five minutes from Nation, a two-roomed apartment of 34.5 square metres (certified in accordance with the *loi Carrez*). Second floor. Fitted kitchen, sitting room, bedroom, bathroom, separate WC. Very light. Parquet flooring. Completely redecorated.

Comment: much clearer but still ambiguous on one important point: what does the five minutes refer to? A car drive, a Métro ride, an RER ride, or walking distance – and in which direction? This is a major consideration. The **loi Carrez** is the recent French law which requires certification of the square metrage of apartments (but not houses) as a basis for sale. If you buy a property and find that you have more than 5% less than the size stated, you are entitled to renegotiate the price. This vendor has already undertaken the necessary official verification and certification process. The fact that it is **refait neuf** might explain a slightly elevated asking price of 20,000FF/square metre, depending on where it is situated. In theory, you will have no extra burden to bear in terms of renovation costs. However, this should be checked carefully. (See also the decision-making checklist below.)

Buttes-Chaumont 3P 2 ch 52m² Parquet, moulures, à refraîchir. 750.000FF

In the Buttes-Chaumont area of the 19th arrondissement of Paris. A three-room apartment including two bedrooms, of 52 square metres. Parquet and moulding/cornices. Needs to be 're-freshed'.

Comment: You need to check on the layout of this apartment. Many Parisian apartments have bedrooms leading one off the other, so that to get to the bathroom for instance you are obliged to cross somebody else's bedroom. It is obviously an older building in co-ownership indicated by the presence of both mouldings and parquet. But the most important point is that it needs to be redecorated. You need to find out just what is involved and then add an estimate figure to the cost of your purchase to get the real total cost.

3ᵉ Bd St Martin 208m² Superbe 6P, possibilitié prof. 3ᵉ asc. excellent plan, travaux, 4.980.000FF

In the 3rd arrondissement of Paris on boulevard St Martin, a superb six-room apartment, which could be converted into office space. Third floor with lift, an excellent opportunity. Needs work.

Comment: Sounds tempting in this up-and-coming well-placed area, but look at the price (nearly 24,000FF/square metres in an area that averages 16,000FF/square metre). Add to that the need to undertake 'works' – what? How much will it cost? Is there even running water and safe electrical wiring? Redecorating a six-room apartment would make this a very costly purchase. The other major concerns are the environment and security. Is it on the boulevard itself? If yes, think about the cost of well-fitted or double-glazed windows, plus the problems of pollution. The area is close to a **quartier chaud** (danger-zone), and there seems to be some ambiguity about what goes on in the building. Is it a purely residential building or are there other offices with clients coming and going, with access to a front-door code and increased security risks? Overall it may be worth a look as a very long-term investment, but you really need to do your homework before deciding to buy.

Pré-St Gervais Loft 143m² prox. Mairie. Etat neuf, gd. vol. 2.80m HsP, soleil. asc. & monte-charge. 1.900.000
In Pré-St Gervais (93), a loft apartment of 143 square metres near the town hall (**mairie).** Perfect condition, large space, 2.8m floor-to-ceiling (**hauteur-sous-plafond**), sunny, lift and goods-lift.
Comment: Depending on you and your lifestyle, it sounds like an interesting proposition. However, you need to check a few things out first. Loft apartments are the latest fashion in Paris, and many people have been tempted into run-down areas such as the Pré-St-Gervais on the north-eastern limits of Paris by opportunities such as this. The first issues you need to think about are security, transport and local environment. In theory you should not be faced with any major works if you really do want to live in a loft in a converted warehouse (note the goods-lift). At more than 13,200FF/square metre in a run-down area, you are paying the price of both fashion and your two lifts. This could turn out to be a costly proposition. How are you going to heat this vast area? The plus side is that it is light and airy, with 2.8 metres from floor to ceiling. But presumably there are no interior walls, except perhaps those separating the bathroom and WC. If you want to create a bedroom, there are costs involved. Also, you have a vast area to decorate, etc. Watch out for the hidden extras with a purchase like this. Note that there is no mention of a parking space; strange considering that this is clearly a factory conversion and that there is a goods lift. Parking may be available at an extra

cost, or you may have to take your chances parking in the street. Which brings you back to the security issue.

OWNING PROPERTY IN FRANCE

If you decide to buy property in France, either as your principal home, or as a second home, the basic process is the same as regards the contracts you will have to sign and the charges you will have to pay.

The distinction between freehold and leasehold does not exist in French property law. Instead, a distinction is drawn between co-ownership and free-standing property.

- **Co-ownership** means that the property (normally an apartment block) is divided into units (**lots**). Each unit has a private area and a proportion of the communal area. The co-ownership regulations are known as **Le Règlement de Copropriété**. These regulations govern boundaries between private and communal areas, conditions for use of the building, etc. An assembly of the co-owners, the **Syndicat de Copropriétaires**, decides on changes to the regulations, and any major building works. The cost of any such works are divided amongst the co-owners.

- If you are buying a distinct property, e.g. you are buying a house with a garden, you will have all the rights of ownership.

- In either case, your purchase will be subject to the complicated French succession laws (see below), and you should discuss these with your French legal advisors when you are planning your purchase.

Decision-making checklist

As you will have seen from the comments on the sample advertisements above, there are a large number of considerations to be made before making an offer on a property and signing any binding documents. These are mainly in addition to the basic questions you need to ask yourself about size, facilities, transport and security.

The checklist below is drawn from a variety of published sources in the specialist French property press. Obviously you need to weigh up the risks quickly, especially in the cases of sought-after areas and types of apartments. But do not allow yourself to be rushed into a wrong and potentially expensive and troublesome choice.

❑ **Check on the surface area**. The price of an apartment is estimated on the basis of a price per square metre. The **loi Carrez** introduced in June 1997 obliges all vendors in buildings owned by **copropriéte** – but not individual house-owners – to detail the exact surface area of the apartment offered within a maximum error margin of 5%. All surface areas with an HSP (hauteur-sous-plafond) of at least 1m80 (c.6ft) must be included in this estimate. Mezzanines (split-levels artificially introduced into a room to create an extra area such as a bedroom), attics and staircases are not therefore included. However cellars (**caves**) may be, depending on the age and style of the building. Garages, balconies, and terraces are not included in the surface area estimation, although they may well influence the price. Terrace areas tend to be noted separately in the advertisements (e.g. + *terrasse de 5m²*, i.e. you could eat out on the balcony if you wanted to hence the higher price for the apartment). If the surface area advertised is less in reality by more than 5% of the figure advertised, you are entitled to have the price reduced by legal ruling if necessary. But all of that is more cost, more trouble, more disappointment, and not what you need in a new home.

❑ **Check on the communal charges**. The communal charges of a building owned by **copropriété** (e.g. lifts, concierges, renovation, etc.) are shared out by the owners according to the size of their **lot** and are estimated in **millièmes** and **tantièmes**. This will have a direct effect on your annual bills. Every year the owners meet to vote new works on the building and the budget for the year. You should make every effort to determine what has already been spent which will also indicate if you are entering a spend-thrift environment), what has been voted but not yet paid for (which will be **your cost** if you buy the apartment before the work is actually carried out **even if you did not vote for it**), and what is planned for the near future. In the worst case scenario, the *copropriété* could have voted for a façade renovation (**ravale-ment**) which has not yet been executed, and could be planning to change the lift(s) in the building the following year. Both of these are very costly exercises. You can demand copies from the vendor of recent minutes (**procès-verbaux**) of the general meetings (**assemblées générales**) of the *copropriété*, and also enquire if a technical survey has been undertaken of the building. If you receive a negative response, there is nothing to stop you organising your survey (**diagnostic technique** or **expertise**) of the building. If in addition to the cost of the façade and the lifts and any personal renovations you need or want to undertake, there is also a problem such as subsidence requiring underpinning, etc. think again.

❑ **Check if the property is correctly valued**. Strangely none of the many regular surveys actually ask this question, perhaps because the wily Gallic character assumes that you will haggle over the price in any case. However, the fact that detailed studies do appear regularly each year in the general press should encourage you to check the price per square metre – the basic cost element – of the property which interests you. Compare prices with comparative sized properties in different agencies. Many factors come into play when pricing a property, but you need to get a feel of the basic value of what you are buying.

❑ **Check on the hidden costs**. Ask the vendors to tell you how much the building **charges** have been over the last two years. Ask how much they have been paying in **impôts locaux** (local housing tax). The cost varies from area to area, according to the size of your apartment, the state of the building, and an official estimation of its market value (which may be out of date). You should also ask the vendor for copies of the bills for major works to the property which in his or her eyes justifies an elevated price; find out just how much it really cost, and what precisely was done. A job half-done badly could be an expensive job to complete successfully.

❑ **Check on precisely what the building is used for**. Are all your neighbours in a co-owned building simply living there and working elsewhere, or are they doing the opposite? If one or more is working in the building, who has the code to the front door? Suppliers, clients, colleagues in other areas? Is it a small one-person independent outfit, or will you be regularly kept waiting for the lift because of streams of clients or because a delivery put it out of action once again? The more people use your building and its facilities, the more wear and tear there is to repair. How safe are you in your own building?

❑ **Check on environmental issues**. If you are buying a house in a rural area or near to the river, what is the likelihood of **flooding** in the area? This has been a real problem in recent years throughout France, and does affect some of the out-lying areas of the Île de France region especially. A rural idyll could turn into a soggy nightmare in a wet winter. Think also about **transport issues**. You may be tempted to buy in an area because of a new high-speed transport link – either rail, road or underground. Make sure it is not going to run under your ground and your foundations, or that you don't have closer access and greater noise pollution than you had bargained on. The local *mairie* will have plans for any such developments, and also will be the place to find out about planned building projects which may change your gracious view into *face-à-face* with new neighbours. Local **schools** normally lead to higher prices as families seek to be near their child's place of education; but they also mean noise and congestion.

❑ **Check on asbestos, lead and pests**. For buildings in collective ownership, **asbestos (amiante)** checks on all common areas and private residential lots are obligatory, and a copy of the statement concerning your chosen building must be given to you no later than the day you are due to sign the **promesse de vente**. You should be able to obtain a copy well in advance in most buildings. For buildings dating from before 1948, a report on the risks of **lead poisoning** from paintwork or pipes is obligatory in Paris, which is considered high-risk zone.

❑ **Pests** such as cockroaches and notably **termites** are becoming a major problem in Paris. Annual rodent and cockroach control exercises are the responsibility of the *copropriété* in a co-owned building, and you will find references to money voted for these works in the minutes of general meetings of the co-owners. For the termites now spreading across Paris (once again classified as a danger-zone), the vendor should attach an **état parasitaire** to the sale contract stating the level of infection, dating from within three months. Once again you should be able to obtain this in advance of the signature date. If the building or property is at risk from any of these three dangers, then you will need to know the costs involved for dealing with the problems, and what if anything has already been voted but not yet paid for by the *copropriété*. Information regarding these problems and contact details for professionals qualified to deal with them can be found on the websites of both the Housing Ministry (www.equipement.gouv.fr) and the Ministry of Health (www.sante.gouv.fr).

SIGNING THE CONTRACTS

When you and the seller have reached an agreement, there is a choice of two kinds of pre-contractual agreements which are possible:

1. **Promesse de vente** This is a unilateral agreement to sell, signed by both the vendor and buyer. Under the terms of such an agreement, the vendor agrees to sell you the property by a certain time, for a set price, and according to set conditions. The buyer is allowed time to reflect on his decision, but must nonetheless pay a deposit, normally about 10% of the full price. The advantage of this kind of agreement, which is very common, is that the vendor cannot withdraw their acceptance of your offer if all the conditions of the agreement are met. The disadvantage is that if you as the buyer withdraw from the agreement, you lose your deposit.

2. **Compromis de vente** Once again, both sides commit themselves to a change in ownership of the property. However, certain 'way out' clauses can be included in the agreement, which are known as **conditions suspensives**. These conditions might include the granting of a mortgage (for which you normally have 40 days), or a town planning report (**certificat d'urbanisme**), etc. All of these clauses must be adhered to, or you are entitled to cancel the agreement and reclaim your 10% deposit.

Once the **notaire** (see below) has all the necessary information, a **projet de l'acte** (draft contract) can be produced. Copies are sent to the buyer and the seller for approval before the final contract is drawn up.

The **Acte Authentique de Vente** is the conveyancing agreement between the two parties. It will reiterate clauses from the pre-contractual arrangement, and will also clarify any further details. The following information must appear:

- Identification of both parties concerned.

- Identification of the property in precise terms and the title to the property (**origine de propriété**).

- The date when you as the new owner will take possession of the property and be entitled to use it (**propriété de jouissance**).

- A **certificat d'urbanisme** which restates any town planning regulations affecting the property, as discovered by the notaire.

- Any guarantees and estimates.

The *notaire* retains the original contract, and copies are given to the buyer and vendor, known as **l'expéditions**. Once the sale has been registered at the **Bureau des Hypothèques**, no-one else has any claim over the building. Finally, the relevant section of the title deed is sent to the Land Registry.

SURVEYING YOUR PROPERTY

Structural surveys are not common in France. Stringent building and construction regulations mean that there is usually no need. The vendor, or in the case of a new house being built, the construction company, are obliged to issue guarantees on the property. Builders must also be insured for work undertaken for ten years thereafter, and even in case of bankruptcy. The ten-year guarantee also applies to older buildings which have been bought and renovated by a builder and then sold off as separate apartments.

The *notaire* can include details of any guarantees on the property and a list of builders involved in your final agreement. A *notaire* or estate agent can carry out a simple survey if required. Otherwise, an **expert géomètre** can check the total surface area of your new property, or you can arrange for a survey by an architect. If you are buying an apartment in a renovated building, be sure to check on precisely what the builder is charging you for, and do not be frightened to check the efficiency of sound-proofing and how well windows actually fit.

LOOKING AT THE LEGAL ISSUES

The role of the *notaire*

According to French law, every property transaction in France must be overseen by a **notaire**. The distinction in the French legal profession is between **avocats** who can appear in the courts (rather like barristers in the UK) and **notaires** who undertake contractual work (such as conveyancing and the writing of wills) rather like solicitors in the UK.

Notaires must be impartial between the two parties of a property sale and are responsible for legally validating the deeds involved, advising clients and drawing up the necessary contracts. They can and sometimes do act as tax consultants, and also as estate agents in certain cases.

The *notaire* is entitled to a legally determined sum as commission when acting as a sale negotiator. Normally this is around 10% of the purchase price. If the building is a new property the *notaire*'s fee is reduced to no more than 3% (as an aid to the French construction industry). A building less than five years old which has never been occupied since construction also qualifies for this reduction in the *notaire*'s fee.

Notaire's fees (**frais**) will eventually include money paid on your behalf, taxes, and dues and contingency duties. Overall costs are high but vary from region to region within a set scale, and depending on the type and value of the property.

The *notaire*'s responsibilities when acting as intermediary for a sale are:

1. To verify the vendor including his/her right to sell the property.

2. To obtain the relevant Land Registry papers, showing any planning objections to the property.

3. To contact anyone with pre-emption rights to the property, and determine whether they plan to exercise these rights.

4. To contact the **Conservation des Hypothèques** (mortgage/ Land Registry) which must issue an **état hors formalité**. This shows any mortgages, securities, etc. on the property. Such debts must be payable and lower than the sale price to avoid redemption proceedings.

If you pay for the property through the *notaire*, they can withhold payment if it is discovered that the vendor has used the property as collateral on a loan, until a negative **état sur formalité** has been issued.

Inheritance issues
It is extremely important that you take good professional advice when buying your property in France, as regards questions of

TOWN & DÉPARTEMENT	L'Express 20/9/00 Old – town centre	L'Express 20/9/00 New – town centre	Le Figaro 27/01/01 Best areas	Challenges Old – appts	Challenges Recent – appts	Challenges New – appts	Challenges Houses 03/01
Asnières sur Seine (92)	11200	16000		10400	11100	14100	10300
Boulogne-Billancourt (92)	15000	24000		17300	18600	23900	22200
Colombes (92)	8900	8900		8400	8400	15000	14300
Courbevoie (92)	12900	18000		12500	13000	16800	12000
Créteil (94)	8000	12000		94000	10500	15900	11700
Enghien-Les Bains (95)	11000	15000	Casino - 16000/20000 new Marché - 13000	12000	14100	17300	12400
Evry (91)	5000	5000		7400	7600	9900	10400
Fontainebleau (77)	9000	9000	Town centre - 17000 Outlying areas - 10000	9500	9800	11400	8800
Fontenay-sous-Bois (94)	Not surveyed	13930 (Village)		13600	14600	18100	13400
Levallois-Perret (92)	16000	21000		16500	19900	25800	24000
Maisons-Lafitte (78)	Not surveyed	Not surveyed	House town centre - c. 24000 Appart. town centre - c. 18000 House St Nicolas - c. 17000 House Petit Parc - c. 23000	12500	14600	19700	11800
Mantes-la-Jolie (78)	6500	10000		7100	9100	11100	8400
Meaux (77)	8500	11500		7800	8100	9400	8300
Mélun (77)	7000	10000		8900	10700	10200	10200
Meudon (92)	See next column	est 11000FF (La Forêt) 14600 (Nr. Clamart) 19000 (Bellevue)		15300	19000	19700	15600

TOWN & DÉPARTEMENT	L'Express 20/9/00 Old – town centre	L'Express 20/9/00 New – town centre	Le Figaro 27/01/01 Best areas	Challenges Old – appts	Challenges Recent – appts	Challenges New – appts	Challenges Houses 03/01
Montrouge (92)	est. 13000	est. 20000		12700	14100	16400	14000 est. 20000 L'Express
Montmorency (95) N	Not surveyed	Not surveyed	Station - est. 14000 Mairie - est. 12500 Fort - est. 10000	9600	10500	13500	9600
Nanterre (92)	9000	12500		10700	12500	15600	10900
Neuilly-sur-Seine (92)	23000	31000		21300	24300	31500	35000
Nogent-sur-Marne (94)	12400	18000		9800	12000	18700	13700
Rambouillet (78)	10000	15000		8900	11000	12000	9600
St Cloud (92)	est. 16000	22000		19900	22500	Unknown	27300
St Germain-en-Laye (78)	14000	14000	Town centre - c. 23-28000 Prieuré, Bel-Air - 15000	14100	16700	20300	13200
St Mandé (94)	17000	23000		17300	19300	19300	21000
St Maur des Fossés (94)	13000	19000		9700	11800	19100	11100
Suresnes (92)	12500	16500		11200	14400	21100	21100
(Gif-sur-) Yvette (78/91)	12000 (région Yvette)	16000 (région Yvette)	Chevreuse - 19000 (new) Villas in the valley - av. 15000	7700 (Gif)	8700 (Gif)	9500 (Gif)	8400 (Gif)
Versailles (78)	21000 (Notre Dame) 18000 (St Louis) 13000 (Aux Chantiers)	N/A	Notre-Dame - c. 23000	15200	15700	20400	12900
Vincennes (94)	17000	23000	St Louis - 21000 Montreuil (south) - 16000	14900	16000	19300	15500

Fig. 4.   Comparative table of purchase prices per square metre published in the French press for the Paris suburbs and commuter towns. Sources: as noted. All figures in French Francs.

ownership and inheritance. You must do this before you sign the contracts; afterwards, it will be too late. You should also bear in mind that the legal system is both very slow and very expensive in France.

The main thing to watch out for is that the *notaire* does not draw up a contract whereby you buy the property **en division**. The much more preferable option is to buy **en tontine**. There are other possibilities (e.g. an **acte de donation**), but you will need to discuss these with your legal advisors.

Problems with buying a property en division
If you and your spouse buy a property **en division**, you will each own half of the property. When one of you dies, the 'half' which belongs to the deceased person will pass automatically to his/her heirs. The situation then is that the surviving spouse owns half a house, with the right of abode for the remainder of their life.

If you have children, you cannot leave your half of your property to your spouse. You can leave part of it to your spouse, but he/she will be liable for Succession Tax on the part they have inherited. If there are more than three children, they automatically inherit three quarters of the deceased person's estate. Succession Tax is then payable immediately, even if the surviving spouse continues living in the house. The house cannot be sold to pay the Succession Tax without the consent of the surviving spouse, nor if one of the children is under 18 years old.

FINANCIAL CONSIDERATIONS

Financing your purchase
Your own personal situation will determine the variety of options open to you for financing your property purchase. Within France, the most common method of obtaining a mortgage is to apply to a high-street bank. A French bank will calculate the amount of money available for your mortgage according to your cash flow. A mortgage should be granted as long as your outgoings plus your mortgage repayments equal less than 30% of your pre-tax income.

Successive French governments in recent years have tried to boost the property market by permitting loans at very low rates. It is worth enquiring widely about the possibilities before taking a decision. Banks and financial institutions vary from being inflexible with anybody but the known and trusted clients, to

ARRONDISSEMENT	L'Express 20/09/00 Average price/sq.m 1st quarter 2000	Challenges 03/01 (apartments only) Average figures for whole arrondissement	Price ranking
Paris I	Les Halles - 19227 Pl Vendôme - 23575	23900	7
Paris II	Opéra - 22948 St Denis - 14971	19350	11
Paris III	Arts & Métiers - 16200 Archives - 21112	18400	13=
Paris IV	Notre-Dame - 31768 Hotel de Ville - 22083 Beaubourg - 19758	29267	3
Paris V	Maubert-Mutualité - 24029 Jardin des Plantes - 22631	25033	5
Paris VI	St Germain - 31479 Montparnasse - 27298	32033	2
Paris VII	Rue du Bac - 31050 Rue Cler - 26144	32066	1
Paris VIII	Champs-Élysees - 30897 Europe - 20851	24867	6
Paris IX	St Georges - 17692 Faubourg Montmartre - 14684	18993	12
Paris X	République - 13326 Louis Blanc - 12161	16166	20
Paris XI	Bastille - 15117 République - 13384	18333	15
Paris XII	St Mandé - 15887 Bercy - 14307	18400	13=
Paris XIII	Gobelins - 18939 Bibliothèque - 14173	17833	16
Paris XIV	Montparnasse - 20975 Plaisance - 17140	21000	10
Paris XV	La Motte Picquet - 19920 Parc G. Brassens - 18078	21800	8
Paris XVI	Trocadéro - 24075 Auteuil - 20857	25300	4
Paris XVII	Ternes - 20762 Batignolles - 16553 Brochant - 12460	21700	9
Paris XVIII	Abbesses - 14413 La Goutte d'Or - 9568	17733	18
Paris XIX	Buttes-Chaumont - 13304 Avenue Flandre - 10948	16766	19
Paris XX	Père-Lachaise - 13305 Belleville - 12147	17767	17

Fig. 5.   Comparative table of purchase prices per square metre
published in the French press for apartments in central Paris.
Sources: as noted. All figures in French Francs.

being more flexible in the face of opposition from high-street competitors. A great deal will depend upon your ability to negotiate and force the hand of lenders.

Negotiating the purchase price

At the time of writing it seems that (according to a survey in the business newspaper *La Tribune*, 10 March 2001), there is generally little room for manoeuvre in negotiating the price of a good property in Paris, with a maximum reduction of about 3.5% in the original price. For poorer quality or less well-situated properties, you can expect to negotiate a reduction of between 5 and 10%, if only because many vendors are testing the waters to see how much they can actually make for their property. But for the moment, after the recent buying sprees of the last couple of years followed by reasonable stability, Paris is a seller's market.

Paying tax on your property

When setting up home in France, you will be liable for the following French taxes:

- **Government registration tax**

  This tax is payable when you are completing your purchase, and when added to the fees of the *notaire* amounts to about 11% of the property's purchase price.

  You will also be required to pay the equivalent of UK Land Registry fees and stamp duty. The rates depend upon the size of the property and its grounds, the type of buildings on the land, and the age of the property. Once you have bought property in France, it must be registered with the tax authorities. If it is a secondary residence, contact the **Centre des Impôts des Non-résidents**. Tax-registration should take place before April 30th of any year.

- **Taxe foncière**

  This is a local tax levied by the commune in which your new property is situated, and levied on you as the owner. Your name will be added to a register at the local *mairie*. The register comprises lists of owners, tax rates paid, and notional letting values of the property concerned. In some cases you will be exonerated from the *taxe foncière* (see the following chapter).

- **Taxe d'habitation**

  Unlike the two taxes above, this local tax is not necessarily payable by the owner of the property, but by its occupant. If you rent a property you will normally be liable for this tax. The rate of tax payable is determined by the building's amenities and size. The basic rate is calculated according to the nominal letting value of property in the local area.

Insuring your property

You are required by French law to take out third-party insurance as soon as you move into your accommodation, or as soon as work has begun on your future home if it is still being built. This is known as **civil propriétaire**.

It is also highly advisable to take out insurance against fire, theft, etc. Comprehensive policies known as **assurances multirisques** are available, as are specific policies. The sum insured should reflect your insurable interest or potential loss according to the contract arranged. Co-owners should already be insured for the building itself and all communal areas. In addition you need to take out insurance on your own belongings.

12

Setting up your Home

Finding and buying or renting a property is, of course, only the beginning. Even if there is seemingly little to be done, or your resources do not permit an immediate start, you still need to set up your services. Also bear in mind that actually moving home is an administrative battle in itself.

MAKING CONNECTIONS

Electricity and gas

Probably the easiest way to deal with gas and electricity contracts, which are administered by the state-run EDF-GDF company (www.edf.fr and www.gazdefrance.fr) is to take over the contracts of the previous residents of your property, be it rented or purchased. Contact your local EDF agency to arrange to have the meter read before you take possession of the property and take over the contract. Otherwise, go to the local EDF store with a copy of your rental agreement or your *acte de vente* if you are an owner, and a piece of official identity (e.g. passport or preferably *carte de séjour* if you have secured this), and you can open your new account. If you do take this option, you will have to pay the rental fee, and arrange to be present on the date that the EDF set.

Bills normally arrive quarterly, and can be paid at the post office using a **mandat** (postal order), or by cheque sent by post. In preparation for the imminent disappearance of the French Franc and the introduction of 'hard' Euros on 19 February 2001, the EDF is already sending out its bills in Euros. Take care to **pay the correct amount in the correct currency**, as you are entitled to pay in Euros (by cheque or standing order) if you wish. However, the French Franc figure is still published beside the figure in Euros. Notices regarding meter readings will be sent to you or posted in your building. You must ensure access on the day of the reading. Normally concierges are willing to help if you live in an apartment and cannot be present.

Collective (central) heating is controlled by the date not the temperature. Normally it is turned on in October and turned off in April. In smaller and older properties, you may well find that it is necessary to install extra electric heaters.

Water
As with electricity and gas, it is probably easiest to take over existing contracts when you purchase a new property. Tenants normally have their water charges included in the general charges they pay with their rent. Water is supplied by private companies. Arrange for a reading of the water meter when taking over a contract. Bills arrive about every three months.

Telephone
In 1998, France Telecom lost its national monopoly in France. However, in reality you still need to take out a France Telecom contract for line rental. It is now locked in price battles with its competitors, many of whom offer very attractive rates for long-distance calls to the UK and the USA. Details of these offers are easily found by looking in *France-USA Contacts (FUSAC)* magazine. You will need to contact each operator to discuss the offers available. If you take out a Cegetel or Le 9 line subscription (**abonnement**), you simply dial 7 or 9 before dialling the standard number.

France Telecom now offer a **toll-free helpline in English on 0800 364 775** Monday – Friday 09h00 – 17h30 (www.paris.francetelecom.fr/anglo). Phones can be rented or bought from France Telecom shops but can also be purchased from major stores such as FNAC or small phone shops. Phone directories – *Pages Blanches* for individuals (www.pagesblanches.fr), *Pages Jaunes* for businesses and services (www.pagesjaunes.fr) – can also be found free of charge at your local France Telecom shop. The websites offer a guide in English to help you find your way around the services on offer, a street plan and even photos of many addresses.

France Telecom offer a number of cost-saving plans for over-seas calls, the numbers most frequently dialled (**Primalistes**), etc., which you can find out about from France Telecom. There is also an internet *Primaliste* with 50% off internet calls at weekends and week-day evenings. Cheap rates for France Telecom 'phone calls are at weekends, French national holidays, and between 7pm and 8am (until 1pm for North America) on weekdays.

The France Telecom internet service is Wanadoo, but all other major companies have sites and access in France. Having emerged from its initial reluctance to accept an Anglo-Saxon cultural invasion, the French are now hooked on the internet and can proudly boast some of the world's experts. They understand anglicisms such as **le web** or **le net**, but they prefer to use the French term **la toile**.

Television

When you buy or rent a television in France, the shop from which you purchase or rent the machine will automatically send your name and address to the TV licence office (**Centre de Redevance Audiovisuelle**). They will then in turn send you an annual bill, normally around January or February each year. You only have to pay a licence fee for one TV per household, so if you buy a second TV for the bedroom or the kitchen, it will be covered under the first licence.

DEALING WITH PROBLEMS

If you are the cause of a problem, such as a leak or a short-circuit, you are obviously responsible for repairing the damage or the problem. Contact your insurance company rapidly in order to establish what help they can offer you in the case of a major problem.

Tenants who are the victims of such problems should inform their landlords immediately. Landlords often have their own plumbers and electricians who deal with such problems for them, and send the bills directly to them. If you cannot contact your landlord, and the situation is an emergency, you will have to arrange and pay for action yourself. Keep copies of the bill, and send the original to your landlord for reimbursement once you have explained the situation.

The *Syndic* of your building will have the names of companies they use in such situations, and whom they can recommend to you. But it is a good idea to try to arrange at least one other estimate in order to keep the costs involved to a minimum. You should note that calling out an electrician or plumber for an immediate visit or at the weekend will normally prove expensive.

Insects, pests and vermin

Unfortunately these may affect you no matter where you live. Your local *mairie* very often will have a department which deals with insect problems such as wasp nests or cockroaches. Call to find out about this service, and check how much it costs. It is not too expensive, and can save a great deal of unpleasant trouble.

Cockroaches unfortunately tend to appear in clean homes as well as dirty ones, mainly due to the fact that you have un-knowingly brought home their eggs on the under-side of packets bought in supermarkets! There are plenty of sprays and traps available for ridding yourself of this problem. Major infestations should be dealt with by professionals.

Vermin can also be dealt with using traps and poison readily available in high-street shops. However, you obviously need to be careful about using these methods if you have children or pets. Follow the instructions carefully.

Regular disinfections should take place of your entire building organised by the *Syndic*. Be careful to note when these are to happen, and arrange for access to your flat even if you do not have a problem. All flats in a building need to be disinfected for the process to be really effective. If you have a problem with vermin, warn your landlord and the *Syndic* so that they can arrange for these measures to be taken.

Problem neighbours

Dealing with problem neighbours is often difficult and unpleasant. In the first instance, you need to try to speak to them about whatever is the source of the problem, be it noise or a leak. Try to remain calm and reasonable, even if your neighbours appear to be the opposite. In the end, your own self-control will work in your favour.

If the problems persist, you will obviously need to speak to them again. Keep a careful note of when you spoke to them, and a brief record of your conversations. If you have persistent problems you are fully entitled to contact your landlord for help since they are obliged to ensure that you can 'peacefully enjoy' the property you are renting.

Eventually, putting your complaints in writing is a useful way of proving you have tried to resolve the situation. Keep a copy of the letter and place the original in your neighbour's post box. Sending a registered letter of complaint with proof of delivery (**lettre**

recommandée avec avis de réception) is an elaborate but sure way of proving you have complained.

The final resort for dealing with neighbours depends on whether they are tenants or owner-occupiers.

- **Tenants** – Speak to the concierge and find out the name of their landlord. You may need to ask your own landlord to help you to find the address. If a landlord receives repeated complaints about tenants, they may be forced to leave the property.

- **Owner-occupiers** – This is a more difficult situation. Ultimately you would need to have a petition signed by the other residents of the building (many of whom will probably refuse even if they are sympathetic) before any definite action could be taken.

In both cases, the police can be asked to intervene. By law, excessive noise before 08h00 and after 22h00 is not permitted. If you own your property in an apartment block, you can also contact the *Syndic* of the building for advice and help.

The Good Neighbour Guide

If all of the above sounds rather drastic and worrying, then remember that there are certain basic courtesies which will at least mark you out as '**correct**' in French eyes and help you avoid problems.

- Always remember the basic courtesies – *bonjour/bonsoir, je vous en prie* (you're welcome), *s'il vous plaît*. The French expect these to be employed with anybody and everybody wandering around the building, be they regular residents or occasional visitors.

- Keep the noise down after 22h00 and before 08h00. Unfortunately this is the hour at which street-works will begin, if you have already survived the dust-cart dawn chorus (which is not normally noticeable except when windows are open).

- If you are going to organise a party – don't do it too often, and place a little explanatory notice in the lift or entrance hall asking your neighbours to excuse the disturbance in advance. They normally do if you are polite.

- If you have building work in your apartment, apart from the common courtesy of warning your neighbours, make sure that your workmen clean up after themselves in the corridors and lifts and do not damage anything.

- Remember to tip the concierge at Christmas or New Year. He or she is the ears and eyes of the building. One wrong foot here could make life difficult.

- The French do not share the Anglo-Saxon custom of popping in to see the neighbours. They may accept to join you for a Christmas drink, but don't expect to drop in for a chat on Saturday mornings.

LOOKING AT HOUSING ASSISTANCE

The **caisse d'allocations familiales** (CAF) administers three different housing benefits for those with limited resources. You cannot receive more than one of these benefits at any given time, and your right to access any of the benefits will almost certainly depend upon the length of time you have lived and worked in France. All the benefits are means-tested.

1. **L'aide personnalisée au logement (APL)** This never covers the total amount of your housing expenses but only one part. It is available to owner-occupiers who have undertaken to improve their property under certain conditions, and also to tenants. For owner-occupiers, the benefit is generally paid directly to your loan agency or bank, whilst for tenants the benefit is normally paid directly to your landlord. In both cases the sum is deducted from your loan or rent.

2. **L'allocation de logement familiale and l'allocation de logement sociale** These benefits are available to tenants in a wide range of situations:

    - if you are already receiving another family benefit

    - if you have a child under 20 years old living at home

    - if you have been married for less than five years and have no children

    - if you are looking after a relative over 65 years of age or are unable to work.

If any of these apply, you may be eligible for this benefit, depending upon your resources. A moving allowance is also available for those with limited resources. Applications should be made for this at your **caisse d'allocations familiales** when you move in.

RENOVATING YOUR PROPERTY

Owner-occupiers who are intending to in some way add to, transform, or renovate their properties should take advice before starting to knock holes in any walls. Be sure to do things the right way and not the wrong way as if you are sued, you will find the French legal system to be cumbersome, slow and expensive.

Basic rules regarding planning permission put a limit on the number of habitable or serviceable square metres which can be added, and all changes in use of the property or exterior appearance require official approval from the local *mairie*.

What you can do without planning permission

- If you are planning to change the interior of your apartment, you can do so as long as it does not change the exterior of the building, or its volume or surface area. So adding another shower room to the existing floor plan, for instance, is not a problem, and there is no need for planning permission.

- If you have a garden and you want to install a patio or terrace, you can do so as long as it is not more than 60cm (2ft) above ground level. The same goes for a greenhouse, potting-shed or summerhouse, as long as it does not cover more than two square metres and is not more than 1.5m high. Anything over these limits requires planning permission.

- You can build a wall in your garden up to 2m high, as long as it is not a dividing wall between yours and a neighbouring property.

What you can do with only a preliminary notification (*déclaration préalable*) at the *mairie*

- You can add less than 20 square metres to your surface living area (e.g. you can convert an attic or a garage into living areas).

- You can build a garage of up to 20 square metres.

- You can build a swimming pool in your garden as long as it does not exceed 20 square metres.

What you cannot do without planning permission

All other building work over these limits, including the construction of a large pool or shed, or adding another floor to your property or a roof garden or terrace, all require planning permission from the local *mairie*. This also applies if you purchase a larger property and convert all or part of it into commercial offices, as you have transformed the nature of the property.

For those people living in **copropriétés**, your plans also have to be approved by your fellow co-owners at the annual general meeting. The rules of the *copropriété* will expressly allow certain building works (e.g. a new bathroom), but other changes (e.g. a roof terrace or attic conversion) will have implications for the building as a whole which everyone has to agree to.

Financial assistance for renovation

There are a number of possibilities which exist for obtaining state aid to renovate your property. Most grants are means-tested and will depend on how long you have lived in France and contributed to the system. However, providing that you are a full resident and paying your social contributions and tax in France, then there is no reason why you cannot successfully apply for these grants if you meet the criteria.

Information regarding all the benefits on offer can be obtained from the Agences Départementales d'Informations de Logement (ADIL) on Tel. 01 42 02 65 95, website www.anil.ord.

A range of benefits exist for those who undertake major structural work in their new homes, and some of these are cumulative.

1. **Le prêt à l'amélioration de l'habitat** This is available to both owner-occupiers and tenants. This loan at a rate of 1% is available for necessary improvements, such as heating or sanitary conditions. It is not means-tested, but you must already qualify for another family benefit. The loan currently limited to 7,000FF, and 80% of the total cost of the works. Repayments take place over 36 months. For more details, you should contact your local *caisse d'allocations familiales*.

2. **Assistance from ANAH (Agence Nationale pour l'Amélioration de l'Habitat)** This is not means-tested. Basically it applies to vacant buildings more than 15 years old which are being made habitable. Normally it is paid only to owners, who commit to renting out the property afterwards. Generally the benefit is around 25% of the total cost of the agreed works, but can be higher. To find out more contact the ANAH at the local *direction départementale de l'équipement*.

3. **La prime de l'amélioration de l'habitat** A means-tested 'bonus' available to owner-occupiers which varies from region to region. This benefit is of particular interest to those adapting homes for people with disabilities amongst other more common measures regarding health and hygiene. The total amount of the bonus cannot exceed 20% of the real costs of the works, within a limit of 70,000FF. However, this bonus can also be added to another bonus worth 50% of the works necessary to allow access for, or conversion for use by, disabled people. The limit on this second bonus is 20,000FF. Hence for works costing a total of 110,000FF, it is possible to be awarded state assistance totalling 34,000FF. Applications for the *prime de l'amélioration de l'habitat* should be made to the *section habitat* of the *direction départementale de l'équipement* (except in Paris where applications should be made to the *préfecture*).

4. **The 0% loan** A means-tested loan on the basis of the previous two years' taxable salary, as a complement to another loan. You have to plan to begin the renovation of a property as soon as you have completed the purchase; be over 20 years old; and the property has to be your principal residence. The cost of the planned works must equal at least 54% of the purchase price of the property, and is limited to 20% of the total cost of the works. The 0% loan is limited to properties which either require extensive renovation, or are brand new. Other limits vary from region to region and also according to how many people will be occupying the property. This is not an easy loan to obtain.

5. **The 1% loan** Limited to employees of companies contributing to the scheme. Find out first if your employer does contribute on your behalf (ask your *direction des ressources humaines*, or *DRH*), and then ask them for details of how to apply.

6. **The 1.5% loan, 'Passe-travaux'** The newest member of the French loan family. Available to employees of even the smallest firms, as long as they are in the private sector and not working in agriculture. The maximum rate is 1.5% when other loans reach a rate of 6–7%. The loan is limited to 60,000FF, reimbursable over ten years. There are very few restrictions on its use, so it can be put towards redecoration, conversions, etc. If your firm contributes to the 1% loan scheme, then they will also operate this loan. If not, you need to contact the local 1% loan contribution collection agency (check with the ADIL above). The *passe-travaux* can easily be used in conjunction with other loans.

Looking at tax advantages

In September 1999, the French government decided on a kick-start for the economy via the building and construction industry, by reducing VAT on work by professional builders from 19.6% to 5.5%. This applies to all home improvements, maintenance and renovation undertaken by professionals. The drop in tax rate also applies to the materials they use, but this is a concession made only to professionals.

If the property you purchase is in an old building which has been renovated by a developer and then sold off apartment by apartment, then the lower rate of VAT applies to all works and purchases for those works undertaken within the habitable areas of the building. Certain *parties communes* such as a boiler for the building or a lift are obviously not covered in the lower rate of tax, but tax breaks are offered of up to 15% against the purchase of this kind of equipment (for which VAT is 20.6%).

Do-it-yourself fans should note that they will still be charged VAT at 19.6% for any purchases they make to deal with household renovations themselves.

Finally, if you have purchased a new property but still decide to undertake some form of reorganisation, etc., then you will be exempted from the *taxe foncière* for two years after completion of the works.

CHANGING ADDRESS

Moving homes in France is not simply a case of finding and securing your new address, and then informing your family and friends where to find you. A great many other people and organisations, listed below, must also be informed. This information applies to both home-owners and tenants.

Moving home action plan

☐ **Tenants** Be careful to respect the notice periods stipulated in your rental agreements.

☐ **Electricity and Gas** Contact your current EDF agency ten days before you move to have your meter read. The cost of terminating your current contract will be sent to your new address. At the same time, contact your new agency to establish the new contract or arrange to take over the existing contract.

☐ **Water** – as above.

☐ **Telephone** Contact your current and future France Telecom agencies. Arrange termination of your existing contract about eight days before the move. In certain cases if you are staying within the same exchange area, you can keep the same number if you wish. A recorded message can also be arranged on the old number for three months informing callers of your new number.

☐ **Post** Organise a **faire-suivre** (forwarding service) at the post office for all your post. This should be done no later than five days before the move. Generally it works well. However, you might wish to consider tipping your current concierge to check that any post does actually reach the new address.

☐ *Carte de séjour* and **passport** After you have moved, the new address must appear on your official documents.

☐ **Driving licence,** *carte grise* **and car registration** You have one month in which to accomplish the change of address on your *carte grise*. If you change départements, your car must also be re-registered.

☐ **Insurance policies** You will need to inform your insurance companies of a change of address. You can either terminate your existing house insurance, or transfer it to your new residence.

☐ **Social security** 15 working days before you move, contact your current and future *caisse d'assurance maladie* to arrange for your new card(s), and the transfer of your files. This is not the most efficient or speedy of services, so allow plenty of time.

☐ **ANPE** If you are registered at the local job centre, inform your old centre of your forthcoming change of address. Visit your new centre as soon as possible after moving in.

☐ **Family benefits** Inform your local *caisse d'allocations familiales* of your intended move 15 working days before the date. They should contact your new *caisse* for you.

☐ **Bank** Inform the bank of your change of address as soon as possible. This will allow them to not only send correspondence to the correct address, but also to print new cheque books for you. You may also wish to change branches.

☐ **Tax Offices** Admittedly, they were probably not on your mailing list for change of address cards. However, they have a nasty habit of finding out where you are in any case. Inform your current tax office before you move of your change of address. The following year, you will send your tax declaration to your old tax office, but marked with your new address on the first page. You must also inform the TV licence centre of your change of address. **Correspondence from tax offices is *not* forwarded by the post office, but sent back to the senders. This can have serious consequences.**

☐ **Municipal crèches** You must enrol your children at your future *mairie* as soon as possible. You must also respect the one month notice period for withdrawing your children from their current crèche.

☐ **Primary schools** Before moving, ask the school for a **certificat de radiation** (this does not mean that your child glows in the dark, but that s/he has been struck off the school register). At the same time, contact the schools office of your new *mairie* to arrange an appointment. They will inform you which school catchment area you now fall under.

☐ **Collège or lycée** Before moving ask the school director for a **certificat de sortie** for your children. The appropriate files should then be transferred directly to the new school.

☐ When you have completed all of the above, sit down, pour yourself a large drink, and swear never to move homes in France again!

13

Finding Employment

THE FRENCH ECONOMY – 'YOU'VE NEVER HAD IT SO GOOD'?

Three years on from *Living & Working in France* (1998), I find myself in the strange position of quoting myself in order to begin analysing the current economic situation. In the early period of the Socialist Jospin government, with unemployment at 12.6%, I wrote, 'The great challenge for the new Socialist government now is to find a compassionate way to balance the books, both creating jobs and safeguarding the present benefits system whilst bringing the financial crisis under control.' Growth industries in 1997 were information technology with the arrival of the Euro and the year 2000, and the advertising sector. The Hauts-de-Seine, Seine-et-Marne (including EuroDisney) and Yvelines regions all showed signs of growth, and the Hauts-de-Seine had the highest average wage in France of 171,600FF in 1997, 50,000FF above the national average.

On March 1st 2001, Prime Minister Jospin announced that unemployment had fallen by over 1 million since 1997, down to 9%. For the government there were three key factors involved in the return to work in France: the linked issues of the 35-hour working week and the reduction in working hours (**réduction du temps de travail**, or **RTT**), and the **emplois-jeunes** offering young job-seekers fixed-term contracts as auxiliaries to the 25% of the French working population still employed by the state. (Workers in the French **administration** and state industries, officially known as **la fonction publique**, are known as **fonctionnaires**). However, this was a scenario bound to produce bumper results in 2000, and government estimates are for a slower unemployment decrease in 2001. The spectacular measures are over, but the outlook is still healthy. One estimate (*L'Entreprise* March 2001) puts job creation in the first half of 2001 at an estimated 230,000 new jobs, although the spate of **plans sociaux** (restructuring plans including factory closures) in the spring of 2001 has perhaps jeopardised the positive impact of new job creations.

Current economic policy

The sudden unexpected departure in a corruption scandal of Jospin's liberal economic mentor Dominique Strauss-Kahn from the key post of Finance Minister left a void not only in the government's balance but also in economic direction. This has been filled by the return of former prime minister Laurent Fabius as Finance Minister. His 2001 budget was based on increased spending power and productivity, with a planned lowest level of public deficit since 1981.

Fabius committed himself to maintaining the state's capacity to intervene in the interests of 'national cohesion' via the public sector, whilst admitting that the capacity to create wealth (and businesses) in France is still too limited. The Jospin-Fabius plan now rests on both reducing the level of social contributions to release more creative capital; and taking the first timid steps in the face of fierce opposition towards **épargnes salariales**, a Gallic form of pension funds.

Fabius' strategies for 2001 are based on a high growth rate of 3.5% (although latest estimates in *L'Entreprise* in March 2001 put growth this year at 2.5%) with capped rather than reduced public deficit, sustained by VAT returns and further minor measures of privatisation at the end of 2000; record tax cuts for individuals and companies, including a petrol price regulatory system; and restrained public spending. For this last area, the major increases are planned in the areas which have been confirmed in the municipal elections as principal French concerns: the environment and the Ministry of the Interior including the penal service and police, covering the general concern over security.

Employment trends

In 1999 Jospin cut VAT on building works from 19.6% to 5.5%, creating a significant building and renovation mini-boom. In one year, up to September 2000, the French construction industry grew by 4.2%, whilst service industries continued to grow by 4.4% continuing the trend of the 1990s. Manufacturing grew by 1.5% and heavier industry grew by 1.3%.

Internet start-ups caught the popular imagination, especially in Paris, where everyone wanted to be in 'Silicon Sentier' once they had found their financiers at 'First Tuesday' meetings. In August 2000, information technology was expected to create anything from 222,000 to 570,000 new jobs in 2001–2004.

Three months later, further evidence supporting this suggestion came from the director-general of the management employment agency, the **Agence Pour l'Emploi des Cadres** or **APEC**. He identified information technology and telecommunications as the sectors with the greatest difficulties in meeting their recruitment requirements, with many jobs going begging, followed by electrical and mechanical engineering, the major chain stores and hypermarkets, banks evolving towards a more commercial approach, and public relations and advertising. All in all, there are not enough candidates for the jobs on offer in all these sectors, with job offers for managers up 41% in 2000 and the number of candidates per post down from 54 to 18 (*L'Entreprise* March 2001).

These trends were confirmed when the new drop in unemployment was announced on 1 March 2001: *Libération* reported that resignations had risen by 17%, whilst the same day *Le Monde* reported that job cuts because of economic cutbacks had diminished.

However, the down-side of Jospin's economic miracle has been an increase in part-time and fixed-term contracts. Nor have record company profits guaranteed jobs. First Michelin, then Renault and now Danone have faced the same public wrath for seeking to increase share-holder value by job cuts at the same time as announcing record profits. The government's condemnation has been clear, and large corporations will find it harder in the future to put their share-holders before their employees.

Jospin has still not balanced the books, with a reduced but still massive debt in the social security budget. But he has given the French back their confidence, and brought a million people back to paid employment.

FOREIGN WORKERS IN FRANCE

Citizens of European Union (EU) member states can stay in France for up to three months without an official *carte de séjour*, for which an employment contract is required. You are entitled to take any position in the private sector providing that security clearance is not required (which you may be granted in any case); but you are generally excluded from positions in **la fonction publique**, with possible exceptions for the health and education sectors. Certain other areas are open to foreigners, but think twice about entering all-French preserves as French unions do not tend to welcome what they see as interlopers in national (i.e. French-only) territory. Anybody considering starting their own business – and this includes in France doctors, lawyers and accountants whether independent or salaried – should see the following chapter on self-employment, as well as checking with their own professional assocaition about practice restrictions.

EU citizens should note that their *carte de séjour* **(which is also their work permit) will be determined by the employment contract(s) they present at their application. If you are on a fixed-term contract, your** *carte de séjour* and social security rights will be limited to that period only.

Commonwealth citizens with residency rights in the UK should note that those rights are only valid in the UK, and do not exempt them from meeting French requirements for citizens of their own country. Residents of the Channel Islands and the Isle of Man should also note that these British dependencies are not full members of the European Union, and different rules also apply. Check with the British Consulate in Paris or the French Consulate in London for details.

US citizens face a major struggle with French bureaucracy similar to the process for a European moving to the States. If you are planning to stay more than 90 days or for purposes other than tourism then you must have a **visa de long séjour** (long-stay). If you do obtain one of these visas, you must apply for your *carte de séjour* **within one week of arrival**.

The basic rule for all visa applications from non-EU nationals – both employment and residential – is that you must start from the outside and work your way in. You cannot avoid returning to your point of origin outside of France in order to successfully apply for your visa. You cannot convert a tourist visa into a long-term visa once in France.

The US Embassy in Paris (www.amb-usa.fr/consul/consulat.htm) states very clearly in all its documentation that it cannot intervene with the French authorities on behalf of US citizens seeking visa exemptions and work permits after arrival. Wannabee Hemingways and fake Fitzgeralds take note . . .

The Embassy goes on to state that unless you fall into one of the privileged categories which basically have already managed to link into the French system and obtain previous visas, 'The only other Americans who have any chance of full-time employment in France are highly-skilled technicians and qualified managerial (cadre) personnel. Some students can qualify for part-time au pair employment, and other students can qualify for part-time or summer employment. There are some voluntary collective work programs.'

US citizens who wish to take a full-time position in France are dependent upon the French employer to take initial steps towards securing both residence and work permits (the latter leading to the former). Authorisations for Americans to work in France rest with the **Service de la Main d'Oeuvre Étrangère** of the Ministry of Labour (127 boulevard de la Villette, 75010 Paris. Tel. 01 44 84 42 86). However, you do have a vital part to play in your own application. The table below shows the parallel processes for visa application once you have found a potential employer:

Once you have passed all the hurdles outlined above, you will be issued with a **carte de séjour temporaire salarié**, valid for one year. It will specify in which départements the permit is valid and the professional activity in which you are employed. This card can be renewed two months before the expiry date or upon presentation of a new work contract.

Three years continued residence in France allows a US citizen to apply for a **carte de résident** valid for ten years and automatically renewable, which is valid for all professional activities. Spouses of French citizens are entitled to the *carte de résident*.

LOOKING FOR WORK

Looking for work is a full-time job in itself. In France, there are a variety of ways in which you can seek work.

1. **Job centres** The state-run job centres are the **Agence Nationale Pour l'Emploi, (ANPE).** You must register in person – applications by post will not be accepted. Proof of permanent residence in France (your **carte de sejour**) will be required, and they may also ask to see your passport. Job advertisements are displayed in the centres, and workshops, counselling and personal interviews are available. The **APEC** job centre (see above) in the 14th arrondissement is open to both **cadre** and non-*cadre* applicants, although it specialises in candidates with *cadre* experience or profiles. There is no set

Employer/French Government departments	Employee
1. Applies to French Ministry of Labour for permission to employ an American citizen. The authorisation will be sent to the chosen French consulate in the USA.	1. Informs the employer of which French Consulate in the USA will receive the visa application in order to receive the Ministry of Labour approval.
2. Provides a copy of the signed employment contract to the French Ministry of Labour for approval.	2. Provides documents required for French visa. The minimum requirements for a French visa are: (i) a valid passport (ii) several passport-size photographs (iii) proof of financial resources to support the applicant and his or her dependants during their stay in France. This can be • bank statements • written confirmation of regular transfers of funds from a US bank account to a French bank account • letters from family or friends guaranteeing regular support • a **certificat d'hébergement** (housing certificate) from a French family or friends with whom the applicant will be staying in France.
3. If the contract is approved, the Ministry of Labour forwards a copy to the **Office des Migrations Internationales (OMI)** who transmit it to the designated French Consulate in the USA.	3. Once you receive your visa and enter France, you must apply at the *Préfecture de Police* for your residence permit (**carte de séjour**) within one week of arrival.
4. **When the French Consulate receives approval from the OMI, the applicant will be informed and can proceed with the visa application (2).**	4. The visa formalities are not completed until the candidate and family have undergone a medical examination by the doctors designated by the OMI.

Fig. 6.   Administrative procedures for Americans intending to work in France.

moment when you can expect to be made *cadre*; it may happen immediately, or it may happen after some years. Further explanations are given below, but do not be afraid to explore *cadre* positions. You do not have to be registered at state job centres in order to reply to advertisements there.

2. **Employment agencies** Although employers are obliged to inform the ANPE of vacancies in their companies, they are much more likely to seek the help of recruitment agencies (**conseils de recrutement**) and head-hunters (**chasseurs de têtes**) to fill vacancies. Most agencies are accessible only by appointment. You therefore need to prepare and send your CV and covering letter (see the section on applying for jobs later in this chapter) in order to open these doors. There are now several agencies in Paris which specialise in bilingual appointments, particularly for secretarial and administrative work. Providing that you do have a good working knowledge of French, your greatest immediate asset in the search for work will be that you are English mother-tongue.

3. **Newspapers and magazines** The most important newspaper for job advertisements in France is *Le Figaro* every Monday. The separate '*économie*' section normally carries a wide variety of jobs of all levels and areas. These are repeated every Wednesday in the job newspaper (*Carrières et Emplois*, which also includes jobs advertised in *Le Parisien*, and sometimes advertisements from *The International Herald Tribune*. *Le Monde* on Mondays and Tuesdays carries a selection of well-paid jobs, and the business newspapers *Les Échos* and *La Tribune* also carry similar job advertisements. *Les Échos* has a reciprocal agreement with *The Financial Times*. This means that you may be able to start your job-search even before you move to France. *Libération* also has a small but developing jobs section each Monday, and magazines such as *L'Express* and *Le Nouvel Observateur* also carry a variety of job advertisements. In Paris, two free magazines, *France-USA Contacts* also known as *FUSAC*, and *The Free Voice* have significant job sections of great interest to English-speakers.

4. **Unsolicited applications (Candidatures spontanées)** composed of your CV and a general covering letter, are the most important method of filling vacancies in France, accounting for 70% of appointments. This approach fits in with the general

'networking' approach which is highly prevalent. A well-presented CV and letter, followed up by a 'phone-call if appropriate can secure you at least a first interview for a post that nobody else knew was even vacant.

5. **The internet** One sign of the changing times in France is that many agencies and firms will now accept applications by internet, allowing you the chance to get out of the otherwise obligatory hand-written letter with the almost inevitable spelling errors! There is a vast choice of internet sites to choose from in well-connected France. Three of the best are www.anpe.fr (extremely well-designed and informative job-centre site with access to all offers); www.apec.fr (the *cadre* job-centre site with access to their regular published magazine); and www.infotaria.com/frans/jobsfrance.htm. This last site gives you a selection of dozens of links to websites for employment in all spheres, regions and categories, from students to temporary workers to permanent management positions.

6. **Professional associations** Certain professions in France have very restrictive rules over practice, such as lawyers, accountants and the medical professions. **Before leaving your home country** you should contact your own professional association to enquire if they have any information to offer you or correspondent associations in France who could offer you guidance on the work available to foreign professionals in a particular field. They may also have contacts with foreign nationals already in the French system who may be willing to offer advice or even a position.

7. **Chambers of Commerce** The Franco-British Chamber of Commerce and Industry (FBCCI) is the oldest foreign chamber of commerce in Paris. The American, Australian, Irish and South African chambers are all also very active, and each chamber offers a wide selection of information and services. Contact details can be found at the end of Chapter 16. Each chamber of commerce also organises regular social events to help new arrivals network with each other and with established members of the expatriate communities. These can be useful forums in which to introduce yourself. The Franco-American Chamber of Commerce at www.faccparisfrance.com, and the Franco-British Chamber of

Commerce and Industry at www.fbcci.com both provide full details of the services offered to job-seekers and new arrivals by both chambers.

REPLYING TO JOB ADVERTISEMENTS

Job advertisements come in a wide variety of shapes and word forms. Figure 7 below contains a number of standard terms. The explanation will help you decode precisely what is being offered.

The basic format is to indicate the name of the company and/or its activity first, then to indicate the post that is being offered, followed by a brief description of the candidate profile the company is seeking. It is important to understand this brief profile – no matter how standard or banal it may seem – in order to compose the correct application letter indicating your suitability for the job.

Two common specifications given in job advertisements are the level of education required of applicants, and whether the position is **cadre** or **non-cadre**. Both of these require explanation.

- **Bac+3** or **Bac+4**, etc. This indicates that graduates are being sought who have at least the level of **baccalauréat** (A-levels), plus three years of further education, or whatever number if

---

Importante société internationale de prêt-à-porter en pleine expansion recherche

Vendeurs/Vendeuses confirmés
pour ses boutiques dans la Région Parisienne.

Jeune et dynamique, vous avez les sens du contact, une première expérience professionnelle réussite dans ce domaine, et vous cherchez maintenant à évoluer dans votre carrière.

Envoyez votre candidature (lettre, CV, photo et prétentions) à DRH, Wear-Well S.A., Service Recrutement, 19, rue Eugene Leblanc, 92300 Levallois-Perret, sous réf. 24679.

Fig. 7.   Basic format of job advertistments.

indicated. Bac+5, for instance, would require an initial higher education degree, plus perhaps a master's degree. A further specialised **cycle** may also be required for certain jobs. **Niveau bac** means A-level education is the minimum.

- **Cadre** This is basically an executive post, unique to France. Advantages include better salaries (in general) and better social security benefits later in life, and a certain 'snob' value. Disadvantages include long hours for no extra pay. **Cadres** are not normally paid over-time, which is obligatory for **non-cadres**.

Decoding the final part of the advertisement is crucial. For the sample advertisement in Figure 7, your complete application must include the following items:

- **Lettre d'accompagnement** This **MUST** be hand-written in impeccable French, well-presented, and no more than one side of A4 paper. Standard forms of letter suitably adapted are perfectly acceptable, but typed letters will simply be ignored. Many firms in France still use graphology as a selection test for candidates, especially for more important jobs.

- **CV** Your curriculum vitae (CV) or résumé must be neatly typed and easy to read, in the French format (see below), and no more than one side of A4 paper. Make sure that you bring out the most important and relevant elements of your experience which suit you for the job for which you are applying. On average, most recruiters spend about two minutes reading what has taken hours to prepare. They need to see your suitability right away.

- **Prétentions** (salary) Some advertisements clearly state salary, some give a salary range according to experience (e.g. 200 – 250-*KF=200,000 – 250,000FF*), and some advertisements ask for your **prétentions**, as in Figure 7. Basically, this is asking you to state what you are willing to accept as a salary – which is a tricky business! You therefore need to know what the 'average' salary is for someone of your experience, and for such a position. Looking at similar advertisements can help. **Only include your *prétentions* if you are asked for them**, or in certain cases when you make a **candidature spontanée**.

Otherwise, *prétentions* will have a much more English meaning!

- **Photo** Despite being the land of *liberté, égalité et fraternité*, the French still tend to preselect their candidates to a large extent on a rather superficial basis. As in the case of our advertisement in Figure 7, appearance is important. Only send a photo when you are asked to do to. Do not use a photo taken in a photo booth. Go to a photo shop and arrange to have a set of four *black-and-white* passport size photos taken in which you are dressed well and appropriately for the position for which you are applying. This should only cost about 40FF, and is money well spent. One photo should then be stapled to the top right-hand corner of your CV.

PREPARING YOUR FRENCH CV

Preparing your French curriculum vitae (or résumé) can be heart-rending, especially if you have spent your university career 'collecting CV points'! You only have one side of A4 on which to cram in the information in a relevant, readable, and eye-catching manner. There is therefore no point in telling potential employers how you captained a cricket team (which the French don't even understand), if it means sacrificing space.

Figure 8 shows you the basic format for preparing your CV. Any of the decent guides available in France will help you to choose one of the variations on this theme which best suits your experience. Contrary to popular opinion, there is no one 'correct' way to present a CV in France. But what is definitely wrong is to produce the kind of detailed CV common in the United Kingdom. Points to remember are:

- Your **état civil** (name, address, telephone numbers, marital status and number of children) always comes in a neat little section at the top of the page. Leave space on the right-hand side for a photo if necessary.

- Start with the most recent/current employment, and work backwards. Arguably you should adopt the same practice with your education.

Paul Williams
75, rue Aristide Briant,
75019 Paris
Tél. 01 47 97 14 39 (Dom.)

État civil
Situation de famille: Célibataire
Nationalité: Britannique
Né le 15 mars 1969 à Bristol (Angleterre)

Formation
1987 – « A Levels » (équivalence baccalauréat) de géographie, français et histoire contemporaine.
1991 – « Bachelor of Arts Honours Degree », University of Warwich (Diplôme d'Histoire Contemporaine en 3 ans).

Langues
Anglais (langue maternelle)
Français (parlé et écrit couramment)

Expérience professionnelle
Depuis septembre 1996: Manager du département de prêt-à-porter masculin auprès de Buyright Limited, Manchester, Angleterre.

– Responsable d'une équipe de cinq vendeurs dans un important magasin au coeur d'une des plus grandes villes de l'Angleterre.
– Responsable des commandes de stock.
– Paritcipation à l'élaboration du plan général du management du magasin.

1994–1996: Assistant au directeur d'exportation auprès de Woolbridge Products Limited, Manchester, Angleterre.

– Réception et suivi des commandes (y compris les clients à l'étranger) et grande expérience du service de facturation.
1992 – 1994: Vendeur, Woolbridge Products, Manchester, Angleterre.
1991 – 1992: Vendeur auprès de Riley Products, Sydney, Australie.

Autres expériences
1987–1988: Voyages en divers pays de l'Afrique du sud.
1991–1992: Séjour en Australie et en Nouvelle-Zélande.
1989–90: Président du « History Society » à l'Université de Warwick
Permis de conduire

Fig. 8. Basic format for a CV.

- Referees are not normally included on a French CV. They may be called for subsequently, but are not normally asked for in advance.

- Companies and consultants receive thousands of CVs. To succeed, yours must stand out. Use a good quality paper, and if possible a similar envelope. Ask French friends to check your spelling, grammar and punctuation. The French are very picky indeed about such things.

'CONVERTING' YOUR QUALIFICATIONS

If you or a potential employer has any doubt over the level of degrees that you hold, a **lettre d'équivalence** can be requested from the Ministère de l'Enseignement et de la Recherche equating your degree to a French degree level.

WRITING YOUR APPLICATION LETTER

Even if you have the perfect CV and are amply qualified for the job, you may well fall foul of a recruiter with a badly written or badly presented letter. Standard form letters are acceptable. However, it is much better to take the standard form and adapt it to the job for which you are applying, bringing out the major points in favour of your application. The letter should not be simply a repetition of your CV. Figure 9 is an example of a typical **lettre d'accompagnement** in response to the advertisement in Figure 7. Examples of standard letters are not only found in CV guides, but also in many good French-English dictionaries, such as *Collins Robert*. Points to remember are:

- The letter must never exceed one side of A4 Paper.

- Begin by stating that you are replying to the advertisement in *X* newspaper, and give the date of the advertisement. If a **réf. (référence)** is given in the advertisement, remember that it must appear in both the letter *and* on the envelope.

- If the name of the person and their gender is not given, begin simply by *Monsieur*. Do not write *Chèr Monsieur*, as this would imply a degree of intimacy.

- As with the CV, the letter must be impeccably written, on good quality stationery.

- Finish the letter with a standard formula. Generally, men assure their correspondants of their *salutations distinguées*, whilst women send their *sentiments distingués*.

GOING TO THE INTERVIEW

The same basic rules apply in France as anywhere else in the world. Dress appropriately and smartly, arrive in good time, shake hands on meeting your interviewer – and smile! As a foreigner newly-arrived in France, you can expect to be asked about your motivation for moving to France, as well as your experience. Prepare yourself in advance as much as possible for the questioning, as your language abilities will be under scrutiny. Allowances will be made for the fact that you are a foreigner, but you must understand at least 95% of what is being said.

DECIDING WHO TO WORK FOR

The French would be the first to admit that the processes described above are what they call a *parcours de combattant*, literally 'a warrior's path', i.e. it is very tough. Whilst to a certain extent 'beggars cannot be choosers', you should not be put off from applying for the best positions available to you according to your age, experience and nationality.

The French perspective

Although joining **la fonction publique** has always been seen by the French as a safe bet with numerous advantages, only 30% of Parisian students in a recent survey (*Le Monde* 18 March 2001) want to join the French civil service in one of its shapes or forms, whilst 47% prefer to work in the **grandes entreprises**, the great French conglomerates which dominate French life and the economy and are increasingly expanding on the international economic stage. Finally, 67% of these same students want to work in the Île de France.

The upsides and downsides of major French employers
In February 2001, *Capital* magazine published its guide and ratings of the 100 best and worst companies to work for in France. Some companies appeared in both categories for different reasons, and other factors also have to be taken into consideration. But overall, the report was revealing, although not surprising, and explained the reasons behind recruitment problems in certain sectors.

The category that came out worst is what is known as **grande distribution** – hypermarkets such as Auchan or Carrefour. Long hours, restrictive working environments and poor career development probably go a long way to explaining the recruitment problems for management candidates for this sector. Unsurprisingly, the sectors linked to the new information technology, economy of computing, internet and telecommunications comes out as one of the best sectors in which to work in terms of conditions and salary.

When you look at career development, the contradictions in company ratings start to emerge. Companies such as the luxury conglomerate Louis-Vuitton-Moët-Hennessy (LVMH) and the renowned beauty products empire of L'Oréal appear at first glance to be excellent choices for those who have the right profiles. L'Oréal has a casual dress code every day, a generous company-wide stock-options scheme and very early on gives important responsibilities to the best employees, whilst LVMH encourages talented young employees to move within their extensive business empire, stretching now from internet to high fashion. But both companies are criticised for the level of stress they place on employees. You have to get it right the first time, because you are rarely offered a chance to redeem yourself. At Proctor & Gamble, every effort is made to fit you into the Proctor mould, which involves daily supervision from your boss. Even if these are gilt-edged companies, working for the best also involves personal sacrifice.

Salary expectations
Probably the most difficult part of a job application in France is stating how much you expect to be paid (your **prétentions**) in your application letter. Put too much and you will rule yourself out of the running before the race even begins; put too little, and you will either be taken for a ride or taken for a fool. Hence the importance of reading carefully all the job advertisements

75 rue Aristide Briant
75019 Paris

Wear-Well,
19, rue Eugène Leblanc,
93200 Levallois-Perret

Paris le 2 juin 2001

Monsieur,
Votre offre d'emploi pour le poste de vendeur auprès de Wear-Well
parue dans Le Figaro Économie du 30 mai (réf. 24679) m'a beaucoup
intéressé.

De nationalité britannique, et doté d'une forte expérience du
domaine du prêt-à-porter, je suis actuellement à la recherche d'un
poste en France qui me permettrait d'évoluer dans ma vie
professionnelle.

Vous trouverez dans le curriculum vitae ci-joint le détail de mes
études et de mes activités professionnelles. Le montant de mes
prétentions s'élève à 13 000 F brut par mois.

Je suis à votre disposition pour vous fournir toute information
complémentaire. Dans l'attente d'un entretien à cet effet, je vous
prie d'agréer, Monsieur, l'expression de mes salutations distinguées.

Paul Williams

P.J.: Curriculum vitae

Fig. 9.   Letter of application for employment.

available to try and pick a good median figure which really does represent your own worth, but also meets your financial needs.

In March 2001, *Le Monde* published a recruitment guide (*Campus*) aimed at recent and near-graduates from France's business schools. A survey of starting salaries at a leading business school recruitment fair in January 2001 showed the following:

Employment sector	Lowest proposed salary	Highest proposed salary
Legal and financial consultancy, accountancy	210KF	300KF
Banking and insurance	180KF	280KF
Hypermarkets and large department stores	190KF	260KF
Heavy industry	200KF	260KF
Service industries	200KF	250KF
New technology	180KF	300KF

Figure 10. Average graduate starting salaries in January 2001 (KF=1,000FF).

For secretaries and personal assistants, the average salary for full-time employment will depend upon experience, capability, and job role. Being bilingual helps increase your 'market value', but the more limited your written and spoken French, the less your value. The major Anglo-Saxon law firms are almost all present in Paris with large prestigious offices, as are the major accountancy firms. All of these have a constant stream of fresh secretarial blood. Salaries range on average from 160KF to 250KF+ for professionals capable of running a top manager or their team. Looking through the advertisements in *FUSAC* will quickly help you decide what the appropriate rate will be for your skills and level.

14

Working in France

LOOKING AT EMPLOYMENT CONTRACTS

The two principal forms of contract for legal employment in France are the fixed-term contract, and the indefinite contract.

- **Contrats à durée déterminée (CDD)** – fixed-term contracts. These can only be applied in certain circumstances, such as a sudden increase in business; or for seasonal work (e.g. at Christmas); or to cover pregnancy or sick leave; or to replace an employee in a position which is being cut, or for which the new employee cannot yet take up the permanent position. They may not exceed nine months, but can be renewed a maximum of twice. After two renewals, the company is obliged to offer you a permanent contract. CDDs are increasingly common in France.

- **Contrats à durée indéterminée (CDI)** – indefinite contracts. These are the most common form of contract in France. They are also the most preferable form of contract for foreigners moving to France, as they will provide you with longer-term residency rights.

Note that your *carte de séjour* will initially be limited to the length of your work contract.

There is no standard model for a contract in France, and surprisingly, there does not even have to be a written contract. However, the following points should normally appear in a written contract:

- name and address of both parties

- job title and description of duties

- place of work

- rate of pay and bonuses, etc.

- hours of work per week

- notice period required by employer and employee

- trial period, normally from one to three months, can be renewed once by the employer; both sides can terminate without notice during this period

- holiday entitlement

- collective agreement (**convention collective**) applicable to the position or company – this is important as it may modify standard working practices

- details of where employer social security payments are made and of complementary retirement fund centres.

Your acceptance for a position is also subject to a general medical examination (**visite medicale**) by the independent firm doctor and being declared **apte** for the position.

You may be in a position of either having to accept a part-time or fixed-term contract when you first arrive if, for example you have a working spouse via whom you will acquire residency and social security rights; or you may be offered a long fixed-term contract of up to nine months, which will provide you with a chance to sample Parisian life (if you are an EU national).

For part-time and fixed-term contracts, the following elements shown in Figure 10 must also be included in your contract by law.

Salary

The minimum hourly wage in France is usually known by the initials **SMIC** (which stand for **Salaire Minimum Inter-professionnel de Croissance**). It is currently 42.02 Francs per hour before social security contributions, making a monthly salary of 7,101.38 Francs for those firms still operating a 39 hour week, or 6,373.17 Francs for those operating the 35 hour week. The **SMIC** is linked to the Cost of Living Index, which is reviewed every six months. When this index rises by 2% or more, the level of the **SMIC** is raised. Pay reviews must take place once a year by law. However, salaries above the **SMIC** do not have to be increased, even if the cost of living has increased.

Salaries are normally quoted in contracts as a total annual figure before social security deductions, but may also be quoted on a monthly or hourly basis. Salaries are usually paid monthly,

CDI part-time	CDD full-time	CDD part-time
1. Your qualifications.	1. The **precise** reason for the CDD. This does not allow the employer to force you into a CDD because 'there is too much work at the moment', etc.	All of the elements outlined in the previous two cases are required by law.
2. Pay.	2. If you are replacing somebody, the name and qualifications of that person.	
3. Number of hours **either** per week **or** per month **or** annually, depending on how your job is organised.	3. Date limit of the contract, renewal date and deadline for renewal.	
4. Method for changing work hours	4. Minimum period if no fixed date is defined, i.e. at least three months.	
5. Number of complementary hours which the employer can request. This is generally limited to 1/10 of the time stated in the contract, and cannot bring the total over the legal limits. NB: This is not overtime (*heures supplémentaires*).	5. All of the general elements outlined under CDI part-time.	

Fig. 10.   French employment contracts.

on around the 26th day of each month. This is to allow the transfer of money into your account to settle bills due at the beginning of the month (notably rent). Payment is normally by standing order to your bank account, except for lower salaries which may be paid by cheque.

Bonuses

Most French firms offer bonuses of a 13th month's pay (**13ème mois**). This is normally paid as one lump sum at one point in the year, usually in December. Bonuses are not, however, obligatory. Other companies offer profit-sharing schemes (**participation des salariés aux résultats de l'entreprise**), which is an obligation in companies with more than 100 employees. Both of these, and any similar benefits, are normally mentioned in your contract. You should note that pay rises are not obligatory. In 1999, half of all **cadres** did not receive a pay rise, whilst those who did averaged pay rises of 11%. Finally, it should be noted that stock options in France are still a limited commodity for the happy few, although some major companies have introduced share purchase schemes to encourage company loyalty whilst leaving the new shareholders at the mercy of the market.

If you are employed under a CDD, you are entitled to an end of contract bonus (**indemnité de fin de contrat**). This is equivalent to 6% of your salary, and is in addition to any other bonuses. CDD employees do not generally receive other bonuses.

WORKING HOURS

Your general working hours should be marked in your contract. *Cadres* only have a notional working week to some extent and are expected to work the hours that it takes to get the job done without extra pay. Non-*cadres* employees should also note that in certain large firms, such as law firms, the lawyers will be classed as **collaborateurs** as they are officially self-employed, so that even if an office has a staff of 50, only 20 may be employees. This could have a significant effect on the length of your working week.

France is in a period of transition at the moment, from a legal working week of 39 hours to 35 hours over a five-day period paid at the same rate as 39 hours. In the year 2000 new legislation introduced by the former Social Security and Employment Minister Martine Aubry began to be applied in French companies.

By October 2000 almost half of private sector employees had seen their working week cut to 35 hours; but small and medium-sized companies with less than 20 employees on the payroll currently have until 1st January 2002 to complete the change-over. From January 1st 2002, hours 36 to 39 must be paid at +25%.

The traditional long French lunch is rarer in Paris than in the provinces. However, government offices still observe a total shutdown between 12h00 and 14h00. Employees can be asked to work paid overtime hours, but cannot be forced to work more than a certain number of overtime hours per year (currently 130). The present government intends to tax overtime hours more heavily to encourage employers to take on extra staff rather than paying existing staff for longer hours. Currently, overtime is paid at 25% more per hour for the first eight hours, and 50% more for every hour in addition to that.

HOLIDAY ENTITLEMENT, LEAVE OF ABSENCE AND RTT

Holiday entitlement is gradually built up on the basis of 2.5 days per month worked, to a total of five weeks annual paid leave. This does not include public holidays. Normally this is taken in segments over the course of the year – one week in winter and spring, and a longer break in the summer months. Some companies still observe the traditional total shut-down in August, when seemingly the whole of France heads for the hills, the coast or the airports. Extra days off are often allowed under the terms of **conventions collectives** (see below) for close family bereavements, weddings or moving house. Check this with your personnel department.

Any existing holiday arrangements are normally honoured when you join a company, but be careful to check this. The 'holiday calendar year' normally runs from 1st May to 30th April. Some companies allow you to carry over some holiday entitlement, but you must be careful not to lose holiday time not taken within the required period.

One important side-effect of the 35-hour week legislation has been the introduction of the **RTT (réduction du temps de travail)**. These are days off each month in order to bring employees into line with the 35 hours. The method used varies from company to company, with some insisting on long weekends whilst others strictly limiting the amount of accumulated RTTs which can be taken at any one time so as not to disrupt office time.

INSURANCE AND PENSIONS

In addition to the regular contributions you will make to the state schemes, you will probably find deductions on your pay slips for additional health insurance via the **mutuelle** to which the firm subscribes, and to a pension scheme.

These contributions, if they are levied, are obligatory. They are very worthwhile, and will cover most if not all of the shortfall in state reimbursements for medical treatment. Ask your personnel department or your colleagues how to apply to the **mutuelle** for supplementary reimbursement. Unemployment insurance (**allocation d'assurance de chômage**) is automatically included in your social security contributions.

In 2000, the government launched a long-awaited and much-criticised reform which offered savings plans (**épargnes**) including plans for what look suspiciously like pension funds (hated by the French left-wing hardliners). These already exist in fact, and come in many shapes and forms, from simple savings plans topped up by employers to share schemes for employees. The new scheme proposed tax exonerations for employers who made larger contributions to the funds on behalf of their employees, and allowed employees either to remove a lump sum after ten years or to receive annuities. The idea of anything resembling a complementary pension payment (excluding the established *mutuelle* system) and diminishing contributions to the social security pension reserves (thus forcing an eventual change) has caused the uproar.

The scheme is planned for the 14.5 million workers in the private sector, but is not limited to long-term employees. It only requires two months' employment in a firm before an employee can start to contribute to the firm's scheme, and also offers the chance to move your savings from one scheme to another as and when you change contracts. It also allows small companies the chance to group together in order to gain advantages for both employees and employers.

Opponents are trying to remove employer tax advantages, fearful of a loss of social security funding and a slump in salary increases as companies opt for tax-reducing saving plan contributions, and the parliamentary jury is still out on the question. The problem will come to a head sooner than everyone wants to believe. The social security budget is already financially the chronically sick man of France. As the unions force early retirement deals (at 55) for a number of transport industries and for the **fonctionnaires** (representing 25% of the active workforce), the private sector is now also faced with the fact that in 2012 half of the current 'baby-boom' *fonctionnaires* will retire. The working population is diminishing, and therefore so are social security contributions. Something has to give soon, but will it be the unions, the employers or the employed?

COLLECTIVE AGREEMENTS

Conventions collectives, as they are known, exist in many varied professions. They cover everything from compassionate leave to the right to union membership, as well as health schemes, loans and rates of pay. They may substantially alter the general conditions of work, and you should note if mention is made of a *Convention* in your contract.

FOOD AND TRAVEL

Many French firms offer either a luncheon voucher scheme (**ticket restaurant**), or a canteen facility. In Paris, the firm will normally reimburse half of the cost of your **Carte Orange** (travel pass) each month. This will be paid directly with your salary, and will be indicated on your pay slip (**fiche de paie**).

PROFESSIONAL TRAINING

French firms with more than ten employees are obliged to set aside 1.2% of their gross annual payroll for **formation continue**. This may be used for advanced training, but also for basic language training. In both cases it could be of great interest to you. However, the allocation is entirely at the discretion of the employer.

WORKER REPRESENTATION TO THE MANAGEMENT

There are three levels of worker representation, all of which may apply in the same company. This depends upon the number of employees.

1. **Délégués du personnel** (employee delegates) Any company with more than ten employees must have *délégués*, with the number of *délégués* increasing in proportion to the size of the workforce. They present employee concerns to the management over individual and collective working conditions, job roles, wages and application of employment laws.

2. **Comité d'Entreprise** (Work council) Both the *délégués du personnel* and the members of the *Comité d'Entreprise* are elected by the employees, by secret ballot, with representatives for the *cadres* and non-*cadres* in a company. There must be more than 50 employees on the payroll for a company to have a *Comité d'Entreprise*. The *Comité* normally also includes a senior management member and a member of the personnel department. The *Comité* discusses in more general terms the same concerns as the *délégués*. However, it should also be informed of general company policies before they are implemented, and is entitled to view the company accounts annually. The *Comité* normally has a budget of its own linked to the number of employees, which is used to enable employees and their families to undertake cultural and leisure pursuits at reduced rates. You may also find that your *Comité* has offers available on the purchase of new spectacles, etc.

UNION MEMBERSHIP

The presence of unions is most heavily felt in nationalised and heavy industry. It is rarer in the private sector, and under the terms of certain *conventions collectives*, simply not allowed. If union membership is allowed, the right to strike is guaranteed under French law (and freely exercised!), except for certain essential public employees.

The rôle and power of the unions

French unions are numerous but are neither as highly organised nor as powerful as those of France's main economic rivals. Union membership, at about 20%, is amongst the lowest in Europe. The power of the unions, however, comes from their strongholds in the public sector, particularly transport, which enables them to cripple the economy rapidly and at will. Strikes are called regularly.

A local branch (**section syndicale**) of a union can be established in any company with at least 50 employees. Union negotiations are carried out at national or regional level between major employers' associations and labour organisations (not all are trades unions). Resulting agreements are then applied throughout that particular industry. In some cases, there may well be 'knock-on' effects in other industries where workers will claim the same rights.

Labour relations are based on a contractual policy (**politique contractuelle**) introduced since the riots of 1968. This provides for renewable and therefore renegotiable labour contracts. This type of collective bargaining not only includes working conditions but also retirement, training, the indexation of wages and prices, and job security.

The main unions

The leading union federations are fragmented and divided along political lines. Most unions are either run by or closely related to political parties. To a very large extent the unions consider themselves to be 'the Fourth Estate' politically, and to have the right to issue political demands – ultimately backed by strike action – to any government.

- The **Confédération Générale du Travail (CGT)**. This is the largest and most belligerent union. The leaders are Communist or Communist-affiliated and controlled. Geographically strongest in the heavy industrialised regions around Paris and Marseilles, and especially in electricity and railways.

- The **Confédération Française Démocratique du Travail (CFDT)** is the most organised and the active of the non-Communist unions. Mostly white-collar workers in the metallurgical, gas and chemical industries.

- The **Force Ouvrière (FO)** is more moderate in tone than the CGT but normally cooperates with the CFT and other left-wing unions in major 'policy' matters. It is the leading federation of workers in the nationalised industries and the civil service. Its strongholds are Paris and the south-west.

The principal unions are principally but not exclusively concerned with workers in the nationalised industries. As such, they are vociferous in their opposition to privatisation, and in defence of their **acquis sociaux** (basically this means 'perks').

Unrest and protest

It seems that scarcely a day goes by without some form of strike (**grève**, sometimes also called a **mouvement social**), protest, demonstration (**manifestation** or **manif'** for short), one-day stoppage or embargo taking place in France. Cynics have commented that ever since 1789, it has been mob rule that has prevailed in France. However, the French generally prefer to regard such behaviour as another form of freedom of expression.

DEALING WITH CONFLICTS AT WORK

If at all possible, it is best to try to contain a problem before it gets out of hand. Speak to the personnel department, and if they cannot or will not help, then try your *délegué du personnel.*

Questions raised by the *délégués* during their confidential meetings with the management are recorded and reviewed annually by the work inspectors (**inspection du travail**), who have the right to pursue an enquiry if they think it necessary. This may also help you in more serious disciplinary cases, or worst of all, in the case of dismissal.

Companies are obliged by law to display the address of the nearest *inspection du travail*, and a telephone number. You can go to them for free confidential advice. You can also find their telephone numbers in the *Pages Jaunes*.

Dismissal

Firing someone in France is almost as difficult for the employer as it is for the employee to find a job in the first place! Nonetheless, it does happen. Strict procedures must be followed, including written warnings. If the procedures are not adhered to, you have a strong case for compensation, especially if you have not been paid your full share of holiday pay, etc.

The two grounds for dismissal are **faute grave** (gross misconduct or incompetence), or economic, in which case you are entitled to 'first refusal' if your job is re-created subsequently. If you intend to contest your dismissal, you can take your employer to an industrial tribunal (**conseil des Prud'hommes**). Winning your case would entitle you to compensation but not reinstatement. Most companies prefer to settle out of court. Legal aid does exist in France (**l'aide juridictionnelle**) for those on low incomes (currently less than 7353FF per month), including the income of your spouse or partner. For further information, contact your local *mairie*.

CROSS-CULTURAL ISSUES

A phrase that often creeps into both French office conversation and job advertisements is *culture générale*, which can be translated quite literally. One of the main differences between British and French culture, for instance, is the emphasis you place upon the rôle and importance of your work.

One French manager working in the UK said recently, '(In the UK) The assumption is that you'll be more productive if you work longer hours but I doubt it. People in France put work in a

The British viewed by the French	**The French viewed by the British**
• Sometimes viewed as aloof, egotistical and silent, to the point of rudeness or arrogance.	• Sometimes seen an undisciplined, rude and arrogant.
• Indirect and unclear.	• Business meetings are unstructured and unproductive.
• Too obsessed by work. Lacking in general culture.	• Over-formal even to the point of being considered comic; too self-important.
• Unable to see 'the big picture' – obsessed by detail.	
• Illogical – gut reaction is not understood by the honed French mind.	• Inexact especially in contractual arrangements which are spelt out to the letter in the UK but 'understood' in France with a legal restraint on both parties.
• Too informal; too lacking in protocol; in too much of a hurry to take decisions.	
• British humour is legendary but perplexing for the French who often fail to grasp subtle understatement.	• Sly, unclear and uncompromising. Compromise is a dirty word in France. The French definition generally seems to be forcing your opponent to capitulate totally in the face of your demands.

Fig. 11.   An Entente Cordiale?

different place in their lives. It's important, but not central. We take our lunch breaks, for example, and even at a business lunch nobody talks about business. You talk about the food because food is also an important part of life' (*The Observer*, July 2, 2000). Whilst this is a little exaggerated, it is generally true.

The FBCCI's millennium publication, *Britain and France, Partners for the Millennium*, included an essay on practical psychology for Franco-British trade relationships by Peter Alfandary, a leading British solicitor.

Overall this is a pretty fair assessment of the problems that both sides face in understanding each other. The key to success is of course the construction of personal relationships based on mutual respect and a willingness to work with one another. Without those relationships, the French tend to withdraw into what the British would regard as 'jobsworth' attitudes, fearful of being exploited if they do somebody else's job rather than seeing it as lending a hand to a colleague and friend-in-need.

Both sides place vital importance on the development of the working relationship, but they have different ways of going about it. The British prefer to call you by your first name but the French prefer to talk to you about your last holiday. The French are also renowned for talking about their personal lives in the office and their business lives at home, whereas the British are perhaps too prone to compartmentalise their lives.

The French are not keen, however, on out-of-office socialising such as you might find in the UK or USA, and the stalwarts of the local bar or office softball team are normally Anglo-Saxons. This reflects the fact that whilst the British in particular are considered too independent and individualistic in their professional practices, the French are once again notoriously individualistic in their private lives and private work domains. This difference might therefore be summed up as the following:

- French – obedient and conformist in public life, policy and method, but highly individual in private.

- British – generally conformist but still highly individual in public life, but greater team spirit in private.

PAYING TAX IN FRANCE

You are liable for tax in France if you reside more than 183 days in France in any one calendar year. A double taxation agreement between France and the UK prevents those who still have tax liabilities in the UK from being taxed twice on the same element of income. This is the Convention for the Avoidance of Double Taxation and the Prevention of Fiscal Evasion with respect to Taxes on Income.

If you do continue to pay tax in your home country (e.g. in the UK where you are taxed at source), then if you have taxable income you should declare the amount of tax you have paid and from what source of income on your French tax declaration. **Take professional advice on this topic**, as some sources of revenue are more highly taxed in one country than in France and vice versa. You might find yourself owing the French tax service an additional sum if they consider you have not fully acquitted your obligations.

A similar double-taxation agreement exists between France and the USA. **US citizens** are required to declare their earnings throughout the world on their Federal income tax returns, and living outside the USA does not remove your obligation to file a tax return. However, living overseas can lead to deductions, exclusions and credits. The US Embassy in Paris offers advice on tax matters at the IRS office at 2 rue St Florentin, 75001, open 09h00–12h00. You can telephone 01 43 12 22 22 from 13h30–15h30 or Fax 01 43 12 47 52. Information can also be found on the Embassy website www.amb.usa.fr, or the IRS website www.irs.ustreas.gov.

Making your declaration

Income tax (**impôt sur le revenu**) is payed in arrears. You will be required to complete a tax declaration, sent directly to your home, in March each year. This will be for the preceeding tax year, which in France runs from 1 January to 31 December. If you send your declaration in late, you risk a fine equivalent to an extra 10% of your allotted tax bill.

If you do not reach your tax threshold by the end of the calendar year (e.g. you start work in September), you will be exempted from income tax for your first year in France. However, you must prepare yourself for your first tax bill when it does arrive, as you will be required to pay this in one lump sum. This is normally in about October or November, and is roughly equivalent to one month's salary. It is advisable to open a deposit account at the bank to prepare for this.

After the first lump sum payment, you will have the choice of paying monthly (**mensuellement**), quarterly (**trimestriellement**), or annually (in one lump sum). You will also have the chance of paying by direct debit, which the tax office will regulate, or by cheque.

The new tax demand will come into effect in January each year. You will be paying tax each year on the basis of your earnings two years previous to the current calendar year. For instance, in March 2001, you declare your revenue for 1 January – 31 December 2000. In the summer or early autumn of 2001, (the French tax authorities are known for their sense of timing; they generally wait until the return from the summer vacations to tell you your new tax bill), you will receive a new **avis d'imposition**, based on the 2000 total, which will take effect in January 2002. If you have opted to pay monthly, your payments will be automatically adjusted over the last few months of the year to take into consideration your new monthly bill.

It is important to bear in mind that you will therefore still have income tax to pay when you leave France, for a limited period after your departure. When you do leave France, you should visit the tax office to 'sign off' their registers, and make the appropriate arrangements.

Working out your declaration

1. On your December payslip for the year ending before the March declaration date (i.e. December 2001 for the March 2002 declaration), you will see a figure supplied by your employer marked **Net imposable**. This is the sum total to declare for the period you have been employed by this company. If you change employers during the year, you will need to take your December payslip figure and the same figure mentioned on your final payslip from your previous employer(s), and add all of these together.

2. Check all personal details recorded on your declaration, e.g. marital status, number of children, etc. This will determine the number of **'parts'** you will have and the attendant reductions.

3. If you have savings accounts or shares at the bank, they should

Amount declared (FF)	2001 tax on 2000 revenue	2002 tax on 2001 revenue	2003 tax on 2002 revenue
Up to 26,230	0	0	0
26,230 – 51,600	8.25%	7.5%	7%
51,600 – 90,820	21.75%	21%	20.5%
90,820 – 147,050	31.75%	31%	30.5%
147,050 – 239,270	41.75%	41%	40.5%
239,270 – 295,070	47.25%	46.75%	46.5%
295,070+	53.25%	52.75%	52.5%

Fig. 12. French tax bands.

supply you with a statement, stating what you owe and in which category on the form this belongs. Certain savings accounts are tax exempt if you keep to the terms of the account.

4. If you receive **shares** as part of your salary remuneration, you will be taxed not only on the dividends from the shares but also on the value of the shares at the date you received them. For stock options, you must take professional advice. At the moment the tax noose is tightening around stock options.

5. If you make **donations** to a church or charitable association that is registered under **sous la loi 1901**, they can issue you with a tax receipt which will lead to a 50% rebate on the value of your donation. These can be accumulated from several different charities.

Tax bands in France

In 2001 new tax bands came into force which will see tax rates come down for everybody up until 2003, with the lower paid benefiting most. The table below explains what you can now expect to pay.

However, there are a variety of rebates and exemptions granted on gross income which moderate the rate of taxation. Most salaried workers receive not only the standard deduction of 10% but also a further deduction of 20% for the remaining figure. The lowest paid category must complete a tax return, and will almost certainly be eligible for a reimbursement of the CSG (one of the social contribution payments withdrawn from your monthly salary). Certain building works will also give you tax breaks; and if you have an adult child under a certain age living at home, they can be included on your declaration if they are studying and you are paying for their general upkeep.

Generally, families are favoured by the French tax system. '**Le quotient familial**' means that taxable income is divided into units reflecting the family status of the family. Hence a single person is taxed on their whole income. A married couple are considered as two units, and their joint income will be divided by two. The first two children each count as a half-unit, and each additional child is counted as a full unit. Couples who sign a PACS at the local *mairie* will qualify for the same tax status as a married couple two years after the signature of their PACS.

Wealth tax

Wealth tax (**impôt sur la fortune** or **ISF**) for French residents is 0.5% if your French assets are worth more than 4,390,000FF. The rate then goes up progressively in bands. Assets worth in excess of 42,520,000FF are subject to a tax of 1.5%. Attempts to revise the wealth tax in 2000 were defeated in Parliament.

Finding help on taxes

Most banks and the vast majority of newspapers and journals will publish free guides in some shape or form when tax declaration time comes around. The Finance Ministry offer a number of possibilities to help you complete your declaration: either by telephone on 08 36 67 10 10, or on www.finances.gouv.fr. You can order tax forms by internet, and even make a 'virtual' declaration (although they still need a hard copy) on www.minefi.gouv.fr/services/formulaires. In the weeks leading up to the declaration deadline, you can ask for help at your tax office, and also now in many local *mairies*.

UNEMPLOYMENT IN FRANCE

Unemployment is dealt with by two agencies in France. The ANPE (www.anpe.fr) is the local job centre, where you must be registered if you are out of work and seeking to claim unemployment benefit. The ASSEDIC (www.assedic.fr) is the agency which actually pays you unemployment benefit, if you qualify.

Job seekers from other EU countries

You have the right to seek work in France for three months before you will have officially 'outstayed your welcome'. During that three month period, if you are registered as unemployed in your home country, you will retain your right to receive unemployment benefits from your home country via the French unemployment service benefit service, the ASSEDIC.

In order to obtain these benefits, you need to complete and bring with you two EU social security forms:

- **The E303** You must present this at your local ANPE (**Agence Nationale pour l'Emploi** – the Job Centre) **within seven days of your arrival**. You must also register at the ANPE at the same time.

- **The E119** This will provide you with full medical cover for the three month period during which you are entitled to stay in France and seek work. To establish your health rights during this period, contact your local **CPAM** (**Caisse Primaire d'Assurance Maladie** – the local health authority), and ask for details of how to contact the nearest **Service des Relations Internationales**.

Unemployment rights for foreign residents

If you are employed in France and are unfortunate enough to lose your job, you will start to appreciate the heavy social charges that you paid when you were in employment.

- If you resign without good reason, are dismissed for a **faute grave** (serious misconduct), or refuse a suitable job offer, you will be refused unemployment benefit on the grounds that you do not wish to work.

- If you resign in order to set up your own business, from 1 July 2001 a new law (still largely undefined) to encourage entrepreneurs will allow for resignations if you intend creating or taking over a business. If that business fails, a new law already in place since January 2001 now provides unemployment benefit for those who tried and failed, as long as they enrol at the ANPE within three years of the end of their last contract.

- To qualify, you must have worked at least three months in the last year, and for two of the last three years. You must also be under 60.

- You must register at the local ANPE, and be both capable of work and actively seeking employment.

The **allocation d'assurance de chômage** (unemployment benefit) you receive depends upon how much you have paid into the system and over what period of time – if you have been working for four years on an average wage, you will receive more than if you have been working on the minimum wage for the last two years. Payments may take some time to come through initially, but are back-dated. Your **allocation** will diminish with time, as you effectively use up the fund you created during the time you were employed. After two years, your situation will be re-assessed and you will receive a reduced **allocation**. The next stage after that, known as the RMI, is the very basic minimum aid which is given out. It is not currently available to anybody under the age of 25. Once that has been exhausted, you are not entitled to any further benefit.

You must be careful to keep copies of job searches and applications during the time that you are **en chômage** (unemployed). This will be required by the ASSEDIC and the ANPE to justify your continued benefit payments.

For over a year, the unions, government and MEDEF (the 'social partners' or **partenaires sociaux**) have sought to create a new plan for returning the unemployed to work. The new **Plan d'Aide au Retour à l'Emploi (PARE)** works as follows:

- When you sign on, you will also sign a PARE and receive a fixed payment.

- The PARE consists of a reminder of your rights and obligations and those of the ASSEDIC; your signature to a Personal Action Plan (PAP); agreement to undergo an examination of your professional competencies if required.

- The PAP detemines the categories of employment in order to orientate your search; decides upon any training required to get you back to work.

- The PAP is activated. If after six months you have refused job offers, you can be reprimanded, or even be struck off the register of benefits altogether.

- After 12 months if you have still not found a job, you will be recategorised and sent for training. An employer who takes you on will receive fiscal benefits for employing a long-term job-seeker, so your chances of employment are higher but your chances of a good salary are probably lower.

Help for the unemployed

Your social security rights, if they are already established, will remain intact throughout the time that you continue to receive unemployment benefits. Even after you have used up the right to the RMI, you will have social security rights under the French system for one further year.

The **Service Social** at your local *mairie* also has a fund at its disposal to help in cases of difficulty and emergency, e.g. the electricity is about to be cut off. The amount of aid available depends entirely on your local *mairie*, and may only be a token contribution towards clearing your debts.

The ANPE offers financial assistance in certain circumstances for travelling expenses incurred to attend interviews, and also for those who accept jobs far from their homes. If you are unemployed and you are forced to move to take up a new position, the ANPE also offers limited financial assistance for moving costs.

Redundancy due to economic cut-backs

If you are made redundant due to cut-backs in the firm, you will have 'first refusal' for your job should it be re-created subsequently. In terms of your financial situation, you can also request a **convention de conversion** which will allow you to draw 80% of your final salary for six months. These conventions allow you to seek a job in the same sector or a similar sector, as long as you have been employed by your previous firm for at least two years. They involve working closely with the ANPE training services, and do not stop you from accepting a new position if you find one during the six-month period.

For further details of the *convention de conversion* speak to the ANPE or check their webside at www.anpe.fr.

15

Au Pairs, Temporary and Student Workers

WORKING AS AN AU PAIR

Traditionally this has been limited to young women in the 18 to 25 year-old age bracket, but young men of a similar age can and do find au pair work in France. The number of people willing to work as au pairs in and around Paris has diminished in recent years. If you are willing and able to consider this option, and you have the correct temperament and skills to cope, you should not find a shortage of opportunities.

Au pairs and nannies

Nannies have formal qualifications in childcare, and are much better paid. Their duties are restricted specifically to childcare, and accommodation is not normally provided. Both nannies and au pairs are often expected to travel with their families.

An au pair is generally a young person with no formal qualification in childcare, who lives as one of the family. The legal age limits are 18 to 30 years old. Au pairs are paid a small sum of 'pocket money' (normally c. 1,500 – 2,000FF/month) in return for looking after the children, *light* housework, and several evenings baby-sitting per week. Accommodation and meals are normally provided by the family. Au pairs normally take a language course during the daytime. This is obligatory for non-EU citizens as regards their residence permits.

EU nationals who can enter and leave France easily are able to take their chances by accepting non declared unofficial positions with families. However, an illegal status leaves you open to abuse – and this does happen. Avoid ad hoc arrangements which may seem a good idea at the time but can go very wrong when you are living on the promise of payment 'tomorrow', and tomorrow never comes. Non-EU nationals who are willing to work as au pairs should definitely not accept illegal contracts. Not only are you not covered if you have an accident cleaning an apartment or minding the children, but you are living and working illegally.

Looking for work
There are a number of agencies which place au pairs and nannies, both in the UK and also in France (principally in Paris). It is quite possible to find a position before arriving in France, through British magazines such as *The Lady*.

In Paris, the magazines *France-USA Contacts* and *The Free Voice* carry regular advertisements. Some agencies which advertise are better than others. Try asking around for the names of the good agencies. You should also check noticeboards including the community noticeboards listed in Chapter 20 for small advertisements, and place advertisements seeking work in the same places.

There are generally more jobs available than au pairs to fill them, so you should not feel stuck if your first family does not prove satisfactory.

Conditions of employment
Au pairing falls within one of the 'grey' areas of French employment. The official title of an au pair in French law is a **stagiaire d'aide familiale**. There are set guidelines, but making sure that these are applied is not always easy. Establishing a good relationship not only with the children but also with 'Monsieur et Madame' is vital to a successful stay.

Generally, you will be employed from September until June, although you may well be asked to stay and help in the summer holiday months. Your employer *should* make a **Déclaration d'Engagement** to the Social Security office. In reality, few employers will do this voluntarily as they fear paying extra taxes to pay for your statutory rights. If you are an EU citizen, make sure you take the E111 form with you to France to cover emergency health care.

Legal requirements for American au pairs are listed below. **Rules and requirements also applying to EU nationals are in bold:**

- **Age limit of 18–30 years old**.
- Fair knowledge of French and/or studying French.
- Minimum stay of 3 months, maximum 18 months. You can

change families during this period but the maximum stay is 18 months.

- Summer au pairs working one to three months are not required to take French classes but must have completed one year of college-level studies in French.

- The recognised objective of au pairing is to share in a French family's life and culture. Foreign families are not normally authorised to hire au pairs.

- **Room and board must be provided, with meals shared with the family and a private bedroom.**

- **The au pair's daily schedule should not exceed more than five hours per day, and should be arranged to allow time for study including classes. Au pairs should have one day off a week, and once a month this should be a Sunday. An au pair should never be prevented from attending Church on Sunday even if this is a working day.**

- American citizens must obtain their au pair visa in the USA from the French Consulate with jurisdiction over their place of residence *before* entering France. You cannot convert tourist visas. This means following the same procedure outlined in chapter 13 for obtaining a **visa de long séjour**, with a contract as a **stagiaire d'aide familiale** approved by the French Ministry of Labour. Your work permit itself is finally granted once you arrive in France after your contract has been approved by the French Ministry of Labour.

- American citizens hoping to au pair in France should enquire about regulations concerning their contracts. The American Embassy website (www.amb-usa.fr/) has useful information.

Accommodation, travel and health cover

If you are lucky, you will have accommodation in the separate **chambre de bonne** – cold and damp in winter, perhaps with a shared toilet – but an oasis of privacy from the children! In Paris, it is customary but not obligatory to pay half the *carte orange* travel pass for all employees. You may have to travel to the family home deep in the country, where you might find yourself looking after more children than you bargained on when the country cousins come to stay too. But the upside is that you could also be taken skiing, for instance.

WORKING WHILE YOU ARE STUDYING

Students are amongst the most sought-after workers on the current French job market and in the new working environment of France. French government restrictions limit the right to work for both student French nationals and foreign students alike, with a limit of 20 hours per week during term-time and 35 hours per week during vacations.

For both employers and employees, the situation tends to work out: extra money and CV material for the students, extra employees without significant extra cost to the employers. Some 170,000 students are now estimated to be enrolled in temporary work agencies (**agences d'intérim**), but thousands of others are also working in contractual situations directly with their employers as au pairs and part-time tutors, waiting in restaurants, operating call centres, or taking their first steps in the **nouvelle économie** of the Net. Foreign students who apply for jobs will normally find that a command of English and another foreign language will give them a cutting edge over competitors.

Every situation is different, and so it is hard to generalise in this field of work. But the main tendencies to note are:

- **Hotels and restaurants** If you can stick the smell and the pace, you will have a good chance of finding a position in this industry. Some 51% of the employees of the 'Quick' chain of restaurants and up to 65% of employees at Pizza Hut are students with CDI contracts. This contract status is a handy extra when it comes round to applying for apartment rentals. The downside is that the fast food environment is hard, and not the most desirable CV material. The hotel industry is apparently suffering from a lack of good staff. If you already have some basic experience and a good approach, you could find yourself moving rapidly from one side of the reception desk to the other.

- **Working with temporary agencies** Working as an **intérimaire** has its advantages as well as its pitfalls. The work on offer will to some extent depend upon your abilities as well as what the agencies have to offer. But at least if you find that you cannot bear where you are working, you know that you can ask your agency to pull you out and place you somewhere else.

- **Call centres** Although the English term has crept into the French language, these are officially known as **centres d'appels**. Advertisements regarding **télémarketing** or seeking **téléoperateurs** or **téléacteurs** will mostly concern working for a call centre. The number of such centres has exploded in recent years, especially with the growth of the mobile phone industry. The sector is expected to employ 300,000 people in France in 2003, in a sector which in the Paris region today has a 30% turnover (*Le Point* 2 February 2001). A limited product training is normally provided, but conditions and contracts vary greatly. You may be offered a **contrat vacataire** which is designed to allow an employer to take on temporary workers to complete a particular project, e.g. launching a new product which requires telephone canvassing or a user hotline. These contracts are pretty basic and swiftly ended by the employer as they please, and pay may be by the hour and/or linked to the number of calls you deal with. It should be noted that *contrats vacataires* do not contribute towards securing residence rights for new arrivals.

- **Working on the web** This is the *luxe* of student employment. You need to be appropriately educated and up to pace to make it in the web world, but if you are, this is where the money is for students: longer contracts, better salaries, and better CV material. Some companies will do their best to keep you on if you prove your worth, so you may even find yourself in the luxurious position of already having a decent CDI when you are finishing your studies and are looking for something better.

Who can work, when, and for how long?

- Students registered at language schools are *not* entitled to work whilst they pursue their studies in France.

- You must be registered and studying at an official French university or Institute of Higher Education which has both obliged and entitled you to be enrolled in the French social security system under the special student *régime* (see chapter 5). This does not mean that you will be exempt from French social charges (**cotisations**) but it does mean that your extra contributions will start to accrue other advantages for you within the social security system.

- Students must complete the first year of their studies before applying for employment.

- The student working week is limited to 20 hours per week in term-time and 35 hours per week in vacations.

- American students are obliged to justify their need to work when applying to the French Ministry of Labour for the **autorisation provisoire de travail**, normally valid for three months and renewable upon production of evidence of continuing studies. Students who receive grants and/or have sufficient financial means to continue their studies are not normally granted a work permit. American students must also produce a valid **carte d'étudiant** and contract from their employer with full personal details and details of working hours and pay. These provisions generally apply to students from non-EU countries, but you should check with your embassy for precise terms and conditions.

- Students from EU countries do not require work permits, but are subject to French legal restrictions. Commonwealth citizens should remember that British residency rights do not equate to British citizenship rights within the EU. You will be governed by the regulations pertaining to your nationality status.

Where to look for work

Most of the French press options outlined in chapter 13 also include job offers specifically aimed at students. French students produce their own magazine, **L'Étudiant**, which is widely available and has its own important employment service (www.l'etudiant-emploir.fr). Other notable websites include www.supjeune.com, www.recrut.com and www.net-work.fr. You should also check out the other sites and links suggested in Chapter 13.

A word of warning

No matter who you work for in France, you and your employer are subject to French law. Your contract and work conditions must conform to French law. Foreign firms have been criticised repeatedly over the last year for failing to observe basic French regulations when employing students and temporary workers.

The official French government website, www.droitsdesjeunes.gouv.fr, will help you draw the line between working hard for your money and working for next to no money at all.

SEASONAL WORK

The major department stores normally advertise for extra help throughout the traditional busy periods up to and after Christmas and during the sales. Every year, the CIDJ (see Chapter 5) organises a special two-day summer recruitment fair to help students find a summer job. The term 'job' is used now in French, but normally implies low/minimum pay for low status work. At the spring 2001 job fair 25% of the jobs were in the lower end of the hotel and restaurant industries, and 21% were in the general commerce sector. Popular choices also include working as **animateurs** (hostesses) in supermarkets, replying to insurance enquiries from holiday-makers during the peak periods on behalf of the major companies, and working in holiday camps for childrens and/or adults as the **gentils organisateurs** invented by the French package holiday industry who are now an institution in France.

You need to start early on the summer job search if you are planning to work. For more information on this area and all areas of student employment, call in at the CIDJ de Paris at 101 quai de Branly, 75015 Paris, M° Bir-Hakeim, www.cidj.asso.fr. The CIDJ also offers advice on rules and regulations covering the employment of students from outside the European Union.

Non-EU students will still be subject to visa formalities, but work for up to three months during the summer vacation period is generally accessible. The Council on International Educational exchange (CIEE) has negotiated reciprocal rights between France and the USA allowing students in full-time American university education or study abroad programmes to obtain temporary work permits. Further details can be obtained from the following addresses:

- Work Abroad, CIEE, 205 East 42nd Street, New York NY10017. Tel. 212 661 1414.

- Work in France, CIEE, 1 place de l'Odéon, 75006 Paris. Tel. 01 44 41 74 74.

16

Setting up your Business in France

Being your own boss in France is not as easy – or as cheap – as you might think it ought to be. Nonetheless, in 1997 there were 500,000 self-employed people in France, representing 6% of the workforce and producing more than 7% of France's Gross Domestic Product, and in 2000, the number of new businesses created was up by 4%.

Becoming either a **travailleur indépendent**, or a **professionnel non salarié**, or a member of a **profession libérale**, (all of which are in fact the same thing), a **commerçant** (independent shopkeeper) or an **artisan** (craftsman) involves certain basic and important steps at the outset to ovoid pitfalls and nasty shocks.

PLANNING YOUR BUSINESS

Many foreign residents may find themselves by choice or professional necessity in the category of self-employment. If this is your case, you must first decide if you are an 'innovator' or an 'operator'. This will help you to establish the correct approach to your business, although many of the basic steps are the same.

Innovators can be defined as either inventing and/or offering a new service (e.g. internet start-ups), or offering an established service in a particular area where there is a gap in the local market – e.g. there are no local cafés but a significant number of local residents.

Operators can be defined as either moving into an established market (e.g. you decide to open a shop or bar in a busy commercial district which has an established commercial draw and clientèle), or you are one more person offering a service to consumers in a particular market (e.g. English-language teaching or one of the 'professional services' of accountancy, law or medicine).

There is also a difference made between what might be termed 'active' and 'reactive' business start-ups. 'Active' business start-ups could be defined as employees who decide to quit their job to start a new business, taking a considerable risk in the process. Previously the self-employed have been left notoriously socially unprotected in a land of great social protection. In 2001, all of that has now changed or is changing. Entrepreneurs are being encouraged, and one of the ways of doing this is to offer them protection should their business fail.

'Reactive' business start-ups could be defined as people who are spurred into creating their own business by forced unemployment. They have not chosen their situation, but the state is willing to guarantee them a certain level of protection and to offer some form of financial aid to help them back to a reasonable level of prosperity. Although many foreigners may feel that they fall into the category of forced inactivity because they have moved to France with their employed spouses, it is highly unlikely that the state authorities would accept applications for state aid from individual foreigners who have not already been working in France and contributed to social security and unemployment funds.

Professional restrictions

Certain professions – most notably lawyers and doctors, but also accountants and architects, for example – may not simply open up their own business in France without the agreement of the appropriate professional organisation. Contact your own professional association before moving to France to find out if you fall into one of these categories.

You should also note that certain professions – accountants, lawyers, and doctors included – are not allowed to advertise their services under French advertising law. Any breach of this law can have very serious sonsequences. This may affect your ability to establish your own practice immediately upon arrival. Even if your natural instinct is to work independently, you need to establish a good reputation and a client base to make a success of your business. If you cannot advertise directly, you need to think carefully about how you are going to do this.

Finally you need to be sure that you have the correct qualifications to operate professionally in France. This is particularly true for English teachers. It is not sufficient simply to have a good command of the language and/or a university degree in English or a related arts subject. You must hold one of the official teaching certificates for teaching English as a foreign language (TEFL). Courses for these certificates are offered very widely in Paris.

Without one of these certificates, you will be at a considerable disadvantage in a very over-subscribed market.

BUDGETING FOR YOUR BUSINESS

For the first two years after establishing your business, you will be assessed for social charges on the basis of set figures for health insurance, pensions and family allowance contributions. Your **CSG (Contribution sociale généralisée) and RDS (recouvrement de la Dette Sociale)** payments are also included in the set figures for the first two years of operating.

In the third year of operating, you will suddenly find that you face higher social charges, and a significant separate CSG and RDS contribution. Since your contributions are based on your net profit from two years previously, you may find yourself heavily out of pocket if you suffer a sudden downturn in business.

You must take all of these factors into account when you are preparing your business plan as you search for funds for your new business. You must also bear this in mind even if you do not intend seeking funds and you only intend to stick to a small-scale one-person independent operation.

FINDING THE FUNDS FOR YOUR BUSINESS

There are a number of different means of seeking funding now available to entrepreneurs in France. All of these come with different restrictions and requirements, but all also require you to put together a solid business plan.

The variety of loans also distinguishes between the 'active' and 'reactive' categories explained above. None of the loans listed below appear to be mutually exclusive, and so it may be possible to accumulate loans from different sources providing you meet the criteria and provide a solid business plan to the loan agencies concerned.

Loans more appropriate for 'active' businesses

- **Le Prêt à la création d'Entreprise (PCE)** Launched in 2000. These loans are for businesses less than three years old whose total financial needs are less than 45,000 Euros. The loans themselves are limited to 3,000 – 8,000 Euros (over five years) but you are not required to provide guarantees or deposits. More details can be found on www.bdpme.fr, or by telephoning 0825 30 12 30.

- **Réseau Entreprendre** A group of local networks of business 'godfathers' backing projects likely to create at least ten jobs in the long-term, and providing interest-free loans repayable over five years. The full list of the 18 networks can be found on www.réseau.entreprendre.org.

- **Business Angels** The Angels have landed in France, and operate in much the same way on an individual basis as the collective Réseau Entreprendre, providing both cash and advice to help you start up your business. Details of how to contact Business Angels in France can be found on www.businessangels.com, where you can also submit your business plan to apply for help.

- **Capital risk investors** Two useful contacts between new businesses and capital risk investors are AFIC (Association Française des Investisseurs en Capital), Tel. 01 47 20 99 09, www.afic.asso.fr, and UNICER (Union des sociétés de capital risque de proximité), Tel. 03 20 68 35 86, www.unicer.asso.fr.

Loans aimed at 'reactive' businesses

- **ADIE** (l'Association pour le Droit à l'Initative Économique) a Network of local associations providing loans of up to 30,000FF repayed over two years at market rates plus deposit. Limited to the unemployed and/or those unable to obtain bank loans. Tel. 01 42 18 57 87, www.adie.org.

- **Le dispositif Éden** Designed for the young unemployed (age limits 18–26), this action plan includes exemption from payment of social charges for the first 12 months, a set of free advice session 'vouchers' with designated specialists (**chéquiers-conseils**) either just before you launch your business or in the 12 months following the start-up; and loans of up to 40,000FF for one-person operations, up to 60,000FF for a multi-partner project, or up to 500,000FF for a group of former employees who buy up their former company should it shut down. The scheme is operated by the Ministry of Employment (**du Travail, de l'Emploi et de la Formation Professionnelle**) and you need to contact the headquarters of your département for further details. A list of their contact details can be found on www.travail.gouv.fr.

- **Fonds France Active** Aimed at the same public as the ADIE, the FFA will stand guarantee of two thirds of a bank loan for business creation, up to a limit of 150,000FF. It also provides a network of advice on finding financial and practical support. The FFA is presided over by the former finance minister Christian Sautter, who is now the Chief Financial Officer of the City of Paris. Tel. 01 52 24 26 26, www.franceactive.org.

Other sources

- **Admical** The website www.admical.org provides a list of those company foundations which provide business start-up funds as well as charitable or arts sponsorship.

- **Former employers** Your future ex-employer can make you a loan at a reduced rate and turn this into a company tax break by deducting up to half the amount loaned as an aid to a former employee seeking to create his or her own business. A new federation known as DIESE (Développement de l'Initiative et de l'Entrepreneuriat chez les Salariés des Entreprises) can also be contacted on 01 42 18 58 58.

- **Fonds de Garantie à l'Initiative des Femmes (FGIF)** Acts rather like the FFA above by standing guarantee for up to 70% of loans to female business entrepreneurs with loans not exceeding 145,000FF over two to seven years. Tel. 01 55 23 07 12.

TAKING THE FIRST STEPS

This falls into two different categories – administrative and financial. Some steps are optional but highly advisable, others are obligatory. The administrative steps will mainly be taken care of for you once you have taken the initial step of registering your business. However, these are important steps as they are not only the most costly, but are almost all linked to providing you and your dependents with social protection including healthcare and pensions.

Visiting the local tax office

This is not an obligation, but a wise precautionary measure. The tax inspector (**inspecteur des impôts**) will be able to tell you if you can open up your business as a self-employed person. He or she will also set out your financial obligations, including those for VAT (known as **TVA** in France).

Registering your new business

You must register your new business with the appropriate authorities, including the **Union de Recouvrement des Cotisations de Sécurité Sociale et d'Allocations Familiales**, more commonly and easily known as **URSSAF**. To register your business, contact the local **Centre de Formalités des Entreprises (CFE)**. For Paris, the main address is URSSAF, 3 rue Franklin, 93518 Montreuil Cedex. Tel. 01 48 51 10 10 or 01 49 20 10 10, Fax 01 49 20 22 04.

The **Chambre de Commerce et de l'Industrie de Paris (CCIP)** also offers CFE facilities. They can be contacted by telephone on 01 53 40 48 48, or by Fax on 01 53 40 48 88. Their Foreign Investment Department & Paris Development Agency with information in English and business creation information is at 2 rue de Viarmes, 75001 Paris (Tel. 01 55 65 33 93, Fax 01 55 65 33 90). NB: Over 3,000 French companies now have 'head offices' (**siège sociale**) outside France in order to pay lower social charges. Many of these are based in the UK. Whilst this complies with European Union law, the French Ministry of Finance is seeking to fight back leagally against the evasion of French social charges. Three years of the French governmental counter-attack has still to come, but as the French themselves say, *c'est une affaire à suivre* (something to watch/follow). No matter where the head office of the company is, it is local French law which applies, just as it will be French services that you draw upon to support you and your dependants.

To avoid paying excess social charges (which are very heavy in any case), the best time to register your new business is at the beginning of a quarterly period (e.g. 1 April). Once you have made the initial **déclaration du début d'activité non salariée** (unwaged activity), the CFE will automatically undertake the next steps for you, which are:

1. The **Déclaration d'existence** to the tax inspector, and enrolment for the **taxe professionnelle**.

2. Your enrolment at the **caisse d'allocations familiales** (family allowance centre), run by URSSAF itself.

3. Your enrolment at the **caisse d'assurance maladie des professions libérales** (local health authority for non-salaried professions). They will offer you a choice of compulsory medical insurance schemes, of which the largest is the Mutuelle de Mans, 18 rue de Londres, 75009 Paris. Tel. 01 40 16 72 72.

4. Your enrolment at the **caisse d'assurance vieillesse** (for pensions). Most professions have their own individual *caisse*. However, if you do not fall into an established category, you will be enrolled at CIPAV, 21 rue de Berri, 75403 Paris Cedex 08. Tel. 01 45 68 28 90.

5. Your registration at **INSEE** – the national statistical office. This acts as a form of business registration, which will lead to your business receiving the necessary SIREN and SIRET numbers.

PROTECTING YOURSELF IF YOUR BUSINESS DOES NOT WORK OUT

Two extremely important new changes to social legislation have become law in 2001. The exact terms and conditions remain unclear at the time of writing but you should definitely make enquiries at your CFE and at the ASSEDIC (who actually pay out unemployment benefit) – www.assedic.fr. Basically for the first time they provide continued limited unemployment rights for those who choose to enter self-employment, changing the traditional French approach that resigning your job also meant resigning your right to unemployment benefit.

- From 1 January 2001 – Every entrepreneur can enroll for unemployment support as long as it is within 36 months of the end of your contract prior to the creation of your business. This includes all business entrepreneurs, including those who had not successfully managed to achieve financing for their start-ups.

- From 1 July 2001 – Entrepreneurs who resign from their existing paid contractual employment to start up their own business will have the same rights. The rules regarding reasons for your resignation have not yet been defined.

Both of these changes clearly only affect those people who have already been employed in France and have contributed to the French social security system, and so are 'activating' the 'points' they have acquired under the system. As these are new rules, it remains to be seen whether in theory it would eventually be possible to transfer to France rights acquired in other EU countries under their social security schemes, although this should be a theoretical possibility.

One other advantage which it is possible for employees to apply for but which is at the discretion of their employers is the **congé de création d'entreprise** for employees who have worked at least 36 months (not necessarily consecutively) in the same firm. This sabbatical period of one year (renewable for a further year if your employer is in agreement) is not paid, but does guarantee your job will still be there for you at the end of the period if you need to return to it. Your social security rights are also guaranteed for up to 12 months. In companies of less than 200 employees the employer can refuse your request. Further details can be found on the employment ministry website, www.travail.gouv.fr.

MAKING THE RIGHT FINANCIAL CHOICES

- **Registering for TVA at your local tax office** This is an optional step which you can take at the tax office. Companies will expect you to charge them TVA (VAT), and you will be able to reclaim TVA on purchases if you are registered. On the other hand, you are not obliged to charge TVA to individuals – hence you can be more competitive in your pricing policy. You should discuss the pros and cons of this choice with the tax inspector when you first visit the tax office.

- **Joining an** *association agréée* This is another optional step to take, but very worthwhile. An **association agréée** offers not only advice and support, but can also offer an important reduction (**abattement fiscal**) in your tax burden. Conditions of membership are simply falling into one of the self-employed categories, conforming to basic accounting rules, and paying an annual membership fee of around 1,000FF. This **abattement fiscal** is achieved by having your annual accounts checked and counter-signed by the association before your tax declaration. In effect, it is worth 20% of your profit figure, as you will only be assessed on 80% of your profit (if it is less than 701,000FF) by the tax authorities if your accounts have been counter-signed by an association.

- **Making banking arrangements** You must have separate bank accounts for private and business accounts. If a bank is aware that one of your accounts is being used for business purposes, you may be required to pay higher bank changes. If necessary, to avoid these higher charges, open your business and personal accounts at different banks.

- **Accounting** You must keep correct accounts which conform to basic French accounting procedures. The easiest way to do this if you already have a computer is to buy an inexpensive personal computer program, which will eventually correspond to the standard French tax form (number 2035).

WORKING ALONE OR IN PARTNERSHIP

One consideration you may wish to make is whether to be truly **indépendant** or to work with a business partner (**associé**). This is a complex issue which requires professional advice, as certain investment and tax issues might favour a 'company' partnership of self-employed workers. Certain clients may also prefer the apparent security of dealing with a company rather than an individual. Amongst the options to explore are:

- Forming a company without any partners, **une Entreprise Unipersonnelle à Responsabilité Limitée** (or **EURL**). This is an alternative to being a **travailleur indépendant**. The minimum capital for an EURL is 50,000FF.

- The 'means of business' – e.g. office premises or furniture, etc. – can be placed in common ownership, whilst each *professionnel libéral* maitains his or her own clientèle. There are several ways of achieving this, for which you should seek professional advice (e.g. from an *association agréée*).

- Associations in France, which are controlled by the law of 1901, can also be of use in making certain economies, as can **Groupement d'Intérêts Économique (GIE)**. It costs nothing to establish an **association 1901**, but in general they are designed to be non-profit making. Any profit will be taxed on the basis of company tax rates. An **association 1901** is not allowed to distribute profits amongst its members. Once again, seek professional advice on this point.

None of these steps should be taken without professional advice. A good **association agréée** should be able to put you in contact with the appropriate professionals to discuss the best way forward.

'MULTIPLE' EMPLOYMENT

Pluriactivité, as it is known in France, has a number of important implications, which make it a generally unproductive option. This is principally because of the level of social charges involved:

- **Several self-employed activities** This will affect which **caisse d'assurance maladie** and which **caisse de vieillesse** you contribute to. If you have chosen to advise a public authority, you contribute to their funds. If you belong to a profession which has an 'order' (e.g. doctors or lawyers), you will contribute to their funds. In other cases, you have a fairly free choice according to the areas of activity in which you are engaged.

- **A self-employed activity and a non-waged, 'non-libéral' activity** You will be obliged to contribute to the same funds as above for the activity which brings you the highest revenue.

- **Self-employment and paid employment** You will be obliged to make payments to the **caisse de vieillesse** in both systems, even if your self-employment is a subsidiary activity. However, you will have rights under both systems. The same applies for the **caisse d'assurance maladie**. The difference is that only those services and rights offered by the *caisse* of your *principal* activity are available to you.

MAKING THE FINAL DECISION

If you are considering self-employment in France, you are probably already aware of the attractions of such a choice, most notably the freedom of being an entrepreneur.

However, listed below are the three main points to consider before taking the plunge:

1. **Professional restrictions** Are you allowed to practise in France, and how will you build up your clientèle if you are not allowed to advertise? Do you have the right qualifications to succeed in the French market?

2. **Heavy social charges** On average, an employee costs a company in total double what he or she receives in their bank account each month. Being your own boss means paying the boss's share of the bill too. French social charges are amongst the highest in Europe. Worse still is the fact that after two years of operating, you are assessed on your profit figure two years ago. If your income suddenly drops, your difficulties will be increased by the fact that your social charges could rise to as much as 90% of your current revenue.

3. **Establishing yourself** You should also bear in mind that a period of one or two years of paid employment in France will bring with it a considerable number of benefits and safe-guards when you do decide to launch your own business. These include unemployment protection but also market knowledge, professional contacts, and a stronger financial position and credit rating. Starting from zero is always a lot harder than choosing to return to zero in order to climb higher and be your own boss, having already established yourself in the local business world.

USEFUL CONTACTS

- American Embassy (US Foreign Commercial Service), 2 avenue Gabriel, 75008 Paris. Tel. 01 43 12 25 32, Fax 01 43 12 21 72, www.amb-usa.fr.

- American Chamber of Commerce, 156 boulevard Haussmann, 75008 Paris. Tel. 01 56 43 45 67.

- Australian Business in Europe/Centre for Commerce, 4 rue Jean Rey, 75015 Paris. Tel. 01 50 69 34 92/22 00.

- British Embassy Commercial Section, 35 rue du Faubourg-St-Honoré, 75008 Paris. Tel. 01 44 51 31 00, Fax 01 44 51 34 01, www.amb-grandebretagne.fr.

- Franco-British Chamber of Commerce, 31 rue Boissy d'Anglas, 75008 Paris. Tel. 01 53 30 81 30, Fax 01 53 30 81 35, e-mail: fbcci@fbcci.com, www.fbcci.com.

- French Embassy in London Economic & Commercial Section, 21/24 Grosvenor Place, London SW1X 7HU. Tel. 0207 235 7080, Fax 0207 235 8598, e-mail: londres@dree.org, www.dree.org/grandebretagne.

- Invest in France/DATAR London agency – same address as the French Embassy commercial section. Tel. 0207 823 1895, Fax 0207 8453, e-mail: info@investinfrance.co.uk, www.investinfrance.co.uk.

- DATAR (Délégation à l'Aménagement du Territoire et à l'Action Régionale) promotes foreign investment in France. 1 avenue Charles Floquet, 75343 Paris Cedex 07. Tel. 01 40 65 12 34, Fax 01 43 06 99 01, www.datar.gouv.fr e-mail: info@datar.gouv.fr. Check the website for details of the nearest Invest in France office. Branches are found in countries around the world.

- APCE (Agence Pour la Création d'Entreprise), the official government agency to aid entrepreneurs in France and to encourage business start-ups, www.apce.com.

- Paris Chamber of Commerce & Industry, 2 rue de Viarmes, 75040 Paris Cedex 1. Tel. 01 45 08 36 00, Fax 01 45 08 35 80, www.ccip.fr. Publications in English available.

- Chambre de Commerce Française de Grande-Bretagne, 21 Dartmouth Street, London SW1H 9BP. Tel. 0207 304 40 40, Fax 0207 304 7034, e-mail: mail@ccfgb.co.uk. Publishes a guide in English on setting up a small business in France.

- ACSEL (Association pour le Commerce et les Services en Ligne), internet businesses. Tel. 01 49 26 03 04, www.acsel-net.org.

- AFA (Association des Fournisseurs d'Accès à des services en ligne et à l'internet), www.afa-france.com.

- 3SCI (Syndicat des Sociétés de Services et des Conseils en Informatique). Tel. 01 47 07 02 99.

- Syntec-conseil en management. Tel. 01 44 30 49 20, www.syntec-management.com.

- Chambre des ingénieurs conseils en France. Tel. 01 44 30 49 30, www.cicf.fr.

The business magazine *L'Entreprise* published an excellent guide in March 2001 on setting up a business in France. Their website is at www.l'entreprise.com. The French Government has created a directory in English of its departmental websites covering all areas of life in France including business life, www.service-public.fr. Many of these websites are partially or totally bilingual. Happy surfing!

17

Shopping in Paris

There are perhaps four major cities in the world which symbolise the art of shopping: London, Milan, Paris and New York, the four poles of the fashion world. But as man and woman do not live on labels alone, you need to think about the needs of the everyday household before getting down to what many consider to be 'the real thing'.

FOOD SHOPPING IN PARIS

Almost every arrondissement and commune in and around Paris has its own market, offering fresh produce from fruit and vegetables, meat and cheese, to household products and clothes (although these will not always be reasonably priced in markets). Shopping at a French market is a real experience, lots of fun and a good way to brush up your language skills whilst choosing your produce.

Market streets will normally include the household suppliers for your daily dietary needs: the **boulangerie** (bakery), where you can also buy **pâtisserie** (cakes); the **boucherie** (butcher's), the **charcuterie** (cold and smoked meats, and pies), and the **poissonnerie** (fish shop), the **épicerie** (grocer's store); the **fromagerie** (cheese shop); the **cave à vins** (wine shop/off-licence); and probably at least one **confiserie** (chocolate/sweet shop).

Remember that France works on the metric system (1lb = c. 0.45Kg). If you tell a butcher or cheese merchant how many people you wish to serve, they will normally suggest what they think is the usual amount. Normally shopkeepers will serve you your items, and then ask, *Et avec ça?/Ça sera tout?* – And with that?/Will that be all?' If you have nothing more to buy, then the answer is simply *C'est tout merci.*

At the *charcuterie* if you are buying ham, you will be asked *Combien de tranches*? (How many slices?). At the *fromagerie*, the shopkeeper will probably show you either the whole cheese or a ready-cut piece and ask you to choose the size of portion (**morceau**) that you want for hard cheeses. Soft cheeses such as Camembert are normally sold either in halves or whole; and certain small and rarer cheeses (e.g. goats cheese, **chèvres**) are only sold whole.

At the baker's if you buy a *baguette*, you will be asked if you want it **coupé en deux** (cut in half). If you buy a small loaf of bread the question will be **Tranché**? ('Sliced?') If you do ask the baker to slice the loaf, it will be produced using a professional machine, presented in plastic with a seal, and charged about 0.50FF extra. If you buy flowers either at the market or in a florist, you will be asked if they are a gift (in which case they will be gift-wrapped automatically) or for the home – *C'est pour offrir ou pour la maison*?

Your concierge and/or your neighbours will be able to tell you where to find your nearest market. Some of the best known are:

- Avenue du Président Wilson (16th), rue Cler (7th) and rue Poncelet (17th) – all excellent markets, especially renowned for being the places where 'ladies who lunch' come to buy their provisions. In rue Poncelet, treat yourself to coffee and central European goodies at Stübli, and throw caution regarding your waistline to the wind.

- Rue Montorgueil (1st and 2nd) – one of the most beautiful market streets with a fine selection of foods and the **plus-hype** clientèle of all Parisian markets. Shopping here is often more like attending a fashion parade as the local 'cool crowd' pick out the best produce or watch you doing the same from the café terraces. Check out the former royal chocolate shop Stohrer for some of the best chocolate in Paris.

- Rue Lepic (18th) – the original Montmartre street market, a favourite and bustling venue for the local stars and fashion crowd who have flocked to the Butte since Christian Dior launched the New Look here in the 1940s. One of the most 'authentic' Parisian street markets.

- Boulevard Raspail (6th) and boulevard des Batignolles (8th and 17th) are both organic food markets, the places to buy 'green greens' but also free-range eggs, meat, cheese, etc.

What if you do not have the time, facility or inclination to shop at the market? Supermarkets are not lacking and there is nothing particularly special about the way in which French supermarkets function – everything is pretty self-explanatory, even if you do not speak French.

The major hypermarkets are to be found outside Paris for reasons of space. They draw both thousands of customers and furious criticism from defenders of neighbourhood shops at the same time. The most well-known hypermarkets are Auchan and Carrefour, both of which also sell clothing, computers and even package holidays. However, they do not offer some of the other services (pharmacies, financial, etc.) which are not found in their British counterparts. The Picard chain of shops specialises in offering frozen (**surgelé**) food, and stores are to be found across central Paris. Details of expat grocery stores and services for the homesick and also for special occasions such as Thanksgiving can be found easily in FUSAC.

The three most famous foodstores in Paris – not for everyday shopping unless you like to stretch your budget – are La Grande Épicierie at Le Bon Marché in the 7th; and Hédiard and Fauchon behind the Madeleine church in the 8th. All of these are luxury stores, but at affordable prices – in small doses! *Á consommer avec modération*, as the French say. Note that the word 'cheap' does not exist in French, only the phrase *pas cher*, which means 'not expensive'!

DISCOVERING DEPARTMENT STORES

The five principal Parisian department stores (**grands magasins**) offering everything from household items to clothes are to be found distributed across Paris in the main shopping areas. In almost all cases the flagship shops in the city centre have now been reproduced elsewhere in the suburbs or in other city shopping centres. But the main shops with the best selections are:

- **Bazar de l'Hôtel de Ville**, rue de Rivoli, 75004 Paris. M° Hôtel de Ville, www.bhv.fr. The **BHV**, as it is usually known, is one of the great department stores, specialising in home furnishings and especially DIY in the basement. For those of us who cringe at the sight of a hammer and a nail, the new Bricolo Café in the basement offers the chance for basic DIY lessons whilst you take a coffee break.

- **Galeries Lafayette**, boulevard Haussman, 75009 Paris. M° Chaussée d'Antin/RER Opéra www.galerieslafayette.com. Also above the Montparnasse station in the 15th. The boulevard Haussmann branch is the best, recently re-vamped to rival its neighbour Printemps. Excellent choice of clothes.

- **La Samaritaine**, rue de Rivoli, 75001 Paris. M° Louvre-Rivoli. Recently renovated, the Art Nouveau masterpiece with a trendy terrace restaurant is one of the two department stores not to branch out into the suburbs. Specialist departments for just about everything; strong on household items.

- **Le Bon Marché**, 75007 Paris. M° Sèvres-Babylone. Right next to the Métro, so impossible to miss. The second main shop not to have branches elsewhere. Trendy and chic like the neighbourhood it serves. Has frequent theme promotions (e.g. British, designers, etc.).

- **Printemps**, boulevard Haussmann, 75009 Paris. M° Havre-Caumartin/RER Opéra. The other great shopping experience. The dome is best seen at Christmas when the Christmas tree is in place. Free fashion shows during the Fashion Weeks. Very *hype* menswear department.

All of these stores have discount card schemes and Galeries Lafayette and Printemps in particular are full of concessionary mini-shops from all the major designers.

SHOPPING FOR THE HOME

If your budget does not stretch to shopping in one of these shops, home furnishings can also be found at Conforama next door to La Samaritaine on the riverbank of the Seine. Castorama at the Place de Clichy (www.castorama.fr) is another DIY/garden centre favourite if you cannot face another afternoon spent wandering around the basement of BHV like a lost soul. You should also check out Leroy Merlin (www.leroymerlin.fr), Habitat, to be found on the avenue Wagram near the Arc de Triomphe and the boulevard de la Madeleine (www.habitat.fr), and Ikea which has four shops in the inner suburbs strategically placed around Paris (www.ikea.fr). Another useful chain who have shops in central and suburban Paris is Mr Bricolage ('Mr DIY'), on www.mr-bricolage.fr.

You should note that the BHV website offers some handy household tips (in French) about what appliances will and will not work in France. For plug adaptors (**adaptateurs**) try the local hardware stores (**drogueries**) or go to the accessories department of the major hi-fi and electrical appliance supplier Darty (avenue des Ternes, Forum des Halles and Madeleine). FNAC, the all-purpose music/book/computer/ticket agencies also stock plug adaptors. Surcouf on avenue Daumesnil in the 12th is a noisy computer warehouse shop. Remember that French keyboards are different to English ones. If you can make the change, it would be as well to move over to a French keyboard so that you can apply the accents where necessary when you write your correspondence.

Interior design and fashionable home furnishing stores abound in Paris, and you would be well advised to check the specialist press and also *À nous Paris* and *Zurban*, who provide weekly updates on the latest and greatest. Areas like Abbesses, Oberkampf or Ménilmontant (the trendy districts) obviously offer the best chances of finding something really original. The Conran Shops in Paris can be found behind Le Bon Marché in the 7th or at La Madeleine in the 9th.

SHOPPING FOR CLOTHES IN PARIS

There is so much to say about this that whole books have been written on the topic, and several weekly columns appear in English detailing the latest places to be seen buying things to be seen wearing. Every magazine and newspaper has its fashion section, and you will quickly catch on to the places that match your budget and style.

The Champs-Élysées remains a popular place to shop, but the real action takes place on rue de Rivoli from La Samaritaine down to Hôtel de Ville, and also the Forum des Halles. Fashion victims can head off to whichever district best reflects their taste, be it hippy chic in the north-east of Paris or ultra-chic in the 'golden triangle' around avenue Montaigne or down in St-Germain-des-Prés.

SHOPPING FOR THE CHILDREN

The major department stores all have good children's departments, as do chains such as Prisunic or Monoprix where

	Men's suits	Men's shirts	Men's shoes
UK/USA	36 38 40 42 44 46 48	14 14.5 15 15.5 16 16.5 17	7.5 8 9 10 11 12
France	46 48 50 52 54 56 68	36 37 38 39/40 41 42 43	41 42 43 44 45 46

	Dress sizes	Women's shoes	Women's tights/stockings
UK	8 10 12 14 16 18	3 4 5 6 7 8	8 8.5 9 9.5 10 10.5
USA	6 8 10 12 14 16	5 6 7 8 9 10	8 8.5 9 9.5 10 10.5
France	36 38 40 42 44 46	36 37 38 39 40 41	0 1 2 3 4 5

Fig. 12.   Clothes size conversion.

kids' and adult clothing are also available. One of the most famous children's shops – and not the cheapest – is Au Nain Bleau, 408 rue St Honoré, 75008 Paris. M° Madeleine. Toys 'R 'Us can be found in the La Défense shopping centre. Probably the best way to find good children's shops, however, is through word of mouth from other parents. The two key guides once again are *Zurban* and *À nous Paris* for the most up-to-date news. According to a recent report in *Zurban*, the rue Vavin in the 14th is now a children's shopping paradise, so it is worth taking a look. The RATP webside (www.ratp.fr) also has some handy links.

BARGAIN-HUNTING IN THE SALES

The **soldes** as they are known are now regulated by the commerce ministry to make sure that sales start across France on the same day, avoiding the previous phenomenon of late-starting towns suffering from shopped-out consumer disinterest. The main sales are still the New Year sales in early to mid January, and there are also summer sales.

Obviously the best bargains go first, but this will only be the first mark-down (**démarque**). There will probably be second and third mark-downs (each should be indicated with the original price on the sale ticket). Sale items are not normally refundable or exchangeable. Items may be marked at any stage in the year as being reduced (**remise de**), but the use of the term *soldes* is now strictly controlled. As a result, 'promotions' advertised as **prix promotionnel** (sales by another name) have limits placed on their time-span and financial impact, to avoid under-cutting the market.

BARGAIN-HUNTING AT FLEA MARKETS

Car-boot sales have yet to appear in France, but flea markets (**puces**) are very popular. The three most well-known are:

- **Porte de Clignancourt** 75018 Paris (Métro of the same name) – Saturdays, Sundays and Mondays. A vast sprawling market of clothes, antiques, furniture, books; you name it, you will probably find it at Clignancourt. The market is a popular venue with tourists and pickpockets, so be careful that you do not end up finding your lost items being sold somewhere further on . . .

- **Porte de Vanves** 75014 Paris (Métro of the same name) – household items in the mornings and clothes in the afternoons at weekends.

- **Porte de Montreuil** 75020, avenue de la Porte de Montreuil – mainly household items.

Paris is one of the acknowledged capitals of second-hand/antique clothing shops. Keep an eye out for **dépôts-ventes** dealers where you can put your clothes in to be sold with the shopkeepers keeping a commission on the sale if and when it happens. This system also applies to furniture. The specialist clothes shops are once again to be found in areas such as Batignolles or Oberkampf, but you should check guides such as the *Time Out* guide for the best tips in English, or magazines such as *Nova* or *Zurban* for tips in French.

18

Discovering Parisian Sporting Life

Parisians, like Londoners, New Yorkers and the inhabitants of most major Western cities, have a sporting life divided between participating (gently or vigorously) and spectating (regularly or occasionally). With the French emphasis on general good living, and the Parisian emphasis on lifestyle linking in to the sport-streetwear culture, the last decade has seen a development of personal opportunities for participation in the capital's sporting life.

The importance of certain spectator sports and events is still central to the French and especially Parisians.

KEEPING FIT IN PARIS

Joining a gym

- The most well-known chain is **Gymnase Club** (www.gymnaseclub.fr), with current annual subscription rates ranging from 5,320–5,920FF/year. Membership of the club entitles you to use any of the clubs across Paris and indeed outside the Paris region also. All the clubs offer cardio training equipment, weight training facilities, sport counsellors on hand for advice and training programmes, and classes for all levels. Some are open on Sundays, and all are packed early evenings during the week at the end of office hours. The club in the 15th arrondissement also has a large swimming pool. Many **comités d'entreprise** subsidise membership for the firm's workers.

- The cheaper rival to Gymnase Club is **Gymnasium** (www.gymnasium.tm.fr). They have about the same number of gyms and work on the same principles. For some reason, Gymnasium is seen as less glamorous than Gymnase Club but really there is not a lot to choose between the two.

- The luxury muscle factories are the **Waou Clubs**, also run by Gymnase Club. An annual subscription here will set you back 7,070FF. There are fewer Waou Clubs, but the quality of the facilities and service is higher. (Tel. 01 53 34 96 60 Paris, 10th or 01 46 51 88 18 Paris, 16th). There is of course also the **Ritz Health Club** (Tel. 01 43 16 30 60) if your blood-pressure can take the membership fee!

- For well-toned fashion victims or those who wish to be, there is also the **Espace Vit'halles** (Tel. 01 42 77 21 71, 48 rue Rambuteau, 75003 Paris, www.espacevithalles.com). Next to the Centre Pompidou, this centre 'voted the best gym in Europe' according to its publicity is known for being Anglo-friendly and very high quality.

SWIMMING IN PARIS

Paris has over 30 municipal swimming pools, but also quite a number of private pools. The municipal pools tend to open early in the morning and then close for school classes during the day. At the weekends you will still need to go early to avoid the crowds. At municipal pools you are normally required to wear a swimming cap (**bonnet de bain**).

The best and most glamorous pool in Paris sank in the early 1990s! This was the famed Piscine Deligny outside the Assemblée Nationale. However, plans are afoot to renovate the old **Piscine Molitor** in the 16th, an Art Deco open-air masterpiece, which will be very popular when and if it does finally open. In the meantime, there are plenty of other good places to cool off and stretch your muscles:

- La Butte aux Cailles, 5 place Paul-Verlaine, 75013 Paris. Tel. 01 45 89 60 05 – another listed masterpiece.

- La Piscine Suzanne Berlioz des Halles, Forum des Halles, 75001 Paris. Tel. 01 42 36 98 44 – the Olympic-size temple of the bodies beautiful. Often packed but stays open late.

- La Piscine Pontoise, 19 rue Pontoise, 75005 Paris. Tel. 01 55 42 77 88 – at the centre of the trendy private *Quartier Latin* sports centre.

- Three pools roll open their roofs in fine weather: Piscine Hébert, 2 rue des Fillettes, 75018 Paris. Tel. 01 42 76 78 24; Piscine Georges-Hermant, 4 rue David d'Angers, 75019 Paris. Tel. 01 42 02 45 10; and Piscine Georges-Vallerey, 148 avenue Gambetta, 75020 Paris. Tel. 01 40 31 15 20.

JOINING A SPORTS CLUB OR CENTRE

If you want to try or practice a number of different sporting disciplines, and also meet new people, the best idea would be to join a sports club. Three of the most well-known clubs are:

- **The Standard Athletic Club**, route Forestière du Pavé de Meudon, 92360 Meudon la Forêt. Tel. 01 46 26 16 09, Fax 01 45 07 87 63, e-mail: standac@aol.com – private British club with a large international membership on the edge of Paris; eight tennis courts, two squash courts, a swimming pool, sports fields with football, rugby, cricket and hockey teams; golf section, snooker, fully stocked bar and large clubhouse facilities home to many social events. Call to arrange a visit. Car necessary for access.

- **Aqua Boulevard**, 4 – 6 rue Louis Armand, 75015 Paris. Tel. 01 40 60 10 00, Fax 01 40 60 18 39. M° Balard – just on the edge of Paris, the great sports centre with centrepiece swimming pools and slides, accessible on day passes. Packed in warm weather. An artificial beach is amongst the attractions, but like most beaches you have to fight your way onto it when the sun shines.

- **Forest Hill**, Tel. 01 47 29 91 91 – a group of private sports centres around the edge of Paris in the nearer suburbs. Much the same concept as Aquaboulevard. More orientated towards membership.

CRICKET, RUGBY AND SOCCER

You can find current contact details for the **British Rugby Club of Paris** on the website www.britishinfrance.com. You need to check for contact details as team captains come and go. The **Standard Athletic Club** (SAC) fields several cricket teams, and other teams are to be found at the **Thoiry Cricket Club** at the Château de

Thoiry. Details of this association are also available on the same website.

Football fans who want to follow the local team will need to discover the Parc des Princes stadium at Porte-St-Cloud, home to the **Paris-St-Germain (PSG)** club. The club has a high media coverage but a low score average despite being First Division players. More details of the club, including ticket sales, on www.PSG.fr or Tel. 0825 075 078. For those who want to play as well as watch football, the SAC fields several teams in a local tournament division. Otherwise, to kick a ball around with your pals, head for Les Invalides in summer, or the wide open spaces of the two Bois to the east and the west.

Both football and rugby fans will want to find their way to the **Stade de France** (RER station of the same name) to the north of the city centre. The masterpiece built for the 1998 World Cup can be visited when matches are not being played, but also provides an excellent venue to watch international matches.

DANCE CLASSES

Probably not what you might think of as sport, but certainly an excellent way to keep in shape. The most well-known place to try is the **Centre de Danse du Marais**, 41 rue du Temple, 75004 Paris. Tel. 01 42 72 15 42, Fax 01 42 77 71 57, www.paris-danse.com. Every conceivable type of dance course seems to be on offer from jazz to classical to contemporary to belly-dancing. Always packed out. The Tex-Mex diner in the courtyard is a cool hang-out and the café-théâtre at the end of the courtyard is a favourite for one-man shows. Music lessons also available.

PLAYING A ROUND OF GOLF

Obviously the main golf courses are outside the city limits, with strong concentrations to the north near Chantilly. The **Fédération Française de Golf** (Tel. 01 44 17 63 00) can provide you with further details of Paris courses and clubs. The SAC also has a golf section which could be a good way for English-speakers to discover the Parisian courses. British expatriates might also try contacting the Royal Society of St George (www.britishinfrance.com) who organise a regular golf tournament.

THE SPORTING YEAR IN PARIS

The great sporting events of the Parisian year fall into two categories. Popular events include the **Paris Marathon** each spring, and the arrival and final lap of the **Tour de France** cycling race each July in central Paris. If you enjoy either sport, then you will be thrilled at the idea that the streets of Paris are full of your fellow-enthusiasts. Naturally the popular viewing grounds are the Champs-Élysées, but traffic will be bad across the city on both days. For details of roller-blading events, see Chapter 3.

The indoor **tennis** championships at **Bercy** remain reasonably accessible if you simply organise yourself well enough in advance to obtain tickets. They draw the great names of tennis, so they are well worth the effort. However, when it comes to the summer outdoor event at **Roland-Garros** on the edge of the 16th arrondissement (the equivalent to Flushing Meadow or Wimbledon), you really need to apply very early and quickly for tickets and/or be prepared to pay for the best tickets – or find the right company to invite you.

Roland-Garros falls into the same category of event as the three great Parisian horse races. Half of the skill of the game is obtaining entry to the best seats; a quarter of the skill is being seen in those seats; and what ever you feel you can muster for the rest goes towards enjoying the event. Roland-Garros, like the **Prix du Président** at the **Hippodrome d'Auteuil** in the 16th on the edge of the Bois de Boulogne (Sunday at the end of April) M° Porte d'Auteuil; or the **Prix de Diane** at **Chantilly** (normally about the third Sunday in June); or the **Prix de l'Arc de Triomphe** at **Longchamp** (first Sunday in October, M° Porte d'Auteuil then free shuttle-bus) forms part of the Parisian 'season'.

Longchamp draws a huge British contingent of weekenders, and many local residents will turn up with cars laden with food and set up picnics in the car parks leading up the edge of the race-track. Much the same happens at dainty Chantilly, through the woods and at 'the bottom of the garden' of the fabulous château. Whereas Longchamp definitely has the atmosphere of the Derby at Epsom, Chantilly has clear pretentions to being the French Ascot. Anybody can enter the stands, but only the select few can enter the sponsors' private enclosures, where the silly hats pay silly money in an effort to be photographed not looking silly . . . In fact, both days out are good fun for all the family, with bands and plenty of space for kids to let off steam. The race tracks at **Maisons-Lafitte** and **St-Cloud** are less pretentious, and the trotting races at the **Hippodrome de Vincennes** in the Bois are a popular venue for **nocturnes** (evening sessions) when you can have dinner whilst watching the races.

19

Catering for Children

The two principal weekly Paris lifestyle guides, *Á nous Paris* (www.anousparis.com), found free in Métro stations each Monday, and *Zurban* (www.zurban.com), available at kiosks every Wednesday, both chose to survey young Parisians in November 2000 on what they liked most and least about the city, and what they could change if they had the chance. Unsurprisingly, the answers were almost identical and reflected adult concerns in similar surveys. But the main points which came out were a fear and/or dislike of public transport and a *ras-le-bol* (fed up with/sick of) pollution in the city. There were two other common themes: a lack of parks to play in, and too many restrictions on children in those parks which do exist.

So what can you do to keep your **mômes** (kids) out of mischief and amused? The answers are not lacking in and around Paris, and the most up-to-date answers can be found each week in the two journals mentioned above, but also in special supplements to the major newspapers and magazines timed to coincide with the school holidays.

The suggestions in this chapter are only a selection of some of the more well-known examples, and you should check the supplements and journals for new ideas. The website www.ratp.fr (in English) also has good regularly updated links and suggestions.

NORTHERN PARIS

- **Parc de la Villette**, 211 avenue Jean Jaurès, 75019 Paris. M° Porte de la Villette or Porte de Pantin. Tel. 01 40 03 75 03, www.la.villette.com. The great cultural activity centre built on the north-eastern edge of Paris with the Cités de la Science, de la Musique, de l'Industrie, and a special Cité des Enfants. Excellently laid out including bilingual exhibition areas. Heavily orientated for children. Giant 360° cinema (la Géode) with natural history films, and an open-air cinema for summer evenings. Lots of lawns designated to be played on by children and adults, and a good place for kids to let off steam after a movie, an exhibition or a workshop.

- **Jardin Sauvage de St-Vincent**, rue St-Vincent, 75018 Paris. M° Larmarck-Caulaincourt. Tel. 01 43 28 47 63. In the heart of old Montmartre just behind the Sacré-Coeur, a place to learn about plants, their uses, and generally about ecology.

- **Parc Astérix**, BP8, 60128 Plailly. Tel. 03 44 62 33 96, Fax 03 44 62 32 94, www.parcasterix.com. Before EuroDisney arrived this was the main Paris theme park. No prizes for guessing what the theme is . . . Accommodation available. To the north of Paris by car.

- **Musée de l'Air et de l'Espace**, (93) Le Bourget. Tel. 01 49 92 71 99. Almost 200 different flying machines on display at Paris, original airport, and a newly-refurbished planetarium with an 8-metre diameter and 3,500 stars.

EASTERN PARIS

It is no wonder that young families are flocking to eastern Paris when you consider the range of opportunities on offer for children, in addition to plenty of excellent housing.

- **Bois de Vincennes** The huge forest has a multitude of resources to amuse the children. The main **Paris Zoo** is at 53, avenue de St-Maurice, 75012 Paris. M° St-Mandé or Porte Dorée. Tel. 01 44 75 20 10, and just beside it is the boating **Lac Daumesnil**. Further to the east stands the original **Château de Vincennes**, with its huge keep and 17th century apartments, open to the public and looking just the way a castle should (M° Château de Vincennes). Only a few yards away lies the **Parc Floral de Paris**, Esplanade du Château, route de la Pyramide, 75012 Paris M° Château de Vincennes. Tel. 01 43 43 92 95, www.parcfloraldeparis.com, a huge activity park for families on the edge of the forest with picnic areas, plenty of space to play and a wide variety of activities. Beyond the Parc Floral lie yet more boating lakes, and across the forest at Joinville-le-Pont lies **La Ferme de Paris** (route de Pesage. Tel. 01 43 28 47 63) with real animals in fields for the infant Parisians to discover. The Bois also boasts sports grounds, and hundreds of acres of forests.

- **Parc de Bercy**, M° Cour St-Émilion or Bercy, the latest arrival on the Parisian park scene, especially planned for children, with a labyrinth, vines, a vegetable garden tended by local children, exhibition areas, and a free-for-all area for families to play on leading up to the terrace overlooking the Seine with its sculptures representing other nations. A really excellent park leading up to the Bercy indoor sports complex, and leading down to the great multi-screen cinema complex at St-Émilion.

- **Disneyland Paris**, Marne la Vallée. Tel. 01 60 30 60 30, www.disneylandparis.com, the big one! RER (and even TGV and Eurostar) direct to Mickey's Magic Kingdom. All the fun of Disney fare. Many different day passes available, plus accommodation and restaurants, regular **spectacles** (shows).

- **Sea Life Paris-Val d'Europe**, Centre Commercial International Val d'Europe, 14 cours de Danube, Serris, Marne La Vallée. Tel. 01 60 42 33 66, www.sealife.fr. A vast aquarium beneath the shopping centre, with sharks swimming around the transparent tube you have to go through to complete your journey once you begin!

SOUTHERN PARIS

- **Jardin des Plantes**, 57 rue Cuvier, 75005 Paris. M° Jussieu or Austerlitz. Tel. 01 40 79 37 94. Paris' botanical gardens, with a small ménagerie to introduce the kids to animal as well as plant life. Herb and flower gardens and exhibition areas.

- **Jardin du Luxembourg**, boulevard St Michel, 75006 Paris. RER Luxembourg. Special children's treats amongst the neat lawns and flowerbeds, including ponies and puppets.

- **Parc Georges Brassens**, rue des Morillons, 75015 Paris. M° Convention. Children's playgrounds and vegetable gardens tended by the pupils of the school leading onto the park.

- **Château de Fontainebleau**, Tel. 01 60 71 50 70. Four free-game-guides are given to children when they visit the château with their parents to help them enjoy their visit.

- **Park du Domaine de Courson**, Courson-Monteloup (91). Tel. 01 64 58 90 12. You will need a car to reach this palatial park, but when you do you can picnic in the park before exploring it on your own or at certain seasons accompanied by students from the local landscape architectural school.

The new town of Sénart is also planning a vast aquarium for some time in the next few years. See also Aquaboulevard in Chapter 18.

WESTERN PARIS

- **Bois de Boulogne** The children of the west are not lacking in amusements either, thanks to their own forest. The most famous site is the **Jardin d'Acclimatation**, Bois de Boulogne, 75116 Paris. M° Les Sablons, Tel. 01 40 67 90 82, www.jardindacclimatation.fr. Open every day, and free for children under three, with entry fees for older children and adults. Radio-controlled boats, merry-go-rounds, mini-motorbikes, puppet shows, a circus and a mini-farm are all on offer. Over at La Muette on the edge of the Bois lies the **Jardin de Ranelagh**, another popular play area, leading up to the two lakes. The **Lac Inférieur** is the smaller of the two and is the real boating lake with an island in the middle and a regular ferry. All around you will find plenty of open space in which to sunbathe, picnic, play games, etc., and the forests run way out to the west. Also try out the **Serres** (greenhouses) d'Auteuil in avenue de la Porte d'Auteuil, opposite the famous Roland-Garros tennis club. Huge 19th century greenhouses reminiscent of Kew Gardens in London offer a variety of fascinating plants.

- **Parc de St-Cloud** the grounds of the former royal palace now provide another favourite Parisian escape overlooking the Seine above the Pont de Sèvres.

- **Château de Thoiry Safari Park**, 78770 Thoiry. Tel. 01 34 87 40 67, www.thoiry.tm.fr. With an American vicomtesse as the lady of the manor, British cricket teams, and wild animals roaming free in the safari park, this has to be one of the most exotic places within easy striking distance of Paris!

- **Espace Rambouillet**, route de Clairefontaine, (78) Rambouillet. Tel. 01 34 83 05 00. A natural park to the west of

Paris leading up to the presidential country retreat. If lions and tigers are not your preferred animal option, try the regular forest inhabitants such as deer in Rambouillet.

CENTRAL PARIS

Children in central Paris are perhaps the most spoilt for choice of all Parisian youngsters. Two favourites, one old and one new, are:

- **Parc Monceau**, 75008 & 017. M° Monceau. Sandpits, swings, a mini-lake and 18th century follies. A classic Parisian play area and extremely popular – but keep off the grass!

- **La Tour Jean-sans-Peur**, rue Étienne-Marcel, 75002 Paris. M° Étienne-Marcel. Tel. 01 40 26 20 28. The last vestige of a medieval fortified palace built in 1411, recently restored and opened to the public. As *Zurban* put it, 'the place to play at knights in the very heart of Paris', with a special learning-game path for children.

CHILDREN'S WORKSHOPS

Every school vacation period sees a flurry of impressive activity from the hundreds of Parisian museums, from the great château at Versailles or the Louvre in the city centre down to the smaller spacialist museums, in order to lay on workshops for young Parisians from age four upwards (depending on the museums and facilities available). Both *Zurban* and *Á nous Paris* review these workshops very regularly, so you should definitely check these two publications for ideas on how to constructively amuse your children.

Theatre groups and dance schools also offer workshops, and many establishments offer workshops throughout the year. The **Académie Américaine de la Danse** (5 rue Rousselet, 75007 Paris M° Vaneau. Tel. 01 47 34 36 22) offers bilingual classes for children aged four and over. The great **Opéra-Garnier** offers back-stage tours to children aged five and over, and the chance to design and create costumes (Tel. 01 40 01 22 46). If your child has a good basic grasp of French then the choices of workshops will be much wider, although a number of museums, etc. offer bilingual classes. Details of French language classes for children at Paris museums can be found on www.monuments-france.fr or by calling

01 44 61 20 00. Finally the main English-language bookshops (Brentanos, and WH Smith) offer special kids' book clubs and activities. Call in at the stores for further details.

SPORT, SCOUTING AND GUIDING

Many of the sports clubs and associations listed in Chapter 18 offer junior sides. Depending on your children's level of French, they might also enrol for a city-sponsored holiday sports course (from the age of seven) at one of the 23 **centres d'initiative sportive** across Paris, offering tennis, diving, judo, canoeing, etc. More details can be found on www.paris-france.org/Parisweb/FR/Sport. British brownie and guide packs can be found in Maisons-Lafitte, Bougival, and at the British Schools of Paris (senior and junior). For more details check www.britishinfrance.com. British scouts have packs at Bougival and Maisons-Lafitte, Chantilly and Fontainebleau. American packs are based at the American School of Paris, and also Marymount School (Tel. 01 46 24 10 51).

SANTA'S LITTLE HELPERS IN PARIS

Paris at Christmas is a magical city. Taking the kids to see the lights and the shop windows is a fun way of building up to the day. Take in the Champs-Élysées in the early evening with their elegant lights, and perhaps the avenues George V and Montaigne. But the essential visits are to the animated window displays of the **grands magasins – Printemps, Galeries Lafayette** (boulevard Haussmann), **La Samaritaine** and **Le Bon Marché**, all of which rival each other in animation, decoration and imagination.

20

Meeting People in Paris

Meeting and making new friends with whom you can share your experiences and to whom you can turn and also offer help is not always easy in the busy and sleek French capital. One of the reasons for this is that the French as a rule are reserved, taking time to get to know newcomers whether foreign or French alike. As a foreigner, you will most likely also suffer from a lack of common experience initially, be it in understanding catch-phrases or popular music or favourite television programmes of the past or present; not to mention not having experienced life in **la France profonde** (the deep backwaters of France), nor having been through the French education system.

Although some French people may admire a perceived total embrace of their culture, many would find it puzzling and ill-advised. The French and especially Parisians believe strongly in **networking**, whether through social, business or culturally-identified groups. Paris is composed essentially of exiles who do not hesitate to call on fellow Auvergnats, Bretons or Corsicans to help them out when they first arrive. Sticking together, at least at first, is normal for the French, so why should expatriates be any different.

THE ANGLOPHONE COMMUNITIES OF PARIS

Anglophone is a word used in French to describe anybody who has English as their mother-tongue, a slightly more global term than Anglo-Saxon which is principally reserved for the Americans and the British. Nonetheless the principal English communities in and around Paris are the American and British, followed by the Irish and Canadian, and a small but visible Australasian community.

Community centres in and around Paris
Anglophone community centres in and around Paris are mainly linked to the churches and their adjoining centres. You will find

information regarding childcare, youth groups, housing, employment, support lines and social organisations.

The American Church, 65 quai d'Orsay, 75007 Paris. M° Invalides/Alma-Marceau. Tel. 01 40 62 05 00. The focal point for Anglophone community activities in Paris, with strong links to groups as diverse as Alcoholics Anonymous, the American University of Paris, and the Montessori Schools. Extensive housing and employment advertising service. The Information Centre operated by the Women of the American Church association offers advice and information on almost any practical topic for newcomers and local residents. They also organise the 'Bloom' Festival. Open every day.

The American Cathedral, 23 avenue George V, 75008 Paris. M° Alma-Marceau/George V. Tel. 01 53 23 84 00. The Episcopalian British-designed and built masterpiece just off the Champs-Élysées. Home to the Junior Service League, housing and employment ads, extensive community and arts groups. Has a (pay) counselling service and one of the best church choirs in Paris.

St George's Anglican Church, 7 rue Augueste-Vacquerie, 75116 Paris. M°/RER Charles-de-Gaulle-Étoile, Kléber George V. Tel. 01 47 20 22 51. A thriving diverse community, 50% British, 50% 'rest of the world'. High Anglican traditional worship, excellent music and thriving Sunday School and crèche. Important community noticeboard.

St Joseph's RC Church, avenue Hoche, 75008 Paris. M°/RER Charles-de-Gualle-Étoile. Tel. 01 42 27 28 56. Modern RC Church served by Irish priests caring for English-speaking Roman Catholics. Diverse congregation of about 2,000 for the Sunday masses. Sunday School, catechism in English, American Catholic Womens' Group all on offer. Useful community noticeboard.

St Michael's English Church, 5 rue d'Aguesseau, 75008 Paris. M° Concorde. Tel. 01 47 42 70 88. This packed Evangelical Anglican church offers modern worship in English. Strong youth/student section, many groups and activities for all ages.

The Scots Kirk. Tel. 01 48 78 47 94. The Kirk is currently being rebuilt but the community continues to meet for worship in friendly French Protestant churches. Small, friendly and dynamic community who will quickly introduce you to the Paris Caledonian Society and things of that ilk.

St Peter's Church, Chantilly, 7a avenue de Bouteiller, 60500 Chantilly. Tel. 03 44 58 53 22. The modern church centre has an English language library, groups for men and women, and an active British Scout group.

Holy Trinity Church, 15 avenue Carnot, 78600 Maison-Laffitte. Tel. 01 39 62 34 97. Home to a busy community of Anglophone locals and offering a full range of family activities, from mother and toddler groups to Scouts and Guides.

St Mark's Church, 31 rue de Pont Colbert, 78000 Versailles. Tel. 01 39 02 79 45. A modern Evangelican Anglican church providing a community focal point to the west of Paris.

The Great Synagogue of Paris is to be found at 44 rue de la Victoire, 75009 Paris. Tel. 01 45 26 95 36. M° Opéra or Le Péletier. Other synagogues can be found across Paris the suburbs.

The main **Paris Mosque** is to be found at 2 place Puits de l'Ermite, 75005 Paris. Tel. 01 45 35 97 33. M° Place Monge. Includes renowned gardens, tea rooms and hammams. Next to the Jardin des Plantes.

Community Communication

France-USA Contacts, www.fusac.fr. 26 rue Bénard, 75014 Paris. Tel. 01 56 53 55 54, Fax 01 56 53 545 55; US office: France Contacts, PO Box 115, Cooper Station, New York, NY 10276. Tel. 212 777 5553, Fax 212 777 5554. Free indispensable magazine available at over 50 Anglo-owned or friendly restaurants, shops, pubs, churches etc. across Paris. Excellent jobs section, useful housing (be careful of inflated prices for foreigners), best place to find out where all the bars, restaurants, etc. are.

The Paris Voice, www.parisvoice.com, 7 rue Papillon, 75009 Paris. Tel. 01 47 70 45 05, Fax 01 47 70 47 72. Started at the American Church. Jobs and housing ads at the end but more news and reviews. Free at the same points as FUSAC. Generally well-informed.

Time Out in Pariscope, www.timeout.com/paris. 100 rue du Faubourg St-Antoine, 75012 Paris. Tel. 01 44 87 00 45, Fax 01 44 73 90 60. Excellent English-language insert in the Pariscope magazine which comes out every Wednesday, available at all newspaper kiosks (3FF). The Time Out team also produce quarterly free listings guides for the forthcoming months, same distribution points as FUSAC. Their annual guide to Paris is probably the best on the market for day-tripping, nightlife, etc.

International Welcome to Paris Insiders Guide, BP 232, 92205 Neuilly Cedex. Fax 01 47 22 31 60/45 02 e-mail: ameline.dominique@wanadoo.fr-. Annual free publication available at churches, consulates and major Anglophone associations. Packed pocket-size English language handbook.

Community events

Bloom where you are planted. At the American Church on quai d'Orsay in the first three weeks of October. Three one-day sessions for new expats. Hugely popular and informative. Strong American dimensions but all nationalities very welcome.

Annual church bazaars/rummage sales. The run-up to Christmas sees a glut of sales to raise church funds and fill Christmas stockings. The main sales are at the American Cathedral, St George's and St Michael's churches.

Community resources

The American Library of Paris, www.ourworld.compuserve.com/homepages/alp. 10 rue du Général-Camou, 75007 Paris. M° École-Militaire/Alma-Marceau. Tel. 01 53 59 12 60.

The British Council Library, 11 rue de Constantine, 75007 Paris. M° Invalides. Tel. 01 49 55 73 00.

Brentanos, 37 avenue de l'Opéra, 75001 Paris. Tel. 01 42 61 52 50, Fax 01 42 61 07 61. www.brentanos.fr-. The main American bookstore just by the Opéra-Garnier also sells American stationery and has book clubs for adults and children.

Children's English Learning Centre, 33 rue de Fleurus, 75006 Paris. M° Rennes. Tel. 01 45 44 11 66, Fax 01 45 44 08 07.

Exactly what it says it is. Offers adult conversation/social groups and kids holiday activities also. A good place to know next to the Alliance Française.

Galignani's, 224 rue de Rivoli, 75001 Paris. Tel. 01 42 60 76 07. The original British bookshop in Paris, still has large English-language section. Busy but refined. (Mme Chirac is a regular).

W.H. Smith, 248 rue de Rivoli, 75001 Paris. M° Concorde. Tel. 01 44 77 88 99, Fax 01 42 96 83 71. www.whsmith.fr-. The English bookshop in Paris opposite the Tuileries at the Place de la Concorde.

The Abbey Bookshop (Canadian, 2nd-hand), 29 rue de la Parcheminerie, 75005 Paris. M° St-Michel.

San Francisco Book Company (2nd hand), 17 rue Monsieur le Prince, 75006 Paris. M° Odéon.

Shakespeare & Co, 75005 Paris, 37 rue de la Bûcherie. M° St-Michel. The most famous 2nd hand English-language bookshop in Paris.

Tea & Tattered Pages, (2nd hand), 24 rue Mayet, 75006 Paris. M° Duroc.

Village Voice, 6 rue Princesse, 75006 Paris. M° Mabillon.

INTERNATIONAL ASSOCIATIONS

A large number of Anglophone associations are open to all nationalities.

British & Commonwealth Womens Association, 8 rue de Belloy, 75116 Paris. Tel. 01 47 20 50 91. www.bcwa.org

Le WIC de Paris/Women's International Club. Tel. 01 40 50 77 23.

The YWCA-Cardew Club, 7 rue Auguste-Vacquerie, 75116 Paris. Tel. 01 47 20 44 02. September-June for young English speakers aged 18-30.

Parents with children in Anglophone or bilingual educational establishments will also find that parents associations' events also provide a good opportunity to meet and make friends.

American associations include:

Association of American Residents Overseas. Tel. 01 42 04 09 38.

Association of American Wives of Europeans. Tel. 01 47 28 46 39.

American Women's Group in Paris. Tel. 01 56 68 04 28.

Australian associations:

Association France-Australie, c/o Australian Embassy. Tel. 01 45 75 19 20.

Association Culturelle Franco-Australienne. Tel. 01 46 03 01 92.

France-Boomerang Association. Tel. 01 69 91 58 11.

British associations (www.britishinfrance.com):
There are over 60 British and Franco-British associations in and around Paris covering all aspects of life and offering one of the most comprehensive expat networks in the world. A free annual digest is available at churches, consulates etc. and from all member associations. Their website also gives full contact details of the member associations and a brief description.

Canadian associations include:

Canadian Women's Association, 5 rue de Constantine, 75007 Paris. Tel. 01 44 43 21 03.

Canadian Club of Paris, c/o The Abbey Bookshop. Tel. 01 46 33 16 24.

France-Ontario Association. Tel. 01 60 66 44 50.

Québec Delegation. Tel. 01 40 67 85 00.

Irish associations include:

Collège des Irlandais, 5 rue des Irlandais, 75005 Paris. Tel. 01 45 35 59 79. The Irish Cultural Centre in the former seminary has its own chapel (popular with the Irish community) and gardens.

Federation of Irish societies. Tel. 01 48 76 62 09.

Association of Irish Women in France, 24 rue de Girenelle, 75007 Paris. Tel. 01 42 22 51 08.

The city's Irish bars also provide good networking points. See FUSAC for addresses and events.

21

Partying in Paris

Partying in Paris is a well accepted tradition dating back centuries. Whether you are an inveterate night-owl and **fêtard** (party-goer) or just an occasional dabbler on the social scene, you need to have a basic grip of what to expect in order to 'pass the first post'. You will soon establish your own rhythms and favourite haunts. Even if the latter turn out to be pretty 'classic' by Parisian standards, there is no shame in that; after all, they would not be well-known if they were not worth going to.

FRENCH DINNER PARTIES

Dinner parties in France are normally held at about eight or nine. Try to be reasonably on time so as not to spoil a carefully prepared meal by leaving it to simmer longer than intended. Written invitations should be acknowledged by written replies. Normally, a French dinner consists of the following elements:

- Starter (**entrée**) normally accompanied by white wine.

- Main courst (**plat**) accompanied by red wine, unless white wine is appropriate.

- Cheese *before* dessert, served either by itself or with a light salad.

- Dessert perhaps accompanied by a special dessert wine.

- Coffee, served at the table. This may or may not be followed by liqueurs.

Very grand dinners will have a sorbet between each course, to clear the taste buds. It is not advisable to take wine as a gift for your host. French people are generally knowledgeable about wine, and will normally have carefully selected what they wish to serve with a particular meal. If you take a gift of wine, it should be good quality and French. Non-French wine is viewed, at best, with caution. Gifts of wine will almost certainly be placed in the store, and served on a later occasion at which you will not be present.

A bottle of champagne is a good present, which need not be expensive. This can also be laid down in a cellar, or chilled during dinner and served with dessert. Flowers are cumbersome for a hostess when she is about to serve dinner. For foreigners, bringing a product or gift from your country is an original idea, and provides a talking point at the table. A small box of good chocolates is also another popular gift, which can be purchased from specialist shops, or even at the *boulangerie*.

If you do not wish to drink alcohol, mineral water is almost always available at French tables and in all restaurants. Smoking is very prevalent in France, and rules regarding smoking at the table – and even between courses – will vary according to the hosts and the company you keep. As with many table manners, it is very much a game of 'follow my leader'. If you object to somebody smoking beside you, a discreet request rather than a loud haughty lecture will achieve the effect you require.

You may well find a rack or block beside your plate, which is a knife or fork rest. In France, it is quite common to keep the same cutlery throughout several courses. Bread is normally in plentiful supply on French tables, and should be broken with your hands, not cut with a knife. Butter is not normally served with bread.

Whilst business associates may well be invited to dinner, there is rarely 'shop talk' at the table. Conversation is more likely to revolve around new films, exhibitions, current events – and probably you as a foreigner in France. French dinner parties, like any other, can either be insufferably formal or very relaxed. If you do not know the rest of the party well, remember that the French are generally conservative and dress accordingly. The fading custom of sending thank-you notes is nonetheless greatly appreciated, and will probably ensure your popularity with your new friends.

Formality and étiquette are part of the French fascination with rules and regulations. If you are worried about making gaffs (**faux pas**), then invest in one of the many etiquette guides available.

EATING OUT IN RESTAURANTS

Finding good restaurants which offer value for money can be difficult. The best Paris restaurant guide in English is the annual *Time Out* guide, but all major newspapers and entertainment guides have regular weekly updates, depending on the style of meal you are looking for. For business lunches note that both *Le Figaro économie, Les Échos* and *La Tribune* all include restaurant reviews both for business lunches and for general guidance on 'how best to spend your money'.

Generally, restaurants offer a choice between meals at a fixed price chosen from a limited menu or **formule**, or allow you to choose from the whole menu, which is known as eating **à la carte**. The formule is normally more economical, and generally involves a selection of the dishes offered in the menu. It may consist of a starter (**entrée**) and main course (**plat**), or a main course and dessert, or all three. A small jug of wine (**pichet**) is also sometimes included. Alternatively, you can ask for a jug of tap water (**une carafe d'eau**), which is free. Mineral water must be paid for. Some restaurants will only offer a lunchtime set menu (**formule de midi**). Be careful to check this before you set out for the restaurant in the evenings, especially if you are on a limited budget.

The menu should always indicate if service is included (**service compris**). This may affect your decision as to whether to leave a tip, especially in expensive restaurants. If you order a meat dish, depending on the meat you will be asked how you like it cooked – *Quelle cuisson?* Your answer might be:

- **saignant** – rare
- **à point** – medium rare
- **bien cuit** – well-done

The French like their meat cooked very rare compared to the British, so you should perhaps over-compensate if you do not like rare meat.

Foreign and regional food

The choice of restaurants available will depend on your location. Non-French food is widely available, and as in the UK the choice reflects France's colonial past. Vietnamese and North African food (such as couscous) are popular, and Chinese and Italian food is widely available. Indian food is rarer, although you should go to the Passage Brady near Strasbourg-St-Denis. British cooking is still eyed with suspicion and/or mirth in France, and there are no truly British restaurants.

What you will find in France is a great choice of restaurants offering regional specialities. It can be great fun when visiting a new area to try not only the local cheese and wine, but also the local dish. Some are now universal, and you will find **boeuf bourguignon** (Burgundy beef stew), for instance, available everywhere.

Fast food and take-aways

Fast food is widely available now in France, and major international chains have outlets in most principal towns and cities. Chinese and Indian take-aways are still not common, but home-delivery services are widespread. Some restaurants do offer **plats à emporter**, but this will mean ordering your food at the restaurant and squeezing up to the counter while you wait. Alternatively, go to a **traiteur** who offers Italian or Chinese/Vietnamese/Thai (the three tend to be mixed together) dishes sold by the portion.

Gastronomic Paris

- **Chinese** The two Paris Chinatowns (but including plenty of Vietnamese and Thai) are in Belleville (19th and 20th) and Place d'Italie (13th).

- **St-Germain des Prés, the Marais, Bastille** A mix of intimate and trendy restaurants of varying quality. Brasserie Lipp at St-Germain remains an institution, and Chez Paul in rue de Charonne is full-hearted French fare with lashings of Gallic arrogance from the staff.

- **Chartiers**, rue du Faubourg Montmartre – the original French canteen, great atmosphere in 19th century decor. The food is good but basic, the prices are reasonable, and the atmosphere guaranteed.

- **The great classics** – La Fermette Marbeuf, avenue George V (fantastic interior, good but not stunning food, excellent service and wines); La Maison Blanche, avenue Montaigne (fashion favourite above the theatre); La Tour d'Argent, quai de la Tournelle (for very special occasions and if you have a golden tower of your own to pay the bill); the Jules Verne restaurant on top of the Eiffel Tower (three months' waiting list for a table, the sky is the limit for the price range).

CAFÉS AND PUBS

Cafés are one of the great traditions of French society, ranging from the high-brow literary **salons** of St-Germain des Prés to scruffy street-corners, and encompassing every style in between.

Drinking at the counter (**comptoir**) is cheaper than at a table (**en salle**) or on a terrace (**en terrasse**). The same rules apply in cafés to ordering alcohol as to ordering coffee or tea. Exploring the local cafés and finding one that suits you, where you can while away half an hour with the newspaper, a book or friends for the price of a coffee, is another of the joys of France.

Those cafés which display a red **tabac** sign also double as tobacconists, offering a wide range of products at the cigarette counter (e.g. phone cards or fiscal stamps). Many also offer a **service restauration** at least at lunchtime, with sandwiches and hot meals available. Some of the terms for these meals include:

- **croque-monsieur** – ham and cheese toasted sandwich

- **croque-madame** – as above, but with a fried egg served on top

- **chèvre-chaud** – hot goat's cheese normally served on toast, with a small mixed salad; either a starter or a main course

- **Francfort-frites** – Frankfurter sausage and chips; sausages such as **saucisse de Toulouse**, are more like a Cumberland sausage and will be served with other vegetables and a sauce

- **garnis avec** – served with: chips (**frites**), mashed potato (**pommes vapeur**), boiled potatoes (**pommes sautées**), pasta (**Pâtes**)

- **salade** – be careful here. In French this means both lettuce, which may be all you receive, or refers to, for example, a **salade de tomates** (a plate of sliced tomatoes). A **salade mixte** will be a side-salad of lettuce plus perhaps chicory (**endives**) and tomatoes. Salads that are served as main courses will normally have a list of their ingredients

- **omelettes** are normally also available in a variety of styles and content.

In Paris, some cafés also become centres of night-life. This café scene is dominated by two brothers, the frères Costes. First they built the Cafe Costes (nicknamed Café Cost-a-lot), in Les Halles, which gave way to the designer masterpiece Café Beaubourg outside the Pompidou Centre. Now they have gone one better and taken over the top floor of the centre itself with Chez Georges, a 'sweetie darling' paradise with stunning views across Paris. They also have Café Marly at the Louvre (the best summer terrace in Paris), L'Esplanade opposite Les Invalides, and La Grande Armée next to the Arc de Triomphe. All Costes cafés offer high but not unaffordable prices; great locations; fantastic modern décor; sultry staff clad in black; and plenty of star gazing. The ultimate is now the Hôtel Costes round the corner from Place Vendôme, where Mick Jagger celebrated his 50th birthday, and the resident DJ has produced three highly successful albums of lounge music. The courtyard restaurant is bliss in summer, even if the majority of the people hanging around it are not.

The other café/bars and café-districts to know are:

- **Abbesses** – La Sancerre and Le Chinon in rue des Abbesses, and La Fourmi in rue des Martyrs

- **Oberkampf** – Le Café Charbon, the Mecano Bar, and all the bars in between on rue Oberkampf

- **Marais** – The Café Trésor in rue du Trésor for trendy night-owls; Le Petit Fer à Cheval on rue Vieille du Temple for its interior and La Belle Hortense bookshop-wine bar opposite; and L'Appartement Café next to the Musée Picasso, with its lazy Sunday afternoons of **jeux de sociétés** (parlour-games and board-games). The **rue des Archives** by Hôtel de Ville is the centre of the gay district, stretching from Les Halles to Bastille.

- **Bastille** – an embarassment of riches. Check out the rue de Charonne, rue de Lappe and du Faubourg-St-Antoine. The Barrio Latino is the place everybody wants to be, but snug little hideouts like the Bar sans nom are really the places for seductive atmosphere.

- **St-Germain-des-Prés** – the great literary cafés are to be found next to the church, but try heading round to La Palette on rue de Seine for a great interior and exterior in fine weather. Round the corner in rue Mazarin is L'Alcazar's AZ Bar, now Paris' top lounge bar, above the restaurant.

- **Latin Quarter** – at one end head for the **Place de Contrescarpe** off the rue Mouffetard with its cafés, or if you prefer lusher surroundings try the chic Closerie de Lilas at Port-Royal.

- **Canal St Martin** – on the quai Jemmapes and quai de Valmy from the Hôpital St Louis down towards République. Try the Antoine & Lili café on a Sunday to see what happened when Bobo and Lili got married . . .

There are over 60 Irish pubs across France in the principal cities, mostly Paris. However, you should note that whilst they appear to be like English and Irish pubs, the prices are very much higher.

A pint normally costs about 40FF in a pub, and spirits are also about 40 to 60FF per glass. The cost of a glass of wine will depend on its size and quality. The standard French person will drink a half-pint (**demi**) of whatever is on tap (**pression**). This is one local custom you should take up quickly!

CABARETS AND CLUBS

The French have been famous for generations for their cabarets and nightclubs. In Paris, the Folies-Bergères, the Lido, the Crazy Horse and the Moulin-Rouge continue to offer high-class – but expensive – entertainment, with a champagne dinner served whilst grand musical shows are performed. Smaller cabarets are also very popular, allowing singers and comedians to perform in a more intimate atmosphere.

Nightclubs, almost by definition, fall in and out of fashion very rapidly and regularly. You should check the style of a club by using a guide, or by asking somebody whom you know already goes to the club. Styles vary widely, even at the same club, depending on the day of the week. The trendiest Paris nightclubs have a very exclusive door policy, so swot up in advance on what to wear and how to act.

At the time of writing, the nightclub scene is thriving in Paris, with self-promotion being the name of the game amongst 'artistic directors' who know little about directing, even less about art, but lots about pulling in the punters with glamorous guest-lists. It all feels a lot more industrial than it used to. Les Bains remains the top club, but one-night events are becoming more and more popular with DJs jetting in from the States and the UK. Flyers can be found in the trendy bars; so find the bars and you will find the info. Otherwise listen to the daily updates on Radio FG, read *Nova* magazine, shave your head and grow a goatee beard (unless you are a woman), and you should soon fit in at most of the top nightclubs. *Time Out in Pariscope* provides a useful and objective view separating the hot from the hype in Paris nightlife.

French nightlife gets going later than in the UK. Bars generally close at 2am, and nightclubs will generally start to fill up from about 1am, and then stay open until dawn. The entry price may include one drink (**une consommation**), but after that be prepared for high prices.

PARTIES

Cocktail parties usually begin about seven, and will last for a couple of hours. Informality over the time of arrival may not be matched by informality over dress, and you should try to find out roughly what is expected of you.

If you decide to organise a more traditional British-style party, do not expect your French guests to bring a bottle with them. In France, the host traditionally provides all the requirements for an evening's entertainment. One way to get around this is to call a party a **soirée à l'anglaise**, literally a British evening, and gently explain the bring-a-bottle concept to your French guests. You should warn both neighbours and the concierge that you will be organising a party, and post polite notes in French in the entrance hall of your building apologising in advance for any inconvenience caused.

Encourage your guests to leave quietly, and be careful of the level of noise. The police may be asked to intervene at rowdy parties after 10pm. Your neighbours will normally be forgiving if you make an excuse such as 'It's my birthday'. However, remember you only have one birthday a year!

BIRTHS, MARRIAGES AND DEATHS

Although these are not leisure activities, it is appropriate to know a few of the social customs of the 'hatched, matched and despatched' business which still thrives in France so that you do not make any blunders. Obviously there is no Court Circular page in French newspapers, but both *Le Figaro* and *Le Monde* carry social announcements, as does *Libération* to a lesser extent. The choice of paper depends entirely on the class pretensions and politics of those concerned.

Births

Births (**Naissances**) are often announced not only by cards as in the UK but also by a small advertisement in one of the papers named above. Typically, a birth announcement will be roughly translated as 'Marie and Pierre are pleased to announce the arrival of their new sister Jeanne' followed by the name and address of the parents.

Infant baptisms are heavily on the decline in France. For Catholic families, they normally take place during the parish mass on Sunday mornings, and will be followed by a family lunch. Coloured sugared almonds (**dragées**) are often distributed, pink for girls and blue for boys.

Weddings

No religious wedding ceremony may take place in France until a civil marriage has first been performed by the mayor at the town hall. This applies to all religions and denominations. If a large religious ceremony is to follow, then normally only close family and friends will attend the wedding at the *mairie*. However, many people choose to stick to civil marriage. Being invited to be a **témoin** (witness) is an honour equivalent to being a bridesmaid or usher.

Wedding lists are very popular in France, and are an easy way of dealing with the problem of presents. The style of the wedding is of course entirely personal to the couple, and may range from the unusual to the strictly traditional. A traditional Catholic wedding will take place in the course of a nuptial mass in the bride's home parish.

As with British weddings, French weddings can be the occasion for a great show of finery. As ever in France, be careful to find out as much about the dress code expected as possible. The wedding invitation may well read like a genealogy of the couple, with grandparents and parents of both sides listed.

The French tradition in wedding receptions is the opposite of the British. Everybody is invited after the wedding to the **vin d'honneur**, to toast the couple's health and happiness. However, after that the reception is limited, ranging from a seated dinner (**dîner placé**) to a **soirée dansante** (dance). A French aristocratic wedding will normally take place at the family château.

Deaths

Generally you will receive a **faire-part** (card announcing a death), including the same genealogical list as you would find on a wedding invitation – only longer. For instance, a *faire-part* announcing the death of a grandmother would begin with her spouse, include any surviving brothers and sisters and their spouses, and then move on to mention each child and their children, sometimes each by name.

The French are very attached to the tradition of writing to express condolence. The *faire-part* will announce when and where the funeral is to take place, if donations should be made in place of flowers, and whether it is a 'family only' affair (**'dans la plus stricte intimité'**).

At a French requiem mass, each mourner will be invited to take place in the ritual of absolution, the **absolution** (springling of holy water) as a final farewell. This is not obligatory if it contradicts with your own faith. If you do wish to participate, move at the instruction of the undertaker, and then 'follow the leader'. Burial is still much the most common end for French men and women, and cremations are rare. It should be noted that French crematoria are to say the least much less 'user-friendly' than British ones.

THE PERFORMING ARTS

France is traditionally very generous in state patronage of the arts. The result is a rich variety in the performing arts, with Paris naturally being centre-stage. Tourist information centres will be able to tell you what forthcoming productions and events are planned in your own area.

Music

Paris naturally has a high concentration of fine concert halls, such as the Salle Pleyel, but the wealth of fine churches provides a secondary source of concert venues. Amongst the most popular church venues are the Église-St-Séverin in the 5th, and La Madeleine in the 8th.

It should be noted that the English-language expatriate communities are very well served by semi-professional musicians in and around Paris. The main bases for these groups and individuals are the American Cathedral with Les Arts George V, and St George's Anglican Church. Many touring British choirs stop off in

Paris and sing in one of the city's great churches, and details can always be found at the Anglophone community centres when these visits are due to take place.

The main popular music concert venues are Bercy, Le Bataclan (11th), La Cigale (18th), and L'Olympia (9th). Tickets and listings can be found at both the Virgin Megastores and the main FNAC stores. See also *Lylo* for concert listings and *Brazuca* for Latino nightlife, both free in bars across Paris.

Opera and ballet

Opera flourishes in Paris, not only in the new Bastille Opera House, but also at the Opéra-Comique in Place Boïeldieu, and sometimes also at the old Paris Opéra (the Palais Garnier), and in other theatres such as the Théâtre Châtelet. Both traditional and modern operas are included in their repertoires. The Paris Ballet is now housed at the grand old Opéra-Garnier, and provides a full programme each season. Visiting ballet companies also regularly appear in Paris.

Theatre

The theatre in Paris thrives, with many small theatres offering the chance for new actors and productions to appear before the public. The most famous French theatre is the **Comédie-Française**, which now has three auditoria.

There are also occasional performances in English in Paris, at the following addresses and by the varying companies:

- The **Shakespeare Garden** in the Bois de Boulogne – open-air summer season with a company from the UK. Tel. 01 42 37 39 54.

- **Théâtre de Nesle**, 8 rue de Nesle, 75006 Paris. Tel. 01 46 34 61 04 – small cellar theatre with regular productions in English, including children's shows.

- **Finnegan's Wake** 9 rue des Boulangers, 75005 Paris. Tel. 01 46 34 23 86 – Irish pub with café-theatre tradition opposite the Jussieu university faculty.

- **Sudden Theatre**, 14bis, rue St Isaure, 76018 Paris. Tel. 01 42 62 35 00 – a repertory theatre providing a welcome to English-language companies and their followers.

- **Dear Conjunction**, Tel 01 42 85 09 57 – Justifiably the Anglo community's favourite company. American and English Paris resident professionals, alternate performances in English and French. Broad range of material performed at various venues. Watch the Anglo press for details and follow the crowd.

- **The International Players**, Tel. 01 39 62 79 64 (see also www.britishinfrance.com). There has been a British amateur dramatic company in Paris since the beginning of the 20th century. The current company is very internatitional but English speaking. Musical productions from Gilbert and Sullivan to *Grease*, with popular pantomimes at Christmas. Normally performs in 'Angloland' Le Vesinet. Generally high standard and a good night out.

- **Paris theatres with productions in English** – The Bouffes du Nord (10th), MC93 in Bobigny (93), and Les Amandiers at Nanterre (92) all occasionally have productions in English, normally of very high quality by visiting directors or companies.

GOING TO THE CINEMA

Cinema is one of the great passions of the French, which they consider to be the 'seventh art'. Paris has two film festivals of its own sponsored by the city, the Paris Film Festival and the *18 heures-18 Francs fête du cinéma*, when anybody can go to the cinema at 6pm for only 18FF. Other festivals take place throughout the year linked to particular themes. There is also an American film festival at Deauville and a British film festival at Dinard each year.

Films in English with French subtitles are widely shown and are marked **v.o. (version originale). V.F. (version française)** means that films have been dubbed. **Premiérs** (first nights) are great occasions, but there are plenty of **avants-premiérs** now advertised in the press. Wednesday is the day that new films come out in France, and is worth avoiding at cinemas if you want a quiet night out. Late-night showings are available at various cinemas across Paris, such as the UGC Ciné-Cité in Les Halles or the Pathé-Wepler at Place de Clichy. For cinema times check *Pariscope, Officiels & Spectacles* or *Zurban*.

Parisians are very attached to their art cinemas, and these in particular have been threatened by the arrival of cinema passes.

The current choice of passes covers the following groups or cinema chains: UGC, Gaumont, MK2, the Rex, Max Linder, a group of Montparnasse cinemas and a group of smaller art cinemas from Passy to Bastille and down to the 5th and 6th arrondissements. Details of the passes can be found in the cinama section of the weekly magazine *Zurban*.

Essential reading

Weekly entertainment guides coincide with new films every Wednesday. Magazines come out on Thursdays. The newspapers publish their reviews on different days. Amongst the best guides are:

In English – *Time Out in Pariscope; The Free Voice; FUSAC* (listings only); *Where* (monthly subscription magazine. Tel. 01 43 12 56 56).

In French – *Pariscope; Zurban; À nous Paris; Officiels & Spectacles; Nova; Aden* (weekly supplement of *Le Monde*); *Libération* (each day); *Le Figaroscope* (weekly supplement of *Le Figaro*); and the Paris supplement to *L'Express*.

Zurban is probably the best observer of what is going on, and *À nous Paris* has an annoying habit of trying to remind you just how **branché** (trendy) and **cool** the reporters and their new-found friends are. *Where* is rather 'preppy' at times, but *Time Out* remains the best guide in English.

The Parisian Party Year Plan
September

La rentrée scolaire (return to school) remains the real starting point of the year. University students start next month. Around the middle of the month you have two antipathetic but supposedly 'cultural cousin' events: **Les Journées du Patrimoine/Portes-Ouvertes** when you can visit the embassies and state palaces normally closed to the public; and the **Technoparade**, which is Paris' limp response to the Love Parade in Berlin. Just to add to the mayhem, the fashion pack fly in for a week of shows and showing-off. Plenty of **soirées** in the Paris clubs . . .

October

Prix de l'Arc de Triomphe at Longchamps – the greatest horse races of the year, equivalent to the Derby takes place on the first Sunday of October. **Halloween** is now popular in Paris with plenty of costume parties in clubs, bars and private homes. *Trick or Treat* is not really accepted practice. Half-term holidays for Toussaint at the end of the month.

November
1 November is **Toussaint**, All Saints Day, 11 November is **Armistice Day**. Both are national holidays when shops and businesses are shut. There is a wreath laying ceremony at the Arc de Triomphe at 11am by the President and Prime Minister, and a service at Notre-Dame for the British community in the afternoon. The third Thursday of the month is **Beaujolais Nouveau**, the festival of a wine too young to drink under any other circumstance except that the more you drink the better it tastes. Parties in bars across Paris, the most famous being in rue du Marché-St-Honoré in the 1st.

December
Only **Christmas Day** itself is a bank holiday in France, and you can legitimately be expected to work on the 26th. The French tradition is for a grand family dinner on Christmas Eve, then off to Midnight Mass, and presents after Mass or early next morning. New Year's Eve in Paris is also known as **St Sylvestre**. Le **réveillon** (name for an evening banquet used at Christmas and New Year) is a special occasion for yet more gluttony. Avoid the Champs-Élysées and Place de la Concorde at these times. Greetings cards are normally sent to wish Happy New Year rather than Happy Christmas, and can be sent between mid-December and the end of January.

January
New Year's Day is a national holiday. 6 January is the **Fête des Rois**. The tradition is to buy a galette of pastry and almonds at the boulangerie, invite family and friends to share it with you, and the person who finds the gift (**fève**) in their slice of cake is the king/queen for the day and wears the supplied paper crown. The youngest person is expected to crawl under the table to announce the distribution of slices.

February
La Chandeleur, the French term for Candlemas (2 February). This is the French pancake (**crêpes**) day. Half-term holidays (**vacances scolaires**) and a popular ski season.

March

According to the date of Easter, you will have **Mardi Gras** (Shrove Tuesday) and Ash Wednesday (**Cendres**). Less observed than in other Catholic countries and cities.

April

Easter festivities across the city after the rigours of Holy Week. **Good Friday** is not a holiday in France, but **Easter Monday** is. The largest Good Friday processions are on the Champs-Élysées and at Sacré-Coeur. Towards the end of the month, the **Prix du Président** at Auteuil race-track is the second great horse race of the year.

May

The favourite month of the year! Three national holidays: **1st Labour day/May Day (Fête du travail); 8th Victory in Europe Day (Fête de la Victoire);** and **Ascension Day** (depends on Easter). On Labour Day, in addition to the traditional trade union marches, the popular tradition is to give a sprig of Lily of the Valley (**un brin de muguet**) to friends and family for good luck. The last Sunday in May is the French **Mother's Day (Fête des Mères)**, with cards available in French in the shops.

June

Ten days after Ascension is **Pentecôte**, and the following Monday (Whit Monday) is a bank holiday. In June the partying starts to really get going about the middle of the month. On the 21 June is the **Fête de la Musique**, with free open-air concerts across Paris. The main venue is at République with top-name billing. Amongst the best areas for free café concerts are the Marais, Les Halles and St-Germain. Check the press for listings. **Gay Pride** on the third Saturday in the month drew 500,000 people in 2001 for a Rio-style carnival. On the upper end of the entertainment market, the end of the month is the **Prix de Diane** at Chantilly, the equivalent to Ascot Gold Cup day.

July

Bastille Day on 14 July is the French National Holiday (**fête nationale**). The parties begin on the 13th in the evening, with free parties at the fire stations (**bals de pompiers**) or on the banks of the Seine. Grand military parade in the morning, and evening fireworks on the 14th at the Eiffel Tower close the celebrations.

August

The **fête de l'Assomption** is celebrated as a national holiday. It is traditionally one of the hottest and quiestest times of the year. There is an open-air mass in front of Notre-Dame, but most Parisians are by now travelling to or from the coast.

22

Escaping from Paris

So, you've read the book, found the job, moved your home, enrolled for your courses, shopped 'til you dropped, partied like there was no tomorrow. What do you do next? The realistic answer is to take a break and head out of Paris before it finally drives you crazy. It is a fantastic place to live, but escaping from the city is essential for your mental health. Thankfully it is not hard to do due to the excellent French transport system.

WHEN SHOULD YOU GO?

The best idea is of course to take a long weekend. With the number and dates of the French bank holidays, this is not too difficult. French bank holidays 'belong' to the date, and are not transferred so if Christmas Day falls on a Saturday, then it is observed on that day and no time off is given in lieu of the weekend celebrations.

However when a *fête* falls on a Thursday or Tuesday, the bridge day is often taken as a holiday by French residents to make a long weekend. The term for this is **faire le pont**, literally to make the bridge. When bank holidays are close together (e.g. *Ascension* and *Pentecôte*, or *Toussaint* and *Armistice*) you will also find that many people will go away between the two to avoid using up too many holidays.

Obviously this creates peak season rates and travel problems, so you need to plan in advance. Friday nights (after 5pm) and Monday mornings are also to be avoided.

WHERE TO GO

Your finances or planning might not allow you to take a whole weekend off, or you might simply wish to take a breather from the Parisian rat-race. There is no shortage of options to choose from for this purpose. The following are just a few suggestions to help you start to explore the nearby regions:

To the north

• **Châteaux** Less than one hour by train from Paris is **Chantilly**, the fairytale jewel-box château at the centre of a forest, equestrian museum and race-course. Across the forest by car lies **Pierrefonds**, another picture-postcard 19th century folly on a lake, whilst royal **Compiègne** boasts a mini-Versailles which was a favourite of Louis XV and Napoléon III.

• **Cathedrals** Both only one hour direct from Paris by train lie **Amiens**, with one of the most stunning Gothic masterpieces in France dominating the pretty town, and **Beauvais**, the unfinished highest Gothic cathedral in the world.

• **Towns Senlis** (for which you need a car) is one of the prettiest and most historic former cities in the Val d'Oise with its tiny cobbled streets, ruined château, ramparts and cathedral. **Lille** is the great metropolis of the north, with a strong Flemish feel. Beautifully restored in the old city centre, excellent restaurants, terrific shopping, a good range of bars, and fine architecture are all combined with new museums in the nearby towns connected by the city's own Métro system. The city centre boasts a fine opera house, theatres and the most important art gallery outside of Paris (**Musée des Beaux-Arts**). You could happily spend a weekend in Lille and come back to Paris feeling much the better for it. English guide books and pamphlets readily available at the Tourist Office.

To the west

• **Châteaux** With direct rail and RER links to central Paris, **Versailles** has a distinctly different feel to it than Paris. If you can't face the maddening crowds at the château, then wander far from them in the parks surrounding the château, and visit the Trianon or Marie-Antoinette's mock farm instead. Another alternative is to head up to **St-Germain-en-Laye** on the RER, visit the castle and wander along the terrace and back through the woods. Two hours direct from Paris by train lies **Tours**, the capital of the Loire valley. From here you could hire a car to visit the Renaissance châteaux which fill the valley, or if you want a really quiet weekend, stop off in **Amboise** or **Blois**. If you head into Normandy, then try the **Château de la Roche-Guyon** if you have a car. Close to Paris, this was Rommel's HQ during World War II.

- **Cathedrals** One hour from Montparnasse will bring you the world-renowned medieval splendours of the stained glass windows (**vitraux**) of **Chartres** Cathedral. Obviously you should try and pick a sunny day to best appreciate the windows. **Rouen**, the attractive capital of Normandy, is dominated by its city-centre cathedral and a cluster of other Renaissance churches and is only one hour by train from St-Lazare.

- **Beaches and Gardens** From May to September, a direct rail link is made from St-Lazare to the Calvados coast of Normandy. **Cabourg** (the home of Marcel Proust) and **Huelgoat** are more laid-back resorts with big sandy beaches, but the jet-set head for **Deauville**, which is packed in the summer months. If you have a car, you could try Monet's home at **Giverny**, but peace and quiet are not assured. Nearby is the Museum of American Impressionists.

To the south

- **Châteaux** The train from Gare de Lyon will take you in about an hour to **Fontainebleau**, the great royal château in the forests to the south of Paris. You will need a car to reach **Vaux-le-Vicomte** but it is worth it to see the château that inspired Louis XIV's jealousy and the creation of Versailles.

- **Towns Provins** is a medieval masterpiece, and feels a million miles from the bustle of Paris. Two hours south of Paris by TGV from the Gare de Lyon lies **Dijon**, the pretty and historic capital of Burgundy, with regular tours of the local vineyards leaving from the city centre.

All the French regions have tourist offices in the centre of Paris (generally **La Maison de . . .**). Check the *Pages Jaunes* for exact details, choose your destination, pack your bags and **bon weekend et bon voyage!**

Useful addresses and contacts

French embassies and consulates

In the UK
www.ambafrance.org.uk.
The French Embassy, 58 Knightsbridge, London SW1X 7JT. Tel. 0207 201 1000.
The French Consulate General – Visas and Immigration services, 21 Cromwell Road, London SW7 2EN. Tel. 0207 838 2000.

In the USA
www.france-consulat.org.
The French Embassy, Consular Services, 4101 Reservoir Road NW, Washington DC. Tel. 202 944 6195.
New York, 934 Fifth Avenue, New York NY 10021. Tel. 212 606 36 89, www.franceconsulatny.org; consulates in Atlanta, Boston, Chicago, Houston, New Orleans, Los Angeles, Miami and San Francisco.

L'Institut Français in London
17 Queensberry Place, London SW7 2DT. Tel. 0207 838 2144, www.institut.ambafrance.org.uk. Tube: South Kensington. Bus: 14, 45a, 49, 70, 74 C1. Open Monday – Friday 10h00–21h30, Saturday 12h00 – 21h30.
For anybody seriously considering moving to France, or finding out about the French language, culture or lifestyle, a visit to the French Institute in London is a 'must' if at all possible. Language lessons, cinema, daily papers and a children's bookshop are amongst the services offered.

The French Travel Centre,
178 Piccadilly, London W1V 0AL. Tel. 0207 491 9996, Fax 0207 491 0600. Open Monday–Friday 10h00–18h00, Saturday 10h00–17h00.

French Railways Ltd, The Rail Europe Travel Centre, 179 Piccadilly. Tube: Green Park or Piccadilly Circus – French Government tourist centre.

For business contacts, see the list of useful contacts at the end of Chapter 16. For education contacts see Chapter 5. Excellent free guide to essential paperwork in French from the Mairie de Paris (www.paris.france.org), *Vivre à Paris* for EU citizens. See also www.service-public.fr for links to French government websites in English.

Consulates and embassies in Paris

The American Consulate, 2 rue St Florentin, 75001 Paris. M° Concorde. Tel. 01 44 96 14 88.

The British Consulate, 18 bis, rue d'Anjou, 75008 Paris. M° Concorde. Tel. 01 44 51 31 00.

The Canadian Embassy, 35 avenue Montaigne, 75008 Paris. M° Franklin-Roosevelt. Tel. 01 44 43 29 00.

The Irish Embassy, 4 rue Rude, 75116 Paris. M° Etoile. Tel. 01 44 17 67 00.

Essential publications

Housing and jobs – *France-USA Contacts*. Tel. 01 56 53 54 54, 1212 777 5553, www.fusac.fr

General lifestyle – *The Paris Free Voice*. Tel. 01 47 70 45 05, www.parisvoice.com

Families – *Living in France* quarterly magazine. Tel. 01 45 44 11 66, www.parisfranceguide.com

Entertainment, shopping and tourism – *Time Out in Pariscope*, available every Wednesday in Paris at kiosks for 3FF. Free quarterly magazines/reviews at Eurostar stations. Also the annual *Time Out Paris* guide, www.timeout.com/paris

Index

LIVING & WORKING IN FRANCE
How to prepare for a successful visit, be it short, long-term, or forever

Alan Hart

'Hart writes with great authority . . . A valuable guide to the country, people and employment situation. Highly recommended.' *Overseas Jobs Express*. 'An in-depth insight into the culture, systems and structures plus many other aspects of life and employment in France – gives the reader a real taste of France before setting a foot outside the UK.' *Careers Europe*.

208 pages. 1 85703 439 2

GETTING A JOB ABROAD
The handbook for the international jobseeker: where the jobs are, how to get them

Roger Jones

Now in its fifth edition, this is the handbook for anyone planning to spend a period of work abroad. Includes a wide range of reference addresses covering employment agencies, specialist newspapers, a comprehensive booklist and helpful addresses. '. . . highly informative . . . lots of hard information and a first class reference section.' *Escape Committee Newsletter*.

336 pages. 1 85703 418 X. 5th edition

SPENDING A YEAR ABROAD
A guide to opportunities for self-development and discovery around the world

Nick Vandome

'Unlike most reference books this one should be read right through, and that is a pleasure as well as being very informative . . . totally comprehensive.' *School Librarian Journal.*

176 pages. 1 85703 544 5

TEACHING ABROAD
How and where to find worldwide opportunities and contacts

Roger Jones

Practical and realistic information including reviews of teaching opportunities in over 180 countries.

192 pages. 1 85703 276 4. 3rd edition

LIVING & WORKING IN LONDON
All you need to know to enjoy this capital city

Joanna Minett

This practical guide covers finding accommodation, whether you're renting, buying or sharing. There is advice for job seekers, guidance on opportunities for work, how to approach the hidden job market or continue your education. Everyday issues are covered too, such as travelling around, socialising on a budget, and understanding this exhilarating city's culture. 'Tips on analysing work opportunities, finding accommodation and retaining your sanity.' *A Guardian Book of the Week.*

128 pages. 1 85703 556 9

GETTING A JOB IN EUROPE
The guide to finding short or long-term employment in Europe

Mark Hempshell

Whether you're seeking executive, professional, skilled or casual work, this information-packed guide is a must. Discover how to job search, how to apply (and prepare Euro CVs), and find out what working life in Europe is really like. It is full of key contacts, sample documents and hard-to-find information.

197 pages. 1 85703 535 6. 4th edition